"Discipline is a subject about which the Scriptures say much—but contemporary authors have been peculiarly silent. Kent Hughes fills a gaping void with this superb volume. You'll be challenged and encouraged as you read. And if there is a spark of spiritual desire in your soul, this book will surely kindle it into a blazing passion for godly discipline."

> —John MacArthur, pastor, Grace Community Church in Sun Valley, California, and author of *Ashamed of the Gospel* and *The Glory of Heaven*

"I enjoyed reading *Disciplines of a Godly Man* because it challenged my spirit. I highly recommend it to men who are not thin-skinned."

> —Mike Singletary, former Chicago Bears middle linebacker and two-time NFL Defensive Player of the Year

"This is a book for men who are eager to learn how to be more effective. It comes from the pen of one who has learned to serve as he has led and who is able to provide the reader with many practical applications of eternal truths."

> —C. William Pollard, Chairman and CEO, The Servicemaster Company

"[This is] one of the best books I've read. . . . What an outstanding volume. . . . I guarantee: Digest this book and you will bid the blahs farewell."

> —Charles R. Swindoll, President, Dallas Theological Seminary

"In *Disciplines of a Godly Man*, Pastor Kent Hughes provides an inspiring and practical guide for men who seek to reflect God's glory in their lives. This book is a challenging text for personal devotions as well as for assisting young followers of Christ to grow in their walk with God."

> —Lieutenant General Howard D. Graves, U.S. Army, retired; former superintendent United States Military Academy, West Point, New York

"The best contemporary book of spiritual guidance I've read in a long time. Usually for this type of food I have to look for a book that is at least 75 years old. This book is a surprising exception. And it has the added advantage of being very relevant to specific needs in today's world."

> —Ajith Fernando, National Director, Youth for Christ, Sri Lanka

"I am so weary of the peculiar therapeutic atmosphere in which we live today that is scared stiff to tell anybody to do anything or to warn anybody of dangerous consequences of failing to take responsibility for his or her life. . . . So to open [*Disciplines of a Godly Man*] and find someone taking seriously the biblical call for 'agonizing to enter the kingdom' and striving like a gymnast to become godly and boxing and sweating like a champion to get victory over sin is the most refreshing thing I could have set my eyes on. So thank you for your courage and for swimming against the stream. May the Lord cause your book to run and the truth in it to be glorified and obeyed."

> —John Piper, pastor of Bethlehem Baptist Church, Minneapolis, and author of *Desiring God* and *God's Passion for His Glory*

DISCIPLINES
of a
GODLY MAN

Tenth Anniversary Edition

Revised Edition

R. KENT HUGHES

CROSSWAY BOOKS

A DIVISION OF
GOOD NEWS PUBLISHERS
WHEATON, ILLINOIS

For my sons
Brian Thomas Hoch,
James Jefferson Simpson,
Richard Kent Hughes II
and
William Carey Hughes

Disciplines of a Godly Man.

10th Anniversary Edition, Revised Edition, copyright © 2001 by R. Kent Hughes.

Original edition copyright © 1991 by R. Kent Hughes.

Published by Crossway Books, a division of
Good News Publishers, 1300 Crescent Street, Wheaton, Illinois 60187.

Cover design: Cindy Kiple

First printing, original edition, 1991; first printing with study questions, 1995

First printing, 10th anniversary edition, revised edition, 2001

Printed in the United States of America

Unless otherwise noted, all Bible quotations are taken from *Holy Bible: New International Version*, copyright © 1978 by the New York International Bible Society. Used by permission of Zondervan Bible Publishers.

Library of Congress Cataloging-in-Publication Data
Hughes, R. Kent.
    Disciplines of a godly man / R. Kent Hughes.—Rev. ed.
       p. cm.
    Includes bibliographical references and index.
    ISBN 1-58134-286-1 (alk. paper)
    1. Discipline—Religious aspects—Christianity. 2. Spiritual life—
Christianity. 3. Men—Religious life. I. Title.
BV4647.D58 H84   2001
248.8'42—dc21   2001004098
                                                            CIP

MV		15	14	13	12	11	10	09	08	07	06	05	04	03
18	17	16	15	14	13	12	11	10	9	8	7			

TABLE OF CONTENTS

RESOURCES

ACKNOWLEDGMENTS

I WOULD LIKE to thank my secretary, Mrs. Sharon Fritz, for her care and pride of workmanship in typing the multiple revisions of the manuscript; Mr. Herbert Carlburg for weekly proofreading and many suggested improvements; Mr. George Grant for his expert editing though busy in far-off England; Mr. Ted Griffin, Managing Editor of Crossway Books, for his discerning eye which has made clear the incomprehensible and for the preparation of the study questions; and my wife, Barbara, who possesses the gracious wisdom to cut through the irrelevant and get to the heart of things with the perpetual James-like question, "So what difference does this make in the way we live?"

INTRODUCTION

1

Discipline for Godliness

SOMETIME IN THE early summer before entering the seventh grade, I wandered over from the baseball field and picked up a tennis racket for the first time . . . and I was hooked! It was not long before I became a ten-year-old tennis bum. My passion for the sport became so intense, I would idly hold a tennis ball and just sniff it. The *pssst* and the rubbery fragrance of opening a can of new tennis balls became intoxicating. The *whop, whop* and the lingering ring of a sweetly hit ball, especially in the quietness of early morning, was to me symphonic. My memories of this and the summer which followed are of blistering black tennis courts, hot feet, salty sweat, long drafts of delicious rubbery tepid water from an empty ball can, the short shadows of midday heading slowly toward the east, followed by the stadium "daylight" of the court's lights, and the ubiquitous eerie night bats dive-bombing our lobs.

That fall I determined to become a tennis player. I spent my hoarded savings on one of those old beautifully laminated Davis Imperial tennis rackets — a treasure which I actually took to bed with me. I was disciplined! I played every day after school (except during basketball season) and every weekend. When spring came, I biked to the courts where the local high school team practiced and longingly watched until they finally gave in and let me play with them. The next two summers I took lessons, played some tournaments, and practiced about six to eight hours a day — coming home only when they turned off the lights.

And I became good. Good enough, in fact, that as a twelve-and-a-half-year-old, one-hundred-and-ten-pound freshman I was second man on the varsity tennis team of my large 3,000-student California high school.

Not only did I play at a high level, I learned that personal discipline is the indispensable key for accomplishing anything in this life. I have since come to understand even more that it is, in fact, the mother and handmaiden of what we call genius.

EXAMPLES

Those who have watched Mike Singletary (perennial All-Pro, two-time NFL Defensive Player of the Year, and member of the Super Bowl XXV Dream Team) "play" — and have observed his wide-eyed intensity and his churning, crunching *samurai* hits — are usually surprised when they meet him. He is not an imposing hulk. He is barely six feet tall and weighs, maybe, 220. Whence the greatness? *Discipline.* Mike Singletary is as disciplined a student of the game as any who have ever played it. In his biography, *Calling the Shots*, he says that in watching game films he will often run a single play fifty to sixty times, and that it takes him three hours to watch half a football game, which is only twenty to thirty plays![1] Because he watches every player, because he mentally knows the opposition's tendency — given the down, distance, hashmark, and time remaining, because he reads the opposition's mind through their stances, he is often moving toward the ball's preplanned destination before the play develops. Mike Singletary's legendary success is testimony to his remarkably disciplined life.

We are accustomed to thinking of Ernest Hemingway as a boozy, undisciplined genius who got through a quart of whiskey a day for the last twenty years of his life but nevertheless had the muse upon him. He was indeed an alcoholic driven by complex passions.[2] But when it came to writing, he was the quintessence of discipline! His early writing was characterized by obsessive literary perfectionism as he labored to develop his economy of style, spending hours polishing a sentence, or searching for the *mot juste*—the right word. It is a well-known fact that he rewrote the conclusion to his novel *A Farewell to Arms* seventeen times in an effort to get it right. This is characteristic of great writers. Dylan Thomas made over two hundred handwritten(!) manuscript versions of his poem "Fern Hill."[3] Even toward the end, when Hemingway was reaping the ravages of his lifestyle, while writing at his Finca Vigia in Cuba he daily stood before an improvised desk in oversized loafers on yellow tiles from 6:30 A.M. until noon every day, carefully marking his production for the day on a chart. His average was only two pages — five hundred words.[4] It was discipline, Ernest Hemingway's massive literary discipline, which transformed the way his fellow Americans, and people throughout the English-speaking world, expressed themselves.

Michelangelo's, da Vinci's, and Tintoretto's multitudes of sketches, the *quantitative* discipline of their work, prepared the way for the cosmic *quality* of their work. We wonder at the anatomical perfection of a da Vinci painting. But we forget that Leonardo da Vinci on one occasion drew a thousand hands.[5] In the last century Matisse explained his own mastery, remarking that the difficulty with many who wanted to be artists is that they spend their time chasing models rather than painting them.[6] Again the discipline factor!

In our own time Winston Churchill has been rightly proclaimed the speaker of the century, and few who have heard his eloquent speeches would disagree. Still fewer would suspect he was anything but a "natural." But the truth is, Churchill had a distracting lisp which made him the butt of many jokes and resulted in his inability to be spontaneous in public speaking. Yet he became famous for his speeches and his seemingly impromptu remarks.

Actually, Churchill wrote everything out and practiced it! He even choreographed the pauses and pretended fumblings for the right phrase. The margins of his manuscripts carried notes anticipating the "cheers," "hear, hears," "prolonged cheering," and even "standing ovation." This done, he practiced endlessly in front of mirrors, fashioning his retorts and facial expressions. F. E. Smith said, "Winston has spent the best years of his life writing impromptu speeches."[7] A natural? Perhaps. A naturally disciplined hard-working man!

And so it goes, whatever the area of life.

Thomas Edison came up with the incandescent light after a thousand failures.

Jascha Heifitz, the greatest violinist of this century, began playing the violin at the age of three and early began to practice four hours a day until his death at age seventy-five — when he had long been the greatest in the world — some 102,000 hours of practice. He no doubt gave his own "Hear, hear!" to Paderewski's response to a woman's fawning remarks about his genius: "Madame, before I was a genius, I was a drudge."

We will never get anywhere in life without discipline, be it in the arts, business, athletics, or academics. This is doubly so in spiritual matters. In other areas we may be able to claim some innate advantage. An athlete may be born with a strong body, a musician with perfect pitch, or an artist with an eye for perspective. But none of us can claim an innate spiritual advantage. In reality, we are all equally *disadvantaged*. None of us naturally seeks after God, none is inherently righteous, none instinctively does good (cf. Romans 3:9-18). Therefore, as children of grace, our spiritual discipline is everything — everything!

I repeat . . . *discipline is everything!*

PAUL ON DISCIPLINE

This being so, the statement from Paul to Timothy regarding spiritual discipline in 1 Timothy 4:7 — "train yourself to be godly" — takes on not only transcending importance, but personal urgency. There are other passages which teach discipline, but this is the great classic text of Scripture. The word "train" comes from the word *gumnos*, which means "naked" and is the word from which we derive our English word *gymnasium*. In traditional Greek athletic contests, the participants competed without clothing, so as not to be encumbered. Therefore, the word "train" originally carried the literal meaning, "to exercise naked."[8] By New Testament times it referred to exercise and training in general. But even then it was, and is, a word with the smell of the gym in it — the sweat of a good workout. "Gymnasticize (exercise, work out, train) yourself for the purpose of godliness" conveys the feel of what Paul is saying.

SPIRITUAL SWEAT

In a word, he is calling for some *spiritual sweat*! Just as the athletes discarded everything and competed *gumnos* — free from everything that could possibly burden them — so we must get rid of every encumbrance, every association, habit, and tendency which impedes godliness. If we are to excel, we must strip ourselves to a lean, spiritual nakedness. The writer of Hebrews explains it like this: "Therefore, since we are surrounded by such a great cloud of witnesses, let us throw off everything that hinders and the sin that so easily entangles, and let us run with perseverance the race marked out for us" (Hebrews 12:1). Men, we will never get anywhere spiritually without a conscious divestment of the things that are holding us back. What things are weighing you down? The call to discipline demands that you throw it off. Are you man enough?

The call to train ourselves for godliness also suggests directing all of our energy toward godliness. Paul pictures this elsewhere: "Everyone who competes in the games goes into strict training. . . . Therefore I do not run like a man running aimlessly; I do not fight like a man beating the air. No, I beat my body and make it my slave" (1 Corinthians 9:25-27). Intense, energetic sweat! We should singularly note that a sentence later in the context of Paul's command to "train yourself to be godly," he comments on the command and the intervening words, saying "for this we labor and strive." "Labor" means "strenuous toil," and "strive" is the Greek word from which we get "agonize." Toil and agony are called for if one is to be godly.

When one seriously trains, he willingly undergoes hours of discipline and even pain so as to win the prize — running 10,000 miles to run 100 yards at one's best. The successful Christian life is a sweaty affair!

No manliness no maturity! No discipline no discipleship! No sweat no sainthood!

WHY THE DISCIPLINES?

Understanding this, we now get down to the reasons for this book, which are two.

First, in today's world and Church, disciplined Christian lives are the exception, not the rule. This goes for men, women, *and* the professional clergy. We cannot excuse ourselves by saying this has always been the case. It has not! As to why this is so, several common-sense reasons could be tendered, such as poor teaching or individual sloth. But underlying much of the conscious rejection of spiritual discipline is the fear of legalism. For many, spiritual discipline means putting oneself back under the Law with a series of Draconian rules which no one can live up to — and which spawn frustration and spiritual death.

But nothing could be farther from the truth if you understand what discipline and legalism are. The difference is one of *motivation*: legalism is self-centered; discipline is God-centered. The legalistic heart says, "I will do this thing to gain merit with God." The disciplined heart says, "I will do this thing because I love God and want to please Him." There is an infinite difference between the motivation of legalism and discipline! Paul knew this implicitly and fought the legalists bare-knuckled all the way across Asia Minor, never giving an inch. And now he shouts to us, "Train [discipline] yourself to be godly"! If we confuse legalism and discipline, we do so to our soul's peril.

The second reason for this book is that men are so much less spiritually inclined and spiritually disciplined than women. A recent study conducted in the United Methodist Church reveals that 85 percent of the subscribers to that denomination's premier devotional booklet, *The Upper Room*, are women. Moreover, the same statistics hold true for their other devotional booklet, *Alive Now*, which has a 75 percent female readership.[9] This is corroborated by the fact that the overwhelming majority of books purchased in Christian bookstores are bought by women.[10] Women simply read more Christian literature!

It is also true that far more women are concerned about the spiritual welfare of their mates than vice versa. The magazine *Today's Christian Woman* has found that articles focusing on the spiritual development of husbands have garnered the highest readership.[11] All this is sustained by hard statistics. A Gallup Poll conducted in June 1990 revealed that 71 percent of the women surveyed believed religion can answer today's problems, while only 55 percent of the men agreed.[12] The typical church service has 59 percent females versus 41 percent male attenders.[13] Furthermore, married women who attend church without their husbands outnumber by four to one the men attending without their wives.[14]

Why? Certainly the pervasive American male credo of self-sufficiency and individualism contributes. Some of this may also be due to the male avoidance of anything relational (which, of course, Christianity is!). But we do not concede that women are simply more spiritual by nature. The parade of great saints (male and female) down through the centuries, as well as spiritually exemplary men in some of our churches today, clearly refutes this idea. But the fact remains that men today need far more help in building spiritual discipline than women.

Men, what I am going to say in this book comes straight from the heart and my long study of God's Word — man to man. In writing this I have imagined my own grown sons sitting across the table, coffee cups in hand, as I try to impart to them what I think about the essential disciplines of godliness. This book is eminently user-friendly. The Church in America needs real men, and we are the men!

COSMIC CALL

We cannot overemphasize the importance of this call to spiritual discipline. Listen to Paul again from 1 Timothy 4:7, 8: "Train yourself to be godly. For physical training is of some value, but godliness has value for all things, holding promise for both the present life and the life to come."

Whether or not we have disciplined ourselves will make a huge difference *in this life*. We are all members of one another, and we are each either elevated or depressed by the inner lives of one another. Some of us affect others like a joyous tide, lifting them upward, but some of us are like undertows to the Body of Christ. If you are married, the presence or lack of spiritual discipline can serve to sanctify or damn your children and grandchildren. Spiritual discipline, therefore, holds huge promise for this present life.

As for "the life to come," spiritual discipline builds the enduring architecture of one's soul on the foundation of Christ — gold, silver, and precious stones which will survive the fires of judgment and remain a monument to Christ for eternity (cf. 1 Corinthians 3:10-15).

Some may minimize the importance of spiritual discipline now, but no one will then! "[G]odliness has value for all things"! The disciplined Christian gives and gets the best of both worlds — the world now and the world to come.

The word *discipline* may raise the feeling of stultifying constraint in some minds — suggesting a claustrophobic, restricted life. Nothing could be farther from the truth! The obsessive, almost manic discipline of Mike Singletary liberates him to play like a wild man on the football field. Hemingway's *angst* over the right word freed him to leave a mark on the English language second only to Shakespeare. The billion sketches of the Renaissance greats set Michelangelo free to create the skies of the Sistine Chapel. Churchill's painstaking preparation freed him to give great "impromptu" speeches and brilliant ripostes. The disciplined drudgery of the musical greats released their genius. And, brothers in Christ, *spiritual discipline frees us from the gravity of this present age and allows us to soar with the saints and angels.*

Do we have the sweat in us? Will we enter the gymnasium of divine discipline? Will we strip away the things that hold us back? Will we discipline ourselves through the power of the Holy Spirit?

I invite you into God's Gym in the following chapters — to some sanctifying sweat — to some pain and great gain.

God is looking for a few good men!

Food for Thought

What is spiritual discipline, and why is it so important? What usually gets in our way (see Romans 3:9-18)? What can a lack of spiritual discipline do to your life?

Reflect on 1 Timothy 4:7, 8 ("train yourself to be godly"). What is the literal meaning of "train" here? Practically, step by step, what does this mean you should do?

What does Hebrews 12:1 say about this? What things are holding you back in your walk with God? Why are you hanging on to them?

Is there a cost to spiritual discipline? Check out 1 Corinthians 9:25-27. What could greater discipline cost you? Are you prepared to pay the price? Why or why not?

"No manliness no maturity! No discipline no discipleship! No sweat no sainthood!" True or not true? How do you feel, deep inside, about this challenge?

How does spiritual discipline differ from legalism? Which do you most often practice? Is a change needed? If so, how can you bring this about?

Application/Response

What did God speak to you about most specifically, most powerfully in this chapter? Talk to Him about it right now!

Think About It!

Can we really become disciplined men of God — a spiritual Mike Singletary or Winston Churchill? Aren't we just setting ourselves up for defeat? Answer this in your own words, without using evangelical clichés.

RELATIONSHIPS

2

DISCIPLINE OF PURITY

ONE NEED TURN on the television for only a few minutes to feel the heat of the oppressive sensuality of our day. Most of the oppression is crude. A boring trip around the TV channels at midday invariably reveals at least one couple wrapped in bed sheets and much sensual monotony. But the heat has become increasingly artful, especially if its purpose is to sell. The camera focuses close up, in black and white, on an intense, lusting male face, over which is superimposed an amber flame, which then becomes a glowing bottle of Calvin Klein's Obsession as the face intones its desire. Newer spots feature subtle cinematic images with prose from D. H. Lawrence — ". . . to know him, to gather him in . . ." — and Flaubert's Madame Bovary as she wanders around her illicit lover's bedroom.[1] The sticky steam of sensuality penetrates everything in our world!

But even with all this, many sensualists want more. Professor David A. J. Richard of New York University Law School, who advocates freedom for hardcore pornography, argues that "pornography can be seen as the unique medium of sexuality, a 'pornotopia' — a view of sensual delight in the erotic celebration of the body, a concept of easy freedom without consequences, a fantasy of timeless repetitive indulgence."[2] Pornotopia? Now there's a word! It sounds like a new section of Disneyland. Autotopia . . . Pornotopia . . . Fantasyland. "Absurd!" we think — and it is — but sadly, Richard's arguments are actually being given serious weight today. It is no wonder we live in a culture that sweats sensuality from its pores!

And the Church has not escaped, for many in today's Church have wilted under the heat. Recently *Leadership Magazine* commissioned a poll of a thousand pastors. The pastors indicated that 12 percent of them had committed adultery while in the ministry — one out of eight pastors! — and 23 percent had done something they considered sexually inappropriate.[3] *Christianity Today* surveyed a thousand of its subscribers who were *not* pastors and found the figure to be nearly double, with 23 percent saying they had had extramarital intercourse and 45 percent indicating they had done something they themselves deemed sexually inappropriate.[4] One in four Christian men are unfaithful, and nearly one half have behaved unbecomingly! Shocking statistics! Especially when we remember that *Christianity Today* readers tend to be college-educated church leaders, elders, deacons, Sunday school superintendents, and teachers. If this is so for the Church's leadership, how much more for the average member of the congregation? Only God knows!

This leads us to an inescapable conclusion: The contemporary evangelical Church, broadly considered, is "Corinthian" to the core. It is being stewed in the molten juices of its own sensuality so that it is:

- No wonder the Church has lost its grip on holiness.
- No wonder it is so slow to discipline its members.
- No wonder it is dismissed by the world as irrelevant.
- No wonder so many of its children reject it.
- No wonder it has lost its power in many places — and that Islam and other false religions are making so many converts.

Sensuality is easily the biggest obstacle to godliness among men today and is wreaking havoc in the Church. Godliness and sensuality are mutually exclusive, and those in the grasp of sensuality can never rise to godliness while in its sweaty grip. If we are to "discipline [ourselves] for the purpose of godliness" (1 Timothy 4:7, NASB), we must begin with the discipline of purity. There has to be some holy heat, some holy sweat!

LESSONS FROM A FALLEN KING

Where are we to turn for help? The most instructive example in all of God's Word is the experience of King David as it is told in 2 Samuel 11.

Life at the Top

As the account begins, David is at the summit of his brilliant career — as high as any man in Biblical history. From childhood he had been a passionate lover of God and possessed of an immense integrity of soul, as attested by Samuel's words when he anointed him as king: "Man looks at the outward appearance, but the Lord looks at the heart" (1 Samuel 16:7). God liked what He saw. God liked David's heart!

His was a brave heart, as was evidenced when he met Goliath and returned the giant's fearsome rhetoric with some spine-tingling words of his own — then charged full-speed into battle, nailing Goliath right between the headlights (1 Samuel 17:45-49).

David had an archetypal sanguine personality brimming with joy, enthusiasm, and confidence and overflowing with irresistible charisma. He was the poet — the sweet Psalmist of Israel — so in touch with God and himself that his Psalms pluck the heartstrings of man even today. Under his leadership all Israel had been united. David hardly seemed a candidate for moral disaster. But the king was vulnerable, for there were definite flaws in his conduct which left him open to tragedy.

Desensitization

Second Samuel 5, which records David's initial assumption of power in Jerusalem, mentions almost as an aside that "after he left Hebron, David took more concubines and wives in Jerusalem" (v. 13). We must note, and note well, that David's taking additional wives was *sin*! Deuteronomy 17, which set down the standards for Hebrew kings, commanded that they refrain from three things: 1) acquiring many horses, 2) taking many wives, and 3) accumulating much silver and gold (cf. vv. 14-17). David did fine on one and three, but he completely failed on number two by willfully collecting a considerable harem.

We must understand that a progressive desensitization to sin and a consequent inner descent from holiness had taken root in David's life. David's collection of wives, though it was "legal" and not considered adultery in the culture of the day, was nevertheless sin. King David's sensual indulgence desensitized him to God's holy call in his life, as well as to the danger and consequences of falling. In short, David's embrace of socially permitted sensuality desensitized him to God's call and made him easy prey for the fatal sin of his life.

Men, it is the "legal" sensualities, the culturally acceptable indulgences, which will take us down. The long hours of indiscriminate TV watching, which is not only culturally cachet but is expected of the American male, is a massive culprit of desensitization. The expected male talk — double entendre, coarse humor, laughter at things which ought to make us blush — is another deadly agent. Acceptable sensualities have insidiously softened Christian men, as statistics well attest. A man who succumbs to desensitization of the "legal" sensualities is primed for a fall.

Relaxation

The second flaw in David's conduct which opened him to disaster was his relaxation from the rigors and discipline which had been part of his active life. David was at midlife, about fifty years old, and his military campaigns had been so successful, it was not necessary for him to personally go off to war. He rightly gave the "mopping up" job to his capable general, Joab — and then relaxed. The problem was, his relaxation extended to his moral life. It is hard to maintain inner discipline when you are relaxing in this way. David was imminently vulnerable.

David did not suspect anything unusual was going to happen on that fatal spring day. He did not get up and say, "My, what a beautiful day. I think I will commit adultery today!" May this lesson not be wasted on us, men. Just when we think we are the safest, when we feel no need to keep our guard up, to work on our inner integrity, to discipline ourselves for godliness — temptation will come!

Fixation

> In the spring, at the time when kings go off to war, David sent Joab out with the king's men and the whole Israelite army. They destroyed the Ammonites and besieged Rabbah. But David remained in Jerusalem. One evening David got up from his bed and walked around on the roof of the palace. From the roof he saw a woman bathing. The woman was very beautiful, and David sent someone to find out about her. The man said, "Isn't this Bathsheba, the daughter of Eliam and the wife of Uriah the Hittite?" (2 Samuel 11:1-3)

It had been a warm day, and evening was falling. The king strode out on the rooftop for some cool air and a look at his city at dusk. As he gazed, his eye caught the form of an unusually beautiful woman who was bathing without modesty. As to how beautiful she was, the Hebrew is explicit: the woman was "beautiful of appearance, very" (v. 2). She was young, in the flower of life, and the evening shadows made her even more enticing. The king looked at her . . . And he continued to look. After the first glance David should have turned the other way and retired to his chamber, but he did not. His *look* became a sinful *stare* and then a burning libidinous sweaty *leer*. In that moment David, who had been a man after God's own heart, became a dirty, leering old man. A lustful fixation came over him that would not be denied.

Dietrich Bonhoeffer made the observation that when lust takes control, "At this moment God . . . loses all reality. . . . Satan does not fill us with hatred of God, but with forgetfulness of God."⁵ What a world of wisdom there is in this statement! When we are in the grip of lust, the reality of God fades. The longer King David leered, the less real God became to him. Not only was his awareness of God diminished, but David lost awareness of who he himself was — his holy call, his frailty, and the certain consequences of sin. This is what lust does! It has done it millions of times. God disappears to lust-glazed eyes.

Men, the truth demands some serious questions: Has God faded from view? Did you once see Him in bright hues, but now His memory is blurred like an old sepia photograph? Do you have an illicit fixation which has become all you can see? Is the most real thing in your life your desire? If so, you are in deep trouble. Some decisive steps are necessary, as we shall see.

Rationalization

From deadly fixation, King David descended to the next level down, which is rationalization. When his intent became apparent to his servants, one tried to dissuade him, saying, "Isn't this Bathsheba, the daughter of Eliam and the wife of Uriah the Hittite?" But David would not be rebuffed. Some massive rationalization took place in David's mind, perhaps very much as J. Allan Peterson has suggested in *The Myth of the Greener Grass*:

> Uriah is a great soldier but he's probably not much of a husband or a lover — years older than she is — and he'll be away for a long time. This girl needs a little comfort in her loneliness. This is one way I can help her. No one will get hurt. I do not mean anything wrong by it. This is not lust — I have known that many times. This is love. This is not the same as finding a prostitute on the street. God knows that. And to the servant, "Bring her to me."⁶

The mind controlled by lust has an infinite capacity for rationalization.

- "How can something that has brought such enjoyment be wrong?"
- "God's will for me is to be happy; certainly He would not deny me anything which is essential to my happiness — and this is it!"
- "The question here is one of love — I'm acting in love, the highest love."
- "My marriage was never God's will in the first place."
- "You Christians and your narrow judgmental attitudes make me sick. You are judging me. You are a greater sinner than I'll ever be!"

Degeneration (Adultery, Lies, Murder)

David's progressive *desensitization, relaxation, fixation*, and *rationalization* set him up for one of the greatest falls in history — and his *degeneration*. "Then David sent messengers to get her. She came to him, and he slept with her. (She had purified herself from her uncleanness.) Then she went back home. The woman conceived and sent word to David, saying, 'I am pregnant'" (vv. 4, 5). David was unaware he had stepped off the precipice and was falling, and that reality would soon arrive — the bottom was coming up fast.

We are all familiar with David's despicable behavior as he became a calculating liar and murderer in arranging Uriah's death to cover his sin with Bathsheba. Suffice it to say that at this time in the king's life, Uriah was a better man drunk than David was sober (v. 13)!

A year later David would repent under the withering accusation of the prophet Nathan. But the miserable consequences could not be undone. As has often been pointed out:

- It was the breaking of the *Tenth* Commandment (coveting his neighbor's wife) that led David to commit adultery, thus breaking the *Seventh* Commandment.
- Then, in order to steal his neighbor's wife (thereby breaking the *Eighth* Commandment), he committed murder and broke the *Sixth* Commandment.
- He broke the *Ninth* Commandment by bearing false witness against his brother.
- This all brought dishonor to his parents and thus broke the *Fifth* Commandment.

In this way he broke all of the Ten Commandments that relate to loving one's neighbor as oneself (Commandments Five through Ten). And in doing so, he dishonored God as well, breaking, in effect, the first four Commandments.[7]

David's reign went downhill from there on, despite his laudable repentance:

- His baby died.
- His beautiful daughter, Tamar, was raped by her half-brother Amnon.
- Amnon was murdered by Tamar's full-brother Absalom.
- Absalom came to so hate his father David for his moral turpitude that he led a rebellion under the tutelage of Bathsheba's resentful grandfather, Ahithophel.
- David's reign lost the smile of God. His throne never regained its former stability.

Men, we must understand that David would never have given more than a fleeting glance to Bathsheba if he could have seen the shattering results. I believe with all my heart that few, if any, would ever stray from God's Word if they could see what would follow.

The record of the tragic fall of King David is God-given and should be taken seriously by the Church in this "Corinthian age" as a warning regarding the pathology of the human factors that lead to a moral fall:

- The *desensitization* which happens through the conventional sensualities of culture.
- The deadly syndrome which comes through moral *relaxation* of discipline.
- The blinding effects of sensual *fixation*.
- And the *rationalization* of those in the grip of lust.

In David's case the cycle included *adultery*, *lying*, *murder*, *familial degeneration*, and *national decline*. The pathology is clear, and so are the horrible effects of sensuality. Both are meant not only to instruct us, but to frighten us — to scare the sensuality right out of us!

THE WILL OF GOD: PURITY

Sometimes people under the Christian umbrella simply do not buy what I am saying in regard to purity. They consider such teaching to be Victorian and puritanical. Victorian it is not. Puritanical it gloriously is — for it is supremely Biblical. In answering such people, I take them to the most explicit call for sexual purity I know, 1 Thessalonians 4:3-8:

> It is God's will that you should be holy; that you should avoid sexual immorality; that each of you should learn to control his own body in a way that is holy and honorable, not in passionate lust like the heathen, who do not know God; and that in this matter no one should wrong his brother or take advantage of him. The Lord will punish men for all such sins, as we have already told you and warned you. For God did not call us to be impure, but to live a holy life. Therefore, he who rejects this instruction does not reject man but God, who gives you his Holy Spirit.

If the reading of this passage is not convincing enough concerning the Biblical ethic, we must understand that it is based on Leviticus 19:2, where God says, "Be holy because I, the Lord your God, am holy" — a command which is given in the context of warnings against sexual deviation. I also want to point out that in 1 Thessalonians we are called to avoid sexual immorality and are three times called to be "holy." To reject this is to sin against the Holy Spirit — the living presence of God — as the Thessalonians passage makes so clear.

As the New Testament scholar Leon Morris has written:

> The man who carries on an act of impurity is not simply breaking a human code, nor even sinning against the God who at some time in the past gave him the gift of the Spirit. He is sinning against the God who is present at that moment, against One who continually gives the Spirit. The impure act is an act of despite against God's good gift at the very moment it is being proffered. . . . This sin is seen in its true light only when it is seen as a preference for impurity rather than a Spirit who is holy.[8]

Therefore, for a professed Christian to reject this teaching regarding sexual purity is to reject God, and this may indicate a false faith!

THE DISCIPLINE OF PURITY

Men, if we are Christians, it is imperative that we live pure, godly lives in the midst of our Corinthian, pornotopian culture. We must live above the horrifying statistics or the Church will become increasingly irrelevant and powerless, and our children will leave it. The Church can have no power apart from purity.

This demands that we live out Paul's dictum: "train yourself to be godly" — holy sweat!

Accountability

An important place to begin our training is with the discipline of accountability. This to be done with someone who will regularly hold you accountable for your moral life, asking you hard questions. If you are married, ideally you should use your spouse, but I also recommend another man, one who will give you no quarter in sensual matters. You need someone of the same gender who will understand your sensuality from the inside out — someone you can be completely honest with, to whom you can confess temptations and attractions. You need someone who will help you toe the mark and keep your soul faithful to God. Mutual accountability is the ideal. In this connection I think of a certain salesman who regularly maintains accountability via phone contact with other Christian salesmen, and even works at scheduling trips to cities at the same time they will be there.

Prayer

Along with this comes the discipline of prayer (more on this in Chapter 8). Pray daily and specifically for your own purity. I am amazed that so few men who are concerned about their lives pray about it. Enlist the prayers of your spouse and friends, and pray for others in this respect. Do not wait to be asked. Pray for the purity of your friends too. They need it, and so do you!

Memorization

Next, fill yourself with God's Word through the discipline of memorization. Our Lord set the example *par excellence* in rebuffing Satan's temptations with four precise quotations from the Old Testament Scriptures (cf. Matthew 4:1-11). The Psalmist said, "How can a young man keep his way pure? By living according to your word" (119:9). And, "I have hidden your word in my heart that I might not sin against you" (119:11). Of course, he was referring to all of God's Word, not just the passages which deal with sensuality. Nevertheless, I have seen the disciplined memorization of 1 Thessalonians 4:3-8 change a man's life. (Other helpful passages include Job 31:1, Proverbs 6:27, Mark 9:42ff., Ephesians 5:3-7, and 2 Timothy 2:22, some of which are commented upon below.)

Mind

The discipline of the mind is, of course, the greatest of challenges (and will be discussed more fully in Chapter 6). And Scripture regularly presents its discipline as a discipline of the eyes. Men, it is impossible for you to maintain a pure mind if you are a television-watching "couch potato." In one week you will watch more murders, adulteries, and perversions than our grandfathers read about in their entire lives.

Here is where the most radical action is necessary. Jesus said, "And if your eye causes you to sin, pluck it out. It is better for you to enter the kingdom of God with one eye than have two eyes and be thrown into hell" (Mark 9:47). No man who allows the rottenness of HBO, R-rated videos, and the various soft-core pornography magazines to flow through his house and mind will escape sensuality!

Job gave us wisdom for our day: "I made a covenant with my eyes not to look lustfully at a girl" (Job 31:1). How do you think Job would live in our culture today? He understood the wisdom of Proverbs: "Can a man scoop fire into his lap without his clothes being burned?" (Proverbs 6:27). Men, Job's covenant forbids a second look. It means treating all women with dignity — looking at them respectfully. If their dress or demeanor is distracting, look them in the eyes, and nowhere else, and get away as quickly as you can!

The mind also encompasses the tongue (see Chapter 11 of this book), for as Jesus also said, "For out of the overflow of the heart the mouth speaks" (Matthew 12:34). Paul is more specific: "But among you there must not be even a hint of sexual immorality, or of any kind of impurity, or of greed, because these are improper for God's holy people. Nor should there be obscenity, foolish talk or coarse joking, which are out of place, but rather thanksgiving" (Ephesians 5:3, 4). There must be no sexual humor, urbane vulgarities, and coarseness, as so many Christians are so prone to do to prove they are not "out of it."

Hedges[9]

Men, put disciplined hedges around your life — especially if you work with women. Refrain from verbal intimacy with women other than your spouse. Do not bare your heart to another woman, or pour forth your troubles to her. Intimacy is a great need in most people's lives — and talking about personal matters, especially one's problems, can fill another's need for intimacy, awakening a desire for more. Many affairs begin in just this way.

On the practical level, do not touch. Do not treat women with the casual affection you extend to the females in your family. How many tragedies have begun with brotherly or fatherly touches and then sympathetic shoulders. You may even have to run the risk of being wrongly considered "distant" or "cold" by some women.

Whenever you dine or travel with a woman, make it a threesome. This may be awkward, but it will afford an opportunity to explain your rationale, which, more often than not, will incur respect rather than reproach. Many women business associates will even feel more comfortable dealing with you.

Never flirt — even in jest. Flirtation is intrinsically flattering. You may think you are being cute, but it often arouses unrequited desires in another.

Reality

Be real about your sexuality. Do not succumb to vain gnostic prattle about your being a Spirit-filled Christian who would "never do such a thing!" I well remember a man who indignantly thundered that he was beyond such sin. He fell within months! Face the truth — King David fell, and so can you!

Divine Awareness

Lastly, there is the discipline of divine awareness. This is what sustained Joseph through the temptations of Potiphar's wife. "How then could I do such a wicked thing," he said, "and sin against God?" (Genesis 39:9) — and he fled. "Flee the evil desires of youth, and pursue righteousness, faith, love and peace, along with those who call on the Lord out of a pure heart" (2 Timothy 2:22).

Men, the heat of our culture oppresses us with its obsessions and pornotopias. Many in the Church have wilted. The statistics tell it all. In order not to become part of those statistics, there has to be some disciplined sweat. Are we men enough? Are we men of God? I pray we are!

Food for Thought

"The contemporary evangelical Church, broadly considered, is 'Corinthian' to the core. It is being stewed in the molten juices of its own sensuality." Do you agree or disagree? Concerning your own church? Concerning your own personal life?

"At this moment [of lust] God . . . loses all reality. . . . Satan does not fill us with hatred of God, but with forgetfulness of God" (Dietrich Bonhoeffer). Have you found this true in your own battles with temptation? What is the most effective way to prevent moral lapses?

Is 1 Thessalonians 4:3-8 too narrow to consider as binding on Christian men today? Why or why not? If not, how can we put this passage to work so we will be victorious in our fight for purity?

What does *God's* holiness have to do with *our* holiness (see Leviticus 19:2)?

Considering the prevalent immorality of our culture, how can we possibly hope to keep our thoughts and behavior pure?

Is the admonition to maintain "hedges" in our relationships with the women in our lives really necessary? Isn't this a putdown of women? Of ourselves?

Application/Response

What did God speak to you about most specifically, most powerfully in this chapter? Talk to Him about it right now!

Think About It!

List at least half a dozen specific, practical applications concerning sexual morality from David's experience in 2 Samuel 11.

3

DISCIPLINE OF MARRIAGE

I REGULARLY HAVE the best view at Christian weddings, as I stand about three feet from the joyous couple. Their skin glows with amber luminosity from the flickering candles behind me. I see everything: the moist eyes, the trembling hands, the surreptitious wink, their mutual earnestness of soul. I hear the words their parents said before them: ". . . for better, for worse; for richer, for poorer; in sickness and in health . . ." They are submitting to the larger logics of life, to the solidarity of the Christian community, to "otherness," to life itself.

Sometimes in my enjoyment I let it all blur for a moment and imagine the ultimate wedding where Christ will officially take us to Himself, and then I blink back to the living parable before me. How will the couple fare over the years? Will she reverence her husband? Will he love his beautiful bride as Christ loved the Church and gave Himself for her? Will he love her with an elevating, sanctifying love? Will he love her as he loves himself? I pray it will be so.

It was and is so in the life of Robertson McQuilkin, the beloved former president of Columbia Bible College, and his wife, Muriel, who suffers from the advanced ravages of Alzheimer's disease. In March 1990 Dr. McQuilkin announced his resignation in a letter with these words:

> My dear wife, Muriel, has been in failing mental health for about eight years. So far I have been able to carry both her ever-growing needs and my leadership responsibilities at CBC. But recently it has become apparent that Muriel is contented most of the time she is with me and almost none of the time I am away from her. It is not just "discontent." She is filled with fear — even terror — that she has lost me and always goes in search of me when I leave home. Then she may be full of anger when she cannot get to me. So it is clear to me that she needs me now, full-time.

Perhaps it would help you to understand if I shared with you what I shared at the time of the announcement of my resignation in chapel. The decision was made, in a way, 42 years ago when I promised to care for Muriel "in sickness and in health . . . till death do us part." So, as I told the students and faculty, as a man of my word, integrity has something to do with it. But so does fairness. She has cared for me fully and sacrificially all these years; if I cared for her for the next 40 years I would not be out of debt. Duty, however, can be grim and stoic. But there is more; I love Muriel. She is a delight to me — her childlike dependence and confidence in me, her warm love, occasional flashes of that wit I used to relish so, her happy spirit and tough resilience in the face of her continual distressing frustration. I do not *have* to care for her, I *get* to! It is a high honor to care for so wonderful a person.

The following month Barbara and I had a brief visit with the McQuilkins and witnessed Dr. McQuilkin's gentle, loving way with his dear wife, who understood little of what was going on. The memory of our visit is one of lingering beauty.

Such beautiful Christlike love did not just happen! It came from the inner resolve of a young husband who had determined forty-two years before to live under the authority of God's directives regarding how a godly man must love his wife — as it is spelled out in Ephesians 5. They are directives every Christian man ought to be familiar with, must understand, and, I think, even commit to memory — as I myself have. They are the foundational discipline of marriage — the bases for holy matrimonial sweat.

To examine the godly man's responsibility, we must fix in our minds the grand truth at the end of Ephesians 5, verse 31, where Paul quotes Genesis 2:24: when a man leaves his father and mother and is united to his wife, "the two will become one flesh." He then adds in verse 32, "This is a profound mystery — but I am talking about Christ and the church." There is an astounding unity in marriage! The assertion that men and women become "one flesh" indicates something of the psycho-spiritual depth of marriage — an exchange of soul.

Marriage *ideally* produces two people who are as much the same person as two people can be! Christians in marriage have the *same* Lord, the *same* family, the *same* children, the *same* future, and the *same* ultimate destiny — an astounding unity. An amazing bonding took place the moment I saw my newborn children and held them in my arms. They are from my flesh. I am close to my children, interwoven with them. Yet, I am not one flesh with them. I am one flesh only with my wife. This, in my opinion, is why old couples possessing extraordinarily different appearances yet often look so much alike — they are "one flesh." There has been an exchange of soul — a mutual appropriation of each other's lives.

This is, indeed, a mystery — which partially illustrates the even deeper marital union of Christ and the Church. And this is why the text often uses descriptive language when speaking of Christ and husbands and the Church and wives at the same time. We must keep the mysterious nature of our union constantly before us if we are to understand the disciplines of marital love as they unfold — the discipline of *sacrificial* love, of *sanctifying* love, and of *self-love.*

SACRIFICIAL LOVE

The opening charge in Ephesians 5 is a clear call to radical, sacrificial love: "Husbands, love your wives, just as Christ loved the church and gave himself up for her" (v. 25). This call to marital love was a bare-knuckled swing at the domestic commitment (or lack of same) of the men of the day — just as it is today. Taken seriously, the naked form of these words, "love your wives, just as Christ loved the church and gave himself up for her," is staggering! And honestly received, the punch it delivers flattens many Christian men . . . because they fall so short!

Death

The reason the punch hurts is because it is a naked call to *love with a willingness to sacrifice, even unto death*. Recognizing this, Mike Mason, author of the classic *The Mystery of Marriage*, says pointedly that marital love is like death — it wants all of us. I agree. If you do not understand this, you do not know what marital love is. It claims everything. Mason goes on by likening marital love to a shark: "And who has not been frightened almost to death by love's dark shadow gliding swift and huge as an interstellar shark, like a swimming mountain, through the deepest waters of our being, through depths we never knew we had?"[1]

The realization of what this call means may at first be frightening, but it is also beautiful, because a man who embraces such a love will experience the grace of death to self. Marriage is a call to die, and a man who does not die for his wife does not come close to the love to which he is called. Christian marriage vows are the inception of a lifelong practice of death, of *giving over not only all you have, but all you are.*

Is this a grim gallows call? Not at all! It is no more grim than dying to self and following Christ. In fact, those who lovingly die for their wives are those who know the most joy, have the most fulfilling marriages, and experience the most love. Christ's call to Christian husbands is not a call to be doormats, but to die. As we shall see, this can mean a death to our rights, our time, our perceived pleasures — all liberating deaths. This is a truly male thing, a masculine thing — for it takes a strong man to die.

Suffering

When Christ "gave himself up" for us, He not only died, He suffered. And His suffering was not only the cross, but it was and is suffering which comes from identification with His bride, the Church. This is why Saul, who was fanatically persecuting the Church, suddenly heard Jesus cry, "Saul, Saul, why do you persecute me?" (Acts 9:4). Christ suffers with His bride, and husbands ought to suffer with and for theirs.

Men, when you properly hitch your life to another, you are in for a wild ride with huge ups and downs. Just as when you really love God you will undergo difficulties foreign to an unloving heart, so it is in marriage. You will share her experienced injustices, cruelties, and disappointments. You will experience her upsets, insecurities, and despairs. But, of course, you will also know an index of joys beyond the range of the unloving. You will ride through some dark valleys, but you will also soar among the stars!

Intercession

On the evening Christ gave Himself up for us, John 17 tells us, He prayed in succession for Himself, for His twelve disciples, and for all of us who would later believe. When He finished praying for His future bride, He went to the cross. Then came His *death*, His *resurrection*, His *ascension*, and His *enthronement* at the right hand of the Father, where He constantly makes *intercession* for us. Thus we understand that giving ourselves for our brides involves prayerful intercession. Men, do you pray for your wives with something more than, "Bless good old Margaret in all she does"? If not, you are sinning against her and against God. Most Christian men who claim to love their wives never offer more than a perfunctory nod to their wives' needs before God. Men, you ought to have a list of her needs, spoken and unspoken, which you passionately hold up to God out of love for her. Praying is the marital work of a Christian husband!

The bare-knuckle command is, "Husbands, love your wives, just as Christ loved the church and gave himself up for her." Men, we are divinely called to *die* for our brides, to take on her *sufferings* as our own, and to make *intercession* for her.

SANCTIFYING LOVE

Marriage under the Lordship of Christ is a mutually sanctifying relationship — it moves us toward holiness. Most of us, by the time we get married, are like a well-furnished home — and a lot of furniture needs to be tossed out to make room for the other person. Marriage helps empty those rooms. Genuine marital love reveals rooms full of selfishness. As these rooms are cleared, one finds other rooms of self-centeredness. Beyond these are autonomy and self-will — an ongoing house cleaning. Marriage certainly did that for me. I had no idea how self-centered I was until I married! George Gilder, in his much-discussed book *Men and Marriage*, even argues that marriage is the one institution which tames the inveterate barbarianism of man.[2] Over the years a good marriage can change us for the better — almost beyond recognition. There is indeed a mutual sanctification in marriage.

But the emphasis in the Scriptures is on the responsibility of a husband's love for his wife: "to make her holy, cleansing her by the washing with water through the word, and to present her to himself as a radiant church, without stain or wrinkle or any other blemish, but holy and blameless" (vv. 26, 27). This is what Christ will do through our divine marriage to Him, for at His return the washed and regenerated Church will be presented to Him in absolute perfection. This is the sealing of the romance of the ages.

Meanwhile, these divine nuptials are a parable of what ought to be the loving husband's elevating effect on his wife. He is to be a man of the Word who lives a godly life, praying and sacrificing for his wife. His authentic spirituality is meant to buoy her onward and upward toward the image of Christ. The man who sanctifies his wife understands that this is his divinely ordained responsibility.

Men (ignoring for the moment our wives' spiritual responsibility to us), do you realize it is your responsibility to seek your wife's sanctification? Even more, honestly, do you accept it? Marriage will reveal something about her which you already know about yourself — that she is a sinner. Marriage reveals everything: her weaknesses, her worst inconsistencies, the things others never see. *Loving your spouse is not to love her as a saint, but as a sinner.* "If we love her for her saintliness, we do not love her at all,"[3] says Mason. You see your wife as you see yourself, and you love her as yourself. You realize your mutual need, and you delve into God's Word, to listen to it with your heart and try, by His grace, to live it out so that she will be encouraged by your life — and thus become an even more beautiful bride for Christ.

This brings up some hard questions: Is my wife more like Christ because she is married to me? Or is she like Christ in spite of me? Has she shrunk from His likeness because of me? Do I sanctify her or hold her back? Is she a better woman because she is married to me? Is she a better friend? A better mother?

Men, our call is clear: sanctifying love.

SELF-LOVE

Greek mythology tells of a beautiful youth who loved no one until the day he saw his own reflection in the water and fell in love with that reflection. He was so lovesick, he finally wasted away and died, and was turned into a flower that bears his name — *Narcissus*.[4] Actually, narcissistic self-love is not a pretty thing! We are repulsed by narcissism and carefully seek to avoid it.

But, incredibly, in Ephesians 5 we are called to a sublime self-love: "In this way, husbands ought to love their wives as their own bodies. He who loves his wife loves himself. After all, no one ever hated his own body, but he feeds and cares for it, just as Christ does the church — for we are members of his body" (vv. 28-30). This loving ourselves by loving our wives is based on the "one flesh" unity we have already talked about — the deep exchange of our souls in marriage which can even make us look alike. It is the love that Shakespeare's Lorenzo celebrates when he says to Jessica she will be placed in "my constant soul."[5] Our marital love is our constant soul!

To love our wives as our own bodies is a grand and great thing. It means granting her the same importance, the same value, "the same existential gravity that we take for granted in ourselves."[6] She becomes as real as we are to ourselves. *She is me.*

How do we love our wives as our own bodies? How do we care for her as we do for ourselves? The answer involves three incarnations.

The first is a *physical* incarnation. Dr. Robert Seizer, in his book *Mortal Lessons: Notes in the Art of Surgery*, tells of performing surgery to remove a tumor and of necessity severing a facial nerve, leaving a young woman's mouth permanently twisted in palsy. In Dr. Seizer's own words:

Her young husband is in the room. He stands on the opposite side of the bed, and together they seem to do well in the evening lamplight, isolated from me, private. Who are they, I ask myself, he and this wry-mouth I have made, who gaze at and touch each other so generously, greedily? The young woman speaks. "Will my mouth always be like this?" she asks. "Yes," I say, "it will. It is because the nerve was cut." She nods and is silent. But the young man smiles. "I like it," he says. "It is kind of cute." . . . Unmindful, he bends to kiss her crooked mouth, and I, so close, can see how he twists his own lips to accommodate to hers, to show her that their kiss still works.[7]

This is the way we must love. Her body is our body, her comfort our comfort, her adornment our adornment, her care our care.

A second way to love our wives as our own bodies is *emotional* incarnation. So many men make the emotional differences between men and women subject to degrading humor. They belittle the female disposition, as if male stoicism were superior. They realize the differences, but make no allowances for them and do not attempt to understand. No man can claim obedience to God and do this! It is a flat-sided masculinity which imagines that understanding another is a feminine trait. Actually such understanding of the complementary natures God gave man and woman is the mark of a fully developed, mature man.

Then, of course, there must be *social* incarnation. Erma Bombeck humorously suggests that some "Archie Bunkers" think their wives spend their day lugging power tools out to the sandbox for their kids to play with, or discarding one sock for every pair in the drawer.

Of course, women have many social settings: the home, the office, the classroom. But I remember a profitable incarnation I experienced when my wife visited her sister in Connecticut for a week, leaving me in charge of our four small children. I fixed the meals, changed thousands and thousands of diapers, fixed hurts, settled quarrels, gave baths, cleaned up catastrophes, and cleaned them up again. I was at work *before* I got up and *after* I went to bed. The experience so marked me that in my mind I invented a new kitchen, modeled after a car wash. The floors slope to a large drain in the middle of the room. A hose hangs on the wall, nozzle ready to spray things down after the meal. It was an incarnation I was not anxious to repeat again, but as my wife says, "It was *good* for you!"

Men, we are called to a divinely appointed self-love: to love our wives as our own bodies, to care for them as Christ does the Church. Loving our wives' bodies as our own demands a triple incarnation: physical, emotional, and social. We are to devote the same energy, time, and creativity to our wives as to ourselves. We are to cherish our constant souls. Envy the woman who is loved like this. Even more, envy the man who loves like this — for he is like Christ.

Men, what a challenge Ephesians 5 presents us — *sacrificial* love (love is like death!), *sanctifying* love (love that elevates), and *self-love* (loving your wife as much as you love your own body). If this calls for anything, it calls for some holy sweat. As Walter Trobisch said, "Marriage is not an achievement which is finished. It is a dynamic process between two people, a relation which is constantly being changed, which grows or dies."[8]

Men, the all-encompassing call to love our wives as Christ loved the Church demands specific disciplines.

COMMITMENT

We must begin with the discipline of commitment. I have grown tougher with the years in my demands on couples who want me to perform their wedding ceremonies. I tell them that wedding vows are a volitional commitment to love despite how one feels. I explain that it is rubbish to think one can break one's vows because one does not "feel" in love. I point out that the Scriptures call us to "put on love" (Colossians 3:14) — and despite the canard about such love being hypocritical, it is never hypocrisy to put on a Christian grace. I tell them that if there is the tiniest thought in the back of their minds that they can get out of the marriage if the other person is not all they expected, I will not perform the ceremony. The truth is, marriages which depend on being "in love" fall apart. Those which look back to the wild promises they vowed in the marriage ceremony are the ones who make it. There is no substitute for *covenant plus commitment*.

FIDELITY

When a man commits himself to love his wife "as Christ loved the church and gave himself up for her," he will ever be faithful to her. One thing the Church can count on is the fidelity of the Bridegroom. And this is the one thing a wife whose husband loves like Christ can rest on. Jeremy Taylor, the great seventeenth-century preacher, in his sermon "The Marriage Ring or the Mysteriousness and Duties of Marriage," gave this charge regarding fidelity:

> Above all . . . let him [the groom] preserve towards her an inviolable faith,
> and an unspotted chastity, for this is the marriage ring, it ties two hearts by
> an eternal band; it is like the cherubim's flaming sword set for the guard of
> paradise. . . . Chastity is the security of love, and preserves all the mysteri-

ousness like the secrets of a temple. Under this lock is deposited security of families, the union of affections, the repairer of accidental breaches.[9]

Men, our wives must be able to rest in the fact of our fidelity. Everything about us: our eyes . . . our language . . . our schedules . . . our passion must say to her, "I am, and will always be, faithful to you."

COMMUNICATION

Next is the discipline of communication. Recently the readers of a popular women's magazine were asked the question, "If you could change your husband, what would you change?"[10] The overwhelming consensus was they would like them to communicate better. They indicated that even more, they would like their husbands to *listen*. Eugene Peterson remarks:

> The stereotype is the husband buried in the morning newspaper at breakfast, preferring to read a news agency report of the latest scandal in a European government, the scores of yesterday's athletic contests, and the opinions of a couple of columnists whom he will never meet rather than listen to the voice of the person who has just shared his bed, poured his coffee, and fried his eggs, even though listening to that live voice promises love and hope, emotional depth and intellectual exploration far in excess of what he can gather informationally from *The New York Times*, *The Wall Street Journal*, and *The Christian Science Monitor* put together.[11]

Men, the discipline of communication demands that you set aside regular time to talk — and that you really do talk, and that you communicate more than facts, that you communicate feelings — that you learn to talk in metaphors and similes with phrases that begin, "I feel like . . ." And it means that you listen. The *Harvard Business Review* recommends that 65 percent of an executive's time should be spent listening.[12] How much more so the wise husband.

ELEVATION

Next, I strongly recommend the discipline of elevation. Winston Churchill once attended a formal banquet in London, where the dignitaries were asked the question, "If you could not be who you are, who would you like to be?" Naturally, everyone was curious as to what Churchill, who was seated next to his beloved Clemmie, would say. After all, Churchill could not be expected to say Julius Caesar or Napoleon. When it finally came Churchill's turn, the old man, the last respondent to the question, rose and gave his answer. "If I could not be who I am, I would most like to be" — and here he paused to take his wife's hand — "Lady Churchill's second husband."[13] The old boy made some points that night. But he also said it for everyone who has a good marriage.

A commitment to building up your wife is of greatest importance. Men, if you think what your wife does is less important than what you do, you are wrong, and you have big problems. Compliments on her kindness and her daily provisions should be commonplace, as should showing her respect by observing common courtesies.

DEFERENCE

Along with this, the discipline of deference must be carefully practiced. Many men never forego a planned pleasure for the sake of their wives. For some men, golf is synonymous to Dante's *Paradiso*, but the entrance to a department store is like the gates of Dante's Hell, bearing the inscription: "Abandon all hope all ye who enter here."[14] But if you love your wife, there must be times when you forsake the heavenly greens because you value her interests and simply love her.

TIME/ROMANCE

Lastly, I must mention the discipline of time and romance. Years ago, in the Midwest, a farmer and his wife were lying in bed during a storm when the funnel of a tornado suddenly lifted the roof right off the house and sucked their bed away with them still in it. The wife began to cry, and the farmer called to her that it was no time to cry. She called back that she was so happy, she could not help it — it was the first time they had been out together in twenty years!

In 1986 *Psychology Today* did a survey of 300 couples, asking them what keeps them together. One of the major "staying" factors was time spent together.[15] Make sure you maintain this priority. Your calendar reveals what is important to you, so write her calendar into yours. Schedule weekly times together that do not just "happen." Be creative. Date! Surprise her. Be extravagant.

Men, when was the last time you opened the door for her . . . said "I love you" . . . complimented her . . . wrote her a loving note . . . sent her flowers . . . "dated" her . . . gave her extraspecial attention?

> 'Tis not love's going hurts my days,
> But that it went in little ways.

— Edna St. Vincent Millay

Many other "disciplines" could be named, most of which are implicit in what we have said — for example, tenderness, sensitivity, patience — but the bottom line is to work at it. In the fire of new love, marriage seems as easy as falling off a log. Actually, it is as easy as *staying* on a log. It requires careful attention, developed skill, and work.

Men, are you working on the second most important relationship of your life (God is first)? Sweat any lately? No perspiration, no progress. No pain, no gain.

Let us bow to God's Word: "[A]ct like men, be strong. Let all that you do be done in love" (1 Corinthians 16:13, 14, NASB) Discipline yourself for the purpose of godliness.

Food for Thought

Do you agree with Mike Mason's analogy between marital love and death? Why or why not? What does your love for your wife demand of you? Are you willing to pay the price?

Do you generally feel what your wife is feeling — her joys and sorrows, her mountain peaks and deep valleys? What can you do to let her know that you want to "connect" with her emotionally and spiritually?

"Praying is the marital work of a Christian husband." Do you agree? How often do you pray for your wife? With her? What can you do to make this more of a habit?

What are you doing currently to help your wife draw closer to Christ? List at least six specific things you will do within the next two weeks to help your wife grow spiritually.

What happens to a marriage if a husband doesn't love himself? What does it really mean to love oneself, biblically? How will such an attitude show itself practically?

How do Colossians 3:14 and 1 Corinthians 16:13, 14 apply to your marriage? Be specific.

Application/Response

What did God speak to you about most specifically, most powerfully in this chapter? Talk to Him about it right now!

Think About It!

Read Ephesians 5:22-33, then write a few paragraphs on the spiritual meaning of Christian marriage. What do the wife's submission and the husband's love have to do with one another? What does the relationship of Christ and His Church teach you about your marriage?

4

DISCIPLINE OF FATHERHOOD

I REMEMBER WITH technicolor clarity when our first child was born — August 10, 1963 — a blazing-hot Southern California night. It had been so hot that I had taken my round little wife to the ocean — Huntington Beach, to be exact — to cool off. There I hollowed out a place in the sand for her tummy, and we stretched out under the sun while the cool breezes of the *Mar Pacifica* refreshed us, as we both unwittingly began to sunburn.

It was midafternoon when we headed back to the heat and smog of L.A., so we rolled back the sunroof of our VW and foolishly baked some more. We soon looked like Maine lobsters.

After dinner, as we lay smarting on the hot sheets of our bed, labor began, and that is about all we remember of our sunburns. My wife was occupied with another kind of pain, and I was so excited I forgot about mine. That night brought one of the greatest events of our lives — for God gave us our firstborn, a beautiful little girl we named Holly. I remember everything, even the color of the hospital walls. It seems like only yesterday.

Another event has lodged in my mind with similar vividness. July 23, 1986, twenty-three years later, in another hospital in far-off Illinois, my baby Holly gave birth to *her* firstborn, a beautiful little boy, Brian Emory, and his father held him with the same rapture.

Both experiences were profoundly supernatural, for I saw God's creation: blood, earth, water, wind and fire. Though just a speck on time's continuum, I felt a sacred solidarity with the past and the present. I also felt *grace*, the unhindered flow of God's goodness to me and my family.

Today, as a grandfather of six (with promises of more to come), it is increasingly apparent that my most treasured possessions, next to life in Christ, are the members of my family. I share the universal reflex that if a fire occurred, after getting the kids out, I would go back for the photographs, the scrapbooks, the birthday cards and notes.

Someday, when all is gone, when I can no longer see or hear or talk — indeed, when I may no longer know their names — the faces of my loved ones will be on my soul.

At mid-life I am finding increasing satisfaction in my family and in their families. All my children are serious Christians and want to make their lives count for Christ. I say this humbly, because parents often take too much blame for their children's problems and too much credit when they turn out well. I realize that my children are what they are by the grace of God and that for me and them the road has not ended.

I have mutually fulfilling relationships with all my children. They are independent of me, but they desire my company and counsel. We have mutual respect. They call me, and I call them, and we all live for the holidays when we can be together.

I have shared all this because, though I have not been a perfect father, I have learned some things along the way which I must pass along, man to man, to those of you in the midst or at the beginning of fathering.

Men, the mere fact of fatherhood has endowed you with terrifying power in the lives of your sons and daughters, because they have an innate, God-given passion for you. Recently, in reading Lance Morrow's *The Chief, A Memoir of Fathers and Sons*, I came across a remarkable expression of this:

> From time to time I have felt for my father a longing that was almost physical, something passionate, but prior to sex — something infantile, profound. It has bewildered me, even thrown me into depression. It is mysterious to me exactly what it is I wanted from my father. I have seen this longing in other men — and see it now in my own sons, their longing for me. I think that I have glimpsed it once or twice in my father's feelings about his father. Perhaps it is some urge of Telemachus, the residual infant in the man still wistful for the father's heroic protection. One seeks to return not to the womb . . . but to a different thing, a father's sponsorship in the world. A boy wants the aura and armament of his father. It is a deep yearning, but sometimes a little sad — a common enough masculine trait that is also vaguely unmanly. What surprises me is how angry a man becomes sometimes in the grip of what is, in essence, an unrequited passion.[1]

Our sons naturally want us! Perhaps, men, you have experienced something like this. You have just finished a run, and you are sitting on the porch sweating like a horse and smelling like one, and your son, or perhaps a little neighbor boy, sits down next to you, leans against you, and says, "You smell good." This is the primal longing for one's father. And our daughters' hearts are naturally turned toward ours with parallel longings.

The terrible fact is, we can either grace our children, or damn them with unrequited wounds which never seem to heal. Our society is awash with millions of daughters pathetically seeking the affection their fathers never gave them — and some of these daughters are at the sunset of their lives. In the extreme, there are myriads of sons who were denied a healthy same-sex relationship with their father and are now spending the rest of their lives in search of their sexual identity via perversion and immorality.[2]

Men, as fathers you have such power! You will have this terrible power till you die, like it or not — in your attitude toward authority, in your attitude toward women, in your regard for God and the Church. What terrifying responsibilities! This is truly the power of life and death.

For these reasons we live in a time of great social crisis. Whole segments of our society are bereft of male leadership. At the other end of the scale, there are strong men who give their best leadership to the marketplace, but utterly fail at home. We are the men! And if God's purpose does not happen with the sons of the Church, it will not happen.

Men, there are few places where sanctified sweat will show greater dividends than in fathering. If you are willing to work at it, you can be a good father. If you are willing to sweat, you will see abundant blessing.

Helpfully, God's Word provides us with an outline for a fatherly workout — in one pungent sentence: "Fathers, do not exasperate your children; instead, bring them up in the training and instruction of the Lord" (Ephesians 6:4). This outline is easiest remembered as a "do not" and a "do." The *"do not"* is: "Fathers, do not exasperate your children"; the *"do"* is: "instead, bring them up in the training and instruction of the Lord."

FATHERHOOD'S "DO NOTS"

The "do not" is perfectly clear, because it literally means, "*do not provoke your children to anger* so they begin to seethe with resentment and irritation." The *New English Bible* captures the idea very well: "You fathers, again, must not goad your children to resentment." The directness and simplicity of this "do not" invites us to do some honest thinking about the ways we goad our children to exasperation.

Criticism

Near the top of most lists has to be criticism. Every year when our family decorates our Christmas tree and I place a tiny red-and-green glass-beaded wreath on the tree, I think of the little boy who gave it to me when I coached soccer. His sarcastic, demeaning father would run up and down the field belittling his boy with words like "chicken" and "woman." He was the only parent I ever told to be quiet or leave the field. I wonder sometimes how that boy, now a man, has fared.

Winston Churchill had such a father in Lord Randolph Churchill. He did not like the looks of Winston, he did not like his voice, he did not like to be in the same room with his son. He never complimented him — only criticized him. His biographers excerpt young Winston's letters begging both parents for his father's attention: "I would rather have been apprenticed as a bricklayer's mate . . . it would have been natural . . . and I should have got to know my father. . . ."[3]

Fathers who criticize their children often bring them to discouragement. The parallel version of this "do not" in Colossians 3:21 indicates that children embittered by nagging and deriding[4] "lose heart" (NASB) — like a horse that has had its spirit broken. You can see it in the way a horse moves, and you can see it in the eyes and posture of a disheartened child.

Criticism comes in many ways besides overt words. Some parents never praise their children on principle — "my praise will mean something when I give it" — only they never give it. Then there is faint praise, backhanded praise like that given to the boy who had just scored a soccer goal: "That was okay, son; now next week do better." Often it is not the words — it is the tone of voice or the distracted eyes which say it all. Why are fathers critical? Perhaps that is the way their fathers treated them. Perhaps they are simply critical people who mask it well in public, but cannot restrain themselves in the heat of domestic relationships. To such fathers, God's Word comes like an arrow headed for the bull's-eye: do not exasperate your children with criticism.

Overstrictness

Some fathers exasperate their children by being overly strict and controlling. They need to remember that rearing children is like holding a wet bar of soap — too firm a grasp and it shoots from your hand, too loose a grip and it slides away. A gentle but firm hold keeps you in control.

We cannot begin to estimate the ravages of overstrictness on the evangelical Christian community over the years. I have had occasion in my ministry to bury people who lived virtually all of their seventy years in reaction to the harsh legalism of their upbringing — lost bars no one could manage to pick up. Others were not so tragic. They came to renounce legalism Biblically and theologically, but still wrestled with it emotionally for the rest of their lives.

Why are some fathers overly strict? Many because they are trying to protect their children from an increasingly Philistine culture — and smothering rules seem the best way to accomplish that. Others are simply controlling personalities who use rules, money, friendship, or clout to rule their children's lives. The Bible, read through their controlling grid, becomes a license to own and dominate. Still others wrongly understand their faith in terms of Law rather than grace. Some men are overly strict because they are concerned about what others will think. "What will they think if my child goes to this place . . . or wears this clothing . . . or is heard listening to that music?" Not a few preacher's kids have been catapulted into rebellion because their fathers squeezed their lives to fit their parishioners' expectations. What a massive sin against one's children!

Rather, we ought to begin our fatherhood by holding the tiny helpless bar snugly, but as it grows, gradually and wisely loosen our grip. As conscientious fathers we have to say "no" to many things. Thus we should try to say "yes" to as much as possible, and save our no's for the really important situations.

We must be Biblical in regard to our no's — and as our children grow, be prepared to discuss the rules Biblically and principially. We must learn to trust God with our children, realizing they must learn to make decisions for themselves.

Fathers, do not exasperate your children by being overly strict. Learn to hold their lives with God's pressure and to mold it with His love.

Irritability

We have all seen it — and perhaps done it! The father walks in the door after a pressured day, preoccupied, with brow furrowed. His three-year-old comes running to him, but Dad is busy unburdening himself to his wife. "Just a moment, Jimmy." Jimmy tugs at his father's trousers — no response. He tugs again! His father explodes, picks him up, and swats him hard for being "rude." Only the Lord knows how many children "lose heart" because their fathers have "hard days."

Life is sometimes like the cartoon where the boss is grouchy toward a worker; his employee, in turn, comes home and is irritable with the children; his son then kicks the dog; the dog runs down the street and bites the first person he sees — the boss!

We fathers must never let our pressures drive us into this unhappy cycle. The costs are too high!

> *Some say you treat your fellow man*
> *on the level.*
> *But when you are home with the wife and kids,*
> *are you mean as the Devil?*

Your kids know!

Inconsistency

Few things will exasperate a child more than inconsistency. Pity the horse that has a rider who gives it mixed signals, digging his heels into its side and pulling the reins at the same time. Pity the child even more who has the rules changed by a capricious father, and who is always exasperated because of the conflicting messages he receives.

Fathers, you may forgive yourself by saying, "I'm so busy . . . Memory isn't my thing . . . I'm just a spontaneous person!" But your children will not.

Be consistent. *Never ever* make a promise to your children you do not keep! Do any unfulfilled promises come to mind? Horseback riding that never happened? Trips to the ice cream store or the ballpark? *You* may forget, but you have a little boy or girl who will remember it eighty years from now.

Favoritism

One of the most exasperating and damning sins a father can commit against his children is favoritism. I say this despite being the last one who would suggest you should treat all your children alike. Some children need more discipline, some need more independence. Some need more structure, some need less. Some need more holding than others. Some need more encouragement. But no child should be favored over another.

Favoritism was the damning sin of Isaac, who favored Esau over Jacob. Ironically, it was also the damning sin of Jacob, who favored Joseph over his brothers. Like favoring father, like rejected son! How crushing, how disheartening to know that you are less favored — less loved.

Men, the great "do not" of fatherhood is, "Do not exasperate your children" — and life tells us what the resulting "do nots" of this are:

- Do not be critical.
- Do not be overstrict.
- Do not be irritable.
- Do not be inconsistent.
- Do not show favoritism.

God has created our children with their hearts turned toward ours. Our power is awesome! We must take God's Word to heart.

FATHERHOOD'S "DO'S"

The comprehensive "do not" of fatherhood is followed by the explicit "do's" — "instead, bring them up in the training and instruction of the Lord" — which, when fully understood, requires three "do's": *tenderness, discipline, and instruction.*

Tenderness

The words "bring them up" mean "to nourish or feed," as in 5:29 which has the same Greek words describing how a man "feeds and cares" for his own body. Calvin translates "bring them up" as "let them be kindly cherished," and goes on to emphasize that the overall idea is to speak to one's children with gentleness and friendliness.[5]

When I was a teenager, my best friend's father was a man's man. He had spent thirty-two years in the Coast Guard as a noncommissioned officer, a chief bosun's mate. He was a big man, and in his prime he had put on the gloves with Joe Louis. Officers greeted him first when he walked down the street. He could be rough and tumble. But do you know what he called his 265-pound son? "David dear." I was "Kent dear," and I did not mind at all. In fact, it made me feel great. He was not hung up on "Real men do not show affection." In fact, he still kisses his grown son — a man's man himself.

We are to be tender. Men are never manlier than when they are tender with their children — whether holding a baby in their arms, loving their grade-schooler, or hugging their teenager or adult children.

Here, a statement from the wise Christian philosopher Elton Trueblood is to the point, extending the principle further. A child, he says,

> . . . needs also to know that his father and his mother are lovers, quite and apart from their relationship to him. It is the father's responsibility to make the child know that he is deeply in love with the child's mother. There is no

good reason why all evidence of affection should be hidden or carried on in secret. A child who grows up with the realization that his parents are lovers has a wonderful basis of stability.[6]

Tenderness — verbal and physical — comes naturally to a father living under God's Word. Men, how do we measure up?

Discipline

Next, there is "training." This is a strong word which means "discipline, even by punishment." Pilate used the same word when he said of Jesus, "I will punish him and then release him" (Luke 23:16). Discipline certainly includes corporal discipline as needed. But it encompasses *everything* necessary to help "Train a child in the way he should go" (Proverbs 22:6).

The tragedy is that so many men have left this to their children's mothers. Not only is this unfair to the mother, but it robs the child of the security and self-esteem which come from being disciplined by the father.[7] Men, do you leave the discipline of your sons and daughters to your wives? If so, that is a sad breach of domestic responsibility. You are not living under God's Word!

Instruction

Last, there is "instruction" — verbal instruction, verbal warning. The word "instruction" literally means "to place before the mind." Often this means to confront and thus is related to the previous topic, discipline. This is precisely where the high priest Eli was such an abysmal domestic failure in raising his sons. First Samuel 3:11-13 tells us:

> And the Lord said to Samuel: "See, I am about to do something in Israel that will make the ears of everyone who hears of it tingle. At that time I will carry out against Eli everything I spoke against his family — from beginning to end. For I told him that I would judge his family forever because of the sin he knew about; his sons made themselves contemptible, and he failed to restrain them."

The Greek word for "restrain" in the Septuagint has the same root as "instruction" in Ephesians 6:4. Eli failed to *confront* his boys. He failed to *instruct* them about their sin. And because of this, they were destroyed.

Clear, forthright instruction is necessary for a proper upbringing. Men, if we are to own up to our responsibilities, we must be:

- Involved in verbally instructing our children.
- Regularly leading them in family devotions and prayer.
- Monitoring and being responsible along with our wives for the input that enters their impressionable minds.
- Taking responsibility to help assure that church is a meaningful experience.
- Above all, we must make sure that the open book of our lives — our example — demonstrates the reality of our instruction, for in watching us they will learn the most.

Late in life Evangeline Booth, age eighty-one and then general of the Salvation Army, was asked when she had first wanted to be a part of the Salvation Army. "Very early," she answered. "I saw my parents [founders of the Salvation Army] working for their people, bearing their burdens. Day and night. They did not have to say a word to me about Christianity."[8]

The "do's" of fathering — *tenderness, discipline, and instruction* — together demand one great thing, as a certain busy doctor came to realize. He would appear at meals, pay allowances, and give advice, often without really listening to the problems of his family before he spoke. One afternoon, as he was preparing an article for a respected journal of medicine, his little son crept into the forbidden sanctuary of his father's study. "Daddy," he appealed. Without speaking, the doctor opened his desk drawer and handed the boy a box of candy.

A few moments later the boy again said, "Daddy," and his father absent-mindedly handed him a pencil. "Daddy," the boy persisted. The doctor responded to this with a grunt, indicating he knew the boy was there but did not want to be bothered. "Daddy!" the boy called out again.

Angered, the busy doctor swung around in his chair and said, "What on earth is so important that you insist on interrupting me? Can't you see I'm busy? I have given you candy and a pencil. Now what do you want?"

"Daddy, I want to be with you!"

The "do's" of fatherhood cannot be lived out by proxy. You need to participate in putting your little ones to bed and praying for and with them. You need to be at their plays, speeches, recitals, and sporting events. You need to schedule *regular time alone* with each of your children. You need to take the lead in planning terrific family vacations and in celebrating and cementing family solidarity.

Now in mid-life I sometimes wistfully think, "Where did the time go between the two indelible memories of the birth of my daughter and the birth of her son?" To be honest, some of the years were long and hard. I thought we would never get through many of the stresses. But when these great events are recalled in all their color, there seems to be no time between them. That is why, whenever I have occasion to hold a baby in my arms, I often encourage the parents to savor every moment and not to rush through the experience — the child will be grown up and gone in no time. The realization that we have only a brief time to raise our children should give us huge motivation to make the most of it and should make Scriptural advice about fathering pulse with importance for us.

Men, time is the chrysalis of eternity — there is no other time but the present. I realize we all go through periods in our lives when we have little time for our families — it is part of the natural rhythm of life. But excessive "busyness" must not be by choice — as it so often is! We must beware of packing our schedules by saying "yes" to things which mean "no" to our families. *Now* is the time to take time. There is no other! Will you do it? Will I?

Men, we must evaluate our fatherhood. What does your heart tell you as you read the questions listed below? Are you weak or strong?

- Do you criticize your children, or build them up?
- Are you overly strict, or reasonably strict — gradually granting your child greater freedom?
- Are you impatient and irritable, or patient and self-controlled, when dealing with your children?
- Are you consistent in your expectations?
- Have you kept your promises?
- Do you show favoritism?
- Are you tender with both your sons and daughters?
- Do you share in the discipline?
- Are you spending time with your children, as a family and individually?

What awesome power we have! Our children all want the "aura and armament" of their fathers. Men, their hearts are turned to us! And our Lord wants our hearts to be turned to them. We hear this truth memorably stated by the angel Gabriel when he announced that part of John the Baptist's mission in making a people ready for the Lord was "to turn the hearts of the fathers to their children" (Luke 1:17). Now that Christ has come, this is a perpetual result of His saving work. When a man truly gives his heart to Christ, it is turned toward his children.

Men, submit to Christ — allow Him to turn your hearts to your children. Ask the Holy Spirit for the power to practice the discipline of fatherhood. Sweat for your children's souls.

Food for Thought

What did you expect or want from your father? Has this happened? Why or why not? What do your children expect or want from you? Is this happening? Why or why not?

Are you living out the "do not" and the "do" of Ephesians 6:4?

As a father, are you too strict or too lenient? What can you do, practically, to become more balanced in this area?

Do you ever make the same mistake as Jacob and Joseph (favoritism)? How can you stop doing this? What should take its place?

What does Proverbs 22:6 teach about parenting? Does this principle of Scripture still work in today's world?

What error did the priest Eli make in relation to his sons? How are you doing in this area? How can you do better?

Application/Response

What did God speak to you about most specifically, most powerfully in this chapter? Talk to Him about it right now!

Think About It!

List some of the attributes of your Heavenly Father, as described in the Bible. Which of these should be emulated by you as an earthly father? List specific ways each of these should be practiced in your life with your children. Then share your findings with your sons and daughters.

5

DISCIPLINE OF FRIENDSHIP

T HERE HAS BEEN an interesting development in suburban architecture. Long gone are the days when homes all had large front porches, with easy access to the front door, enabling one to become quickly acquainted with others in the neighborhood.

In the 1990s we have architecture which speaks more directly to our current values. The most prominent part of a house seems to be the two- or three-car garage. Inside are huge bathrooms with skylights and walk-in closets larger than the bedroom I grew up in. Modern architecture employs small living and dining rooms and now smaller kitchens as well, because entertaining is no longer a priority. Today's homes boast smaller yards and an increasing incidence of high fences.

The old adage that "a man's house is his castle" is coming true today. His castle's moat is his front lawn, the drawbridge his driveway, and the portcullis his automatic garage door through which he passes with electronic heraldry. Once inside, he removes his armor and attends to house and hearth until daybreak, when he assumes his executive armament and, briefcase in hand, mounts his steed — perhaps a Bronco or a Mustang — presses the button, and rides off to the wars.

Today's homes reflect our modern values of individualism, isolation, and privatization.

> There is this cave
>   In the air behind my body
> That nobody is going to touch
> A cloister, a silence
>   Closing around a blossom of fire.[1]

It is no longer unusual to not even know the families immediately surrounding one's own house! The average American family moves four times, even
when the job does not force it. People move from house to house looking for the
elusive "something." We lack roots, continuity, and community — all of which
is to say that friendship, especially deep friendship, has fallen on hard times.

This is especially true for men. Alan Loy McGinnis, author of the best-sell-
ing *The Friendship Factor*, says that America's leading psychologists and ther-
apists estimate that only 10 percent of all men ever have any real friends.[2] The
decade-long research of 5,000 men and women by Michael McGill, published
in 1985, corroborates this. He reports:

> To say that men have no intimate friends seems on the surface too harsh. . . .
> But the data indicates that it is not far from the truth. Even the most inti-
> mate of friendships (of which there are few) rarely approach the depth of
> disclosure a woman commonly has with many other women. . . . Men do
> not value friendship.[3]

Why is this? we wonder.

We all know that men, by nature, are not as relational as women. Men's
friendships typically center around activities, while women's revolve around
sharing. Men do not reveal their feelings or weaknesses as readily as women.
They gear themselves for the marketplace, and typically understand friendships
as acquaintances made along the way, rather than as relationships. Also, men
fear being suspected of deviant behavior if they have an obviously close friendship with another man. And, of course, there are some who suffer from the John
Wayne delusion that "real men do not need other people."

Tragically, those who think this way rob themselves, their wives, their children, and the Church because they will never be all God wants them to be.

Such thinking ignores the wisdom of both Scripture and life. Soon after
Adam's creation, God said, "It is not good for the man to be alone" (Genesis
2:18). While this relates directly to the creation of Eve, it is also a primary ontological statement about the nature of man, who is, whether he admits it or not,
a relational being. His growth and significance are worked out in relationships.

Christ is our example. His ministry was centered in deep friendships with
the Twelve, whom He repeatedly called "friends" (John 15:13-15), and there
was also the inner circle of three with whom He formed an even deeper friendship and to whom He bared His heart.

Being a Christian is a relationship with the Triune God through Christ and with His Body, the Church. God becomes our Father; we become eternal brothers and sisters. *Relationship!* The warning to not "give up meeting together, as some are in the habit of doing" (Hebrews 10:25) was, and is, a call to relationships and friendships with other believers. Friendship is not optional.

Men, if you are married, your wife must be your most *intimate* friend, but to say, "my wife is my best friend" can be a cop-out. You also need Christian male friends who have a same-sex understanding of the serpentine passages of your heart, who will not only offer counsel and pray for you, but will also hold you accountable to your commitments and responsibilities when necessary. We will now consider a prime example of this kind of friend.

A GREAT FRIENDSHIP

If there ever was a "man's man," it was Jonathan; and if there ever was a man who felt the need of a friend, it was Jonathan. The Philistines' domination of Israel in that day was so complete that they allowed no blacksmiths in the land for fear they would make swords and spears for the Israelites. In fact, there were only two swords in the entire nation, those of King Saul and his son Jonathan.

All Israel was in a dark funk of depression and despair — all, that is, except Jonathan. Jonathan saw matters differently. He believed that if God willed it, Israel could be saved, even by a few. While others looked down, he looked up and saw a great and glorious God who could deliver him anytime He saw fit.

Armed with this conviction and his sword, Jonathan and his armor-bearer attacked a Philistine detachment alone. His sallying words say it all: "Come, let's go over to the outpost of those uncircumcised fellows. Perhaps the Lord will act in our behalf. Nothing can hinder the Lord from saving, whether by many or by few" (1 Samuel 14:6).

Assured that God would deliver them into his hand, Jonathan launched a horrifying single-handed attack. It was *mano a mano*, hand-to-hand, man-to-man. Blood ran to the dust and white bone gleamed in the sun as Jonathan sliced and hacked attacker after attacker, until twenty Philistines lay spread over a terrible half-acre. Blood-covered Jonathan was one tough *hombre!*

Jonathan's heroics put some steel into his people, and a rebellion followed — and some good days for Israel. But with Saul's subsequent sin and rejection, Israel fell to even darker days than before (chapters 15 — 17), and Jonathan was more alone than ever. Even *his* great heart was affected, as he too trembled before Goliath. There was no one of like mind, he thought — until he encountered David. He could not believe his ears as David called out to the giant:

"You come against me with sword and spear and javelin, but I come against you in the name of the Lord Almighty, the God of the armies of Israel, whom you have defied. This day the Lord will hand you over to me, and I'll strike you down and cut off your head . . . and the whole world will know that there is a God in Israel. All those gathered here will know that it is not by sword or spear that the Lord saves; for the battle is the Lord's, and he will give all of you into our hands." (17:45-47)

Then David ran full-speed at Goliath and nailed him right between the eyes! Blood-smeared David stood holding the great gory head, talking calmly with Jonathan's father, Saul. At last Jonathan had found someone whose heart was in tune with his — a *friend*.

What followed was the flowering of a deep male friendship, one of the most celebrated friendships in all of literature. As such, it provides the essential elements and wisdom for all genuine friendships

Friendship's Mutuality

The initial element in Jonathan and David's great friendship was mutuality of soul. As the account so plainly states, "After David had finished talking with Saul, Jonathan became one in spirit with David" (18:1). Literally, "The soul of Jonathan bound itself to the soul of David."[4] Jonathan saw that David viewed life from the same divine perspective (God is sovereign and does as He pleases, and all of life is to be lived for Him). And when he saw this, his soul reflexively clung to David's. Here was a man whose heart beat with his!

This is the way it is with deep friendships. It is not that friends think alike on everything. Often it is quite the opposite. But they do share the same worldview and approach to life. And this is why a Christian friendship exceeds anything that exists between nonbelievers — for such a friendship is founded on a supernatural mutuality of soul. The Holy Spirit makes your souls chorus the same cries.

- You assent to the same authority.
- You know the same God.
- You are going the same way.
- You long for the same things.
- You dream mutual dreams.
- You yearn for the same experiences of holiness and worship.

Jonathan's soul bound itself to David's soul. You know when this happens, and it is wonderful.

Friendship's Love

Mutuality of soul is followed by love, as the next phrase indicates — "and he [Jonathan] loved him [David] as himself" (v. 1). This is an amazing statement because of its immediacy. This love did not develop in a month or even a day, but in a flash! It was because David's sizzling soul met such a deep need in Jonathan's — "At last I have found someone who lives like me!" He really did love him as himself, and in doing so was loving his neighbor as himself — and he was thus fulfilling the Law of God.

This love would pay great dividends because honest, unselfish love has irresistible drawing power. David would be drawn to the same love, as we shall see.

Friendship's Commitment

Jonathan's astonishing mutuality of soul and the immediacy of his love was followed by profound commitment — "And Jonathan made a covenant with David because he loved him as himself. Jonathan took off the robe he was wearing and gave it to David, along with his tunic, and even his sword, his bow and his belt" (vv. 3, 4).

What sublime spiritual theatre — symbolism of a noble soul! Jonathan, the king's son, stands humbly in his undergarment, while the shepherd boy dons the prince's robe and armament. Jonathan's act was one of *honor*, *equality*, and *vulnerability*. To wear the robe of a king was an immense honor, as testified by Haman's fateful request to wear the Persian king's robe and parade through the streets (cf. Esther 6:6-9). Jonathan's symbolic divestiture formally abolished David's status as a shepherd and placed him side by side as an equal. His disrobing was a conscious display of vulnerability and real risk. The Shakespearean gesture meant, "My life for your life" — and he meant every bit of it.

We may wonder, is such friendship really possible outside the sacred pages of Scripture? After all, these men were spiritual giants. But consider what happened when a twenty-year-old Anne Sullivan arrived in Tuscumbia, Alabama, to tutor the blind and deaf seven-year-old Helen Keller, who could only utter animal-like sounds and often fell into destructive rages. For weeks Anne Sullivan tried to break through to the girl's consciousness, until the famous fifth of April 1887 — a day Helen Keller described sixty years later — when the girl was holding a mug under the spout while Anne pumped water into it, using her other hand to repeatedly spell w-a-t-e-r — and Helen suddenly understood! She later said, "Spark after spark of meaning flew from hand to hand and miracu-lously, affection was born."[5]

Anne Sullivan gave almost her entire life to Helen Keller. By ten, Helen was writing to famous persons in Europe — in French. She mastered five languages and displayed far greater gifts than her teacher. Still, Anne Sullivan was devoted to Helen, sitting beside her famous pupil at Radcliffe, spelling the lecture into her hand. Anne Sullivan's devotion never changed. She was satisfied to be Helen's friend and encourager — to make her a queen.

The deepest of friendships have in common this desire to make the other person royalty. They work for and rejoice in the other's elevation and achieve-ments. There are no hooks in such friendships, no desire to manipulate or con-trol, no jealousy or exclusiveness — simply a desire for the best for the other. Dostoyevski had the idea when he wrote: "To love a person means to see him as God intended him to be."

Do you have the great fortune to have such a deep friend? Men, are we kingmakers?

Friendship's Loyalty

Jonathan maintained a fierce loyalty to David as their friendship grew. This is most remarkable, because after the first flush of dramatic commitment he was reminded by his father (no doubt more than once!), "As long as the son of Jesse lives on this earth, neither you nor your kingdom will be established" (20:31). Yet, when Saul maligned David, we read that "Jonathan spoke well of David" (19:4), and on one occasion even persuaded his father to make an oath not to harm David (an oath Saul did not keep).

Loyalty is indispensable to the survival of friendship. How many once-pros-perous friendships have faded because of disloyal talk? Pascal put it pointedly: "I set this down as a fact, that if all men knew what each other said of the other, there would not be four friends in the world." You will never know a deep friendship unless there is mutual loyalty and trust.

Friendship's Encouragement

Constant flight from Saul produced some down times for David. For example, when he delivered the town of Keilah from the Philistines, he learned that the citizens of the town were plotting to turn him over to Saul — and so off to Horesh in the desert he fled, disheartened and terribly discouraged. But Jonathan came to the rescue: "And Saul's son Jonathan went to David at Horesh and helped him find strength in God" (23:16). What a friend! "A friend loves at all times, and a brother is born for adversity" (Proverbs 17:17).

Jonathan's encouragement was more than "everything is going to be okay." The verse quoted above literally reads, "He strengthened his hand in God." Jonathan pointed David upward to the grand perspective which had first drawn him to the shepherd boy. This undoubtedly involved instruction, prayer, and mutual worship.

The Apostle Paul experienced similar comfort from his friend Titus: "But God, who comforts the downcast, comforted us by the coming of Titus . . . so that my joy was greater than ever" (2 Corinthians 7:6, 7). This is the "Titus Touch" — the golden touch of an encouraging friend.

As we have catalogued the beautiful elements of Jonathan and David's deep friendship — *mutuality, love, commitment, loyalty,* and *encouragement* — we have observed that they came largely from Jonathan. But it did not remain one-sided. Repeated mutual commitments began to mark the friendship of these two remarkable men. The apex of their commitment was the mutual promise to care for one another's family, should one be taken (cf. 20:14-17) — "I'll take care of yours, and you take care of mine." They bound their lives and their children's lives to one another. Later, when they reaffirmed their promises, "David wept the most" (20:41, 42). It appears that Jonathan's friendship had drawn David to unexpected heights of devotion.

Male friendship has reached Heaven when men make such promises to each other. I treasure a sacred moment when my old childhood friend, married and with family, met my wife and me on vacation in the Colorado mountains and said, after a late-evening meal, "If anything happens to you, Kent, Judy and I will look out for Barbara and the children." It was a sacredness I gladly reciprocated.

A GREAT LOSS

David was destined to be king, and he and Jonathan planned to be side by side as David ruled. But that was not to be, for Jonathan and his brothers died with their father on Mount Gilboa at the hands of the Philistines. David was crushed with sorrow. In grief he wrote a lament, and commanded that all the men of Judah be taught it. The lament ends with these words:

> How the mighty have fallen in battle!
> Jonathan lies slain on your heights.
> I grieve for you, Jonathan my brother;
> you were very dear to me.

Your love for me was wonderful,
more wonderful than that of women.
How the mighty have fallen!
The weapons of war have perished!

(2 Samuel 1:25-27)

That David felt Jonathan's love was "more wonderful than that of women" would not have been said if he had a good monogamous marriage! This is testimony to the poverty of his relationships with his wives, an inevitable result of the sin of multiplying wives (cf. Deuteronomy 17:17). However, there is no hint of sensuality here, but simply a celebration of a deep friendship — Jonathan's mutuality of soul, Jonathan's commitment, Jonathan's loyalty, and Jonathan's encouragement — elements David would never know in any other relationship.

David and Jonathan's friendship shows us what a deep friendship can and ought to be. C. S. Lewis said, "Friendship . . . is the instrument by which God reveals to each the beauties of all others."[6] This is certainly what the friendship of David and Jonathan does for us. It reveals the beauties that can be ours in a deep male relationship grounded in God and sets the standard for all deep friendships.

DISCIPLINE OF FRIENDSHIP

Today friendship has fallen on hard times. Few men have good friends, much less deep friendships. Individualism, autonomy, privatization, and isolation are culturally cachet, but deep, devoted, vulnerable friendship is not. This is a great tragedy for self, family, and the Church, because it is in relationships that we develop into what God wants us to be. But deep friendships and friendships in general (close friendships, good friendships, and casual friendships) are there to be made if we value them as we ought — and if we practice some simple disciplines of friendship.

Prayer
We must pray specifically for God's help in effecting inward changes that will expand our capacities for friendship. And we must pray for the opportunity to develop friendships. Such relational requests may not occur naturally to the minds of most men, but they are prayers which God delights to answer, as my own experience, and that of many other Christian men, amply testifies. Need some good friendships? Spiritual logic demands that prayer is the place to begin.

Friendliness

A wise old farmer was working beside the road when a family moving to a nearby town stopped and asked him if that town was "friendly." The farmer said he could not really say. But the people pressed him for an answer, so he asked them what the town was like that they came from. They answered that it was terrible — the people were rude and small-minded. The old farmer replied, "That is just how you will find this town."

No matter what our disposition, we need to work at friendliness. We need to be *consciously cheerful*. We need to *ask questions*. We need to *place ourselves in situations where friendships happen*. If you are a regular church attender but do no more than attend morning worship, you are depriving yourself and the church of the friendship so desperately needed by all. Men, we must place ourselves in the ways of friendship: an adult Sunday school class, a home Bible study, a men's Bible study, a men's breakfast group, men's retreats, and, especially, service in some ministry of the church. Women are so much better at this than men. We must learn from them to take the initiative.

Work

Few of the truly valuable things in life just happen. Usually when they do, it is because we recognize their value and go for it. You can have just about anything you want if you work for it. If you want to make a million dollars badly enough, you can very likely do it. If you want to earn a Ph.D. and are willing to pay the price, you can do it. We generally get what we set our sights on. It is the same with friendship. Those who have friends place importance on them. This is why women have more friends than men.

Affirmation

If we will work at affirming others, we will have friends. Mark Twain said, "I can live for two months on a compliment." He is right! I have a friend who sends me a note every two or three months that is meant to affirm me and encourage my steadfastness. Compliments have huge buoying power. Be liberal with honest affirmations, and you will have friends.

Listening

Even more, men, if you will work at being a good listener, you will develop friends. The epigram "Eloquence is with the audience" is not only true of public speaking but of general conversation. Listen well, and you will be pronounced a "brilliant" conversationalist! What's more, people will discover they are important to you, which is key to any friendship.

Acceptance

Life is filled with small rejections — a sarcastic smile, innuendos, awkward silences, club atmospheres — so that many walk through the day with their guard up. If we discipline ourselves to be accepting, others will see the sparkle of our eyes, the tilt of our head, the ethos of our voice — and will know that acceptance is there. An open, accepting soul is like a well-lit home on a cold dark night.

Hospitality

When we think of the Scriptural command to practice hospitality, we reflexively imagine a feminine mandate — "This is something my wife should excel at, or my mother, or my daughter. Women, hear God's Word!" And they do, much to their souls' benefit. But the command is for both genders. Men, you ought to take the initiative in practicing hospitality (see 1 Peter 4:9), whether you are single or married. If you do, you will not only begin to build friendships, but may even host some "angels without knowing it" (Hebrews 13:2).

We must set ourselves against the cultural consensus and pursue and practice friendship if we are to be all God wants us to be. God's Word demands a countercultural manliness which is capable of deep friendship.

We need to put some holy sweat into our relationships, resist the lure of our architecture with its moats, drawbridges, and descending doors, and overcome the technology of autonomy — the isolating lure of our televisions and VCR's.

Most of all, we must overcome our privatized hearts — for Christianity is a relationship with God *and His people*. God's truth is most effectively learned and lived in relationships. Friendships hold the promise of grace!

Food for Thought

What can we learn about friendship from Christ's statements about us being His friends (John 15:13-15)?

"If you are married, your wife must be your most intimate friend." Do you agree, really? How would such a friendship show itself (apart from sexuality) . . . grow . . . weather the stresses of the relationship?

What truths of Christian friendship are evident in the relationship between David and Jonathan (1 Samuel 14 — 18)? List as many as you can.

Have you experienced the "Titus Touch" (2 Corinthians 7:6, 7)? In your own words, what is the "Titus Touch"? How can you become more like Titus? Why would some men choose not to?

What does prayer have to do with your friendships? God won't force someone to be your friend, will He?

What do 1 Peter 4:9 and Hebrews 13:2 teach about friendship? How can you apply these Scriptures to your life?

Application/Response

What did God speak to you about most specifically, most powerfully in this chapter? Talk to Him about it right now!

Think About It!

List those whom you consider good or close friends. After each name, tell why you see that person as a friend. Then summarize what you are looking for in friends and why you value such relationships.

SOUL

6

DISCIPLINE OF MIND

T HE COMPLEX CAPACITY of the human brain is the subject of ever-widening scientific wonder. Its twelve to fourteen billion cells are only a shadow of its complexity, for each cell sends out thousands of connecting tendrils so that a single cell may be connected with 10,000 neighboring cells, each of which is constantly exchanging data impulses. These twelve to fourteen billion brain cells times 10,000 connectors make the human mind an unparalleled computer. The mind's activity has been compared to 1,000 switchboards, each big enough to serve New York City, all running at full speed as they receive and send questions and orders. Put another way, there is more electronic equivalent in one human brain than in all the radio and television stations of the entire world put together!

The human brain does not miss a thing. It is capable of giving and receiving the subtlest input — from imagining a universe in which time bends, to creating the polyphonic texture of a Bach fugue, or transmitting and receiving a message from God Himself — feats no computer will ever accomplish.

The dizzying potential of the human mind reaches its apex in the possibility of possessing the mind of Christ through the ministry of the Holy Spirit — a possibility affirmed by Paul when he said, "But we have the mind of Christ" — a mind which is constantly renewed (cf. 1 Corinthians 2:16 and Romans 12:2). No computer will ever be able to think God's thoughts, nor will any device ever be able to know the heart of God or do His works. But the mystery which resides between our ears has this capacity. Indeed, it was created for this — to have the mind of Christ.

This cosmic potential of the believer's mind introduces the great scandal of today's Church: *Christians without Christian minds*, Christians who do not think Christianly — a tragic fact which is far more true of professing Christian men than women, as we shall see.

Some prophetic voices have been sounding the alarm for some time now, like that of former United Nations Secretary General Charles Malik, who told the distinguished audience at the dedication of the Billy Graham Center at Wheaton College: "Believe me, my friends, the mind today is in profound trouble, perhaps more than ever before. How to order the mind on sound Christian principles, at the heart of where it is formed and informed, is one of the . . . greatest themes that can be considered."[1]

Harry Blamires, in his much discussed *The Christian Mind*, has said that while Christians may worship and pray as Christians, they do not *think* as Christians: "[T]he Christian mind has succumbed to the secular drift with a degree of weakness and nervelessness unmatched in Christian history."[2] Elsewhere he sees our generation as suffering from religious anorexia (*anorexia religiosa*), a loss of appetite for growth in Christ.[3]

The bottom line is: this grievous scandal comes from a declining willingness to properly program the amazing instruments God has given us. Christians leave their twelve billion cells unguarded and unthinking — and undisciplined.

When we turn to God's Word, we are aware that the Biblical writers understood the problem in a less technical, though more personally beneficial, way. "Above all else, guard your heart," says Proverbs, "for it is the wellspring of life" (Proverbs 4:23). "For as he thinks within himself, so he is" (Proverbs 23:7, NASB). The Scriptures tell us rightly that input determines output — that our programming determines production.

THE DIVINE PROGRAM

In the New Testament no one understood this better than the Apostle Paul. In fact, in his letter to the Philippians, after alluding to guarding the heart Paul prescribed his personal program in one sublime sentence: "Finally, brothers, whatever is true, whatever is noble, whatever is right, whatever is pure, whatever is lovely, whatever is admirable — if anything is excellent or praiseworthy — think about such things" (Philippians 4:8).

Each of Paul's ingredients is explicitly positive. The true, the noble, the right, the pure, the lovely, the admirable all defy negative exposition. Each ingredient was, and is, *a matter of personal choice* — and our choices make all the difference in the world. We all can *choose* a thought program which will produce a Christian mind.

I have great sympathy for those whose past has been a series of bad choices. I understand that if over the years one has chosen the impure and the illusory and the negative, it is very difficult to change. But as a Biblical thinker I give no quarter to myself or anyone else who rationalizes his present choices by the past. Brothers, *as Christians we are free to have a Christian mind*. It is within our reach, and it is our duty.

As we consider how Paul's program should affect our minds, the sheer weight of its positives demands a determined rejection of negative input: "Finally, brothers, whatever is untrue, whatever is ignoble, whatever is wrong, whatever is impure, whatever is unlovely, whatever is unadmirable — if there is anything shoddy or unworthy of praise — do not think about these things." It was not that Paul was a naive Pollyanna. He knew the dark side of human experience. Romans 1 proves that. But he chose not to make such input a part of his mental programming.

So we must lay down as fundamental to our Christianity this truth: *a Christian mind demands conscious negation; a Christian mind is impossible without the discipline of refusal*.

Charles Colson tells of sitting at dinner with a president of one of the three major television networks. Colson felt he had a tremendous opportunity to influence the man, so he told him how millions of Christians were offended by the networks' programming. Knowing that TV executives have an intense interest in profit, Colson suggested that it would be good business to air wholesome family entertainment. "After all," added Colson, "there are fifty million born-again Christians out there." The gauntlet was down, and as Colson tells it:

> He looked at me quizzically. I assured him that was Gallup's latest figure.
>
> "What you are suggesting, Mr. Colson, is that we run more programs like, say, *Chariots of Fire*?"
>
> "Yes!" I exclaimed. "That's a great movie with a marvelous Christian message."
>
> "Well," he said, "CBS ran it as a prime-time movie just a few months ago. Are you aware of the ratings?"
>
> All at once I knew I was in trouble.
>
> He then explained: That night NBC showed *On Golden Pond*; it was #1 with 25.2 percent of all TV sets in America tuned in. Close behind was *My Mother's Secret Life*, a show about a mother hiding her past as a prostitute. It was #2 with 25.1 percent.
>
> And a distant third — a big money loser — was CBS with *Chariots of*

Fire — 11.8 percent. In fact, of the sixty-five shows rated that week, "Dallas" was #1, *Chariots of Fire*, #57.

"So," my companion concluded, "where are your fifty million born-again Christians, Mr. Colson?"

Good question. Where are we?

If even half of Gallup's fifty million born-again Christians had watched the show with the Christian message, *Chariots of Fire* would have topped the ratings. But the disturbing truth, as studies by the secular networks as well as the Christian Broadcasting Network show, is that the viewing habits of Christians are no different than those of non-Christians!

Since TV is a business, it gives its customers — the public — what they want. It is but a mirror image of us.[4]

The Christian community is putting the same input into its collective computer as is the rest of the world. According to A. C. Nielsen, the TV set in the average home is on seven hours and seven minutes a day, and the average viewer watches four and one half hours each day.[5] The statistics for religious homes is just a half hour less.[6]

A renowned media expert, Professor Neil Postman of New York University, says that between the ages of six and eighteen, the average child spends some 15,000 to 16,000 hours in front of the TV, whereas he spends only 13,000 hours in school.[7] Postman says that during the first twenty years of an American child's life, he will see some one million commercials, at the rate of about 1,000 per week![8]

As to television's effects, the results are infamous:

• Shortened attention span.

• Diminution of linguistic powers.

• Reduced capacity for abstraction.

• Homogenization of adulthood and childhood.

To attract and hold its audience, the TV industry feels it has to parade the taboos of culture: adultery, promiscuity, homosexuality, incest, violence, and sadism.[9] As a result the lowest of activities become commonplace, and even morally cachet.

There is a distinct connection between these things and the background of TV executives as compared with the viewing public. Only 7 percent attend church regularly, as compared to 55 percent of the viewing public; 44 percent have no religious affiliation, as compared to only 10 percent of the viewers having no such affiliation.[10] To deny there is a conscious assault on the Christian mind and its traditional values is like believing Saddam Hussein is building a "kinder, gentler world."

I am aware of the wise warnings against using words like "all," "every," and "always" in what I say. Absolutizing one's pronouncements is dangerous. But I'm going to do it anyway. Here it is: *It is impossible for any Christian who spends the bulk of his evenings, month after month, week upon week, day in and day out watching the major TV networks or contemporary videos to have a Christian mind.* This is *always* true of *all* Christians in *every* situation! A Biblical mental program cannot coexist with worldly programming.

If we are to have Christian minds, there are things we must put out of our minds — and this extends beyond TV, to what we read, listen to, and laugh at.

My advice? Stop watching television. I mean that sincerely! Not watching TV will liberate so much time, it will become virtually impossible not to become a deeper person and a better Christian. Even if you play poker with your friends, you will be better off, because you will be *relating to human beings*!

I am not suggesting a new legalism which forbids TV and the cinema. (There are many worthwhile things to view; moreover, while Christianity is by nature countercultural, it is not anti-cultural.) But I am calling for believers to take control of their minds — what comes in and what goes out. If you cannot control what you watch and read, perhaps it needs to go. "If your right eye causes you to sin, gouge it out and throw it away," says Jesus (Matthew 5:29). My wife and I chose to raise our children without a television for this very reason, and we have no regrets. What we did is not for everyone, but it may be for you.

The Psalmist gives sage advice for those living in the media age: "I will walk in my house with blameless heart. I will set before my eyes no vile thing" (Psalm 101:2, 3). We need to allow Christ to be Lord of our prime time.

Some of you need to schedule a confidential conference with your spouse and prayerfully seek God's will regarding this. And you single men who have so much trouble with your minds need to likewise seek God's will — and someone to hold you accountable. Let us not settle for being like other Christians or for having a church that is like other evangelical churches. May we be different because we have *Christian* minds.

INTENTIONAL PROGRAMMING

In the text we have been considering, Paul recommends that we focus our minds on truth, nobility, rightness, purity, loveliness, admirability, excellence, and praiseworthiness, and ends with this loaded charge: "*Think* about such things" (Philippians 4:8, italics added). The word he uses is *logidzamai*, from which we get the mathematical computer-like word *logarithm*. It means a ". . . deliberate and prolonged contemplation as if one is weighing a mathematical problem."[11] The way I handle my mail gives an example. Frankly, most of it gets tossed. I read the return address to see if it is an ad, perhaps open it, scan a few lines — and away it goes. But if it is an outdoor catalog, say the Orvis catalog, it gets deliberate and prolonged contemplation — especially the Superfine graphite fly rods. We are to think about the wonderful elements God wants us to put into our computers. God calls us in His Word to a massive and positive discipline of the mind.

Scripture

This can only happen through a profound exposure to and continual immersion in God's Word, accompanied by the illumination of the Holy Spirit — an exposure that is within the reach of all literate and semiliterate Christians.

Lt. General William K. Harrison was the most decorated soldier in the 30th Infantry Division, rated by General Eisenhower as the number one infantry division in World War II. General Harrison was the first American to enter Belgium, which he did at the head of the Allied forces. He received every decoration for valor except the Congressional Medal of Honor — being honored with the Distinguished Silver Cross, the Silver Star, the Bronze Star for Valor, and the Purple Heart (he was one of the few generals to be wounded in action). When the Korean War began, he served as Chief of Staff in the United Nations Command — and because of his character and self-control was ultimately President Eisenhower's choice to head the long and tedious negotiations to end the war.

General Harrison was a soldier's soldier who led a busy, ultra-kinetic life, but he was also an amazing man of the Word. When he was a twenty-year-old West Point Cadet, he began reading the Old Testament through once a year and the New Testament four times. General Harrison did this until the end of his life. Even in the thick of war he maintained his commitment by catching up during the two- and three-day respites for replacement and refitting which followed battles, so that when the war ended he was right on schedule.

When, at the age of ninety, his failing eyesight no longer permitted his discipline, he had read the Old Testament seventy times and the New Testament 280 times! No wonder his godliness and wisdom were proverbial, and that the Lord used him for eighteen fruitful years to lead Officers Christian Fellowship (OCF).[12]

General Harrison's story tells us two things. First, it is possible, even for the busiest of us, to systematically feed on God's Word. No one could be busier or lead a more demanding life than General Harrison.

Second, his life remains a demonstration of a mind programmed with God's Word. His closest associates say that every area of his life (domestic, spiritual, and professional) and each of the great problems he faced was informed by the Scriptures. People marveled at his knowledge of the Bible and the ability to bring its light to every area of life.

He lived out the experience of the Psalmist:

Oh, how I love your law!
I meditate on it all day long.
Your commands make me wiser than my enemies,
for they are ever with me.
I have more insight than all my teachers,
for I meditate on your statutes.
I have more understanding than the elders,
for I obey your precepts.

(119:97-100)

You must remember this: You can never have a Christian mind without reading the Scriptures regularly because *you cannot be profoundly influenced by that which you do not know*. If you are filled with God's Word, your life can then be informed and directed by God — your domestic relationships, your child-rearing, your career, your ethical decisions, your interior moral life. The way to a Christian mind is through God's Word!

Again, we must be careful not to create a Bible-reading legalism — "good Christians read the Bible through once a year." The Bible nowhere demands this. Some simply cannot read well, or fast, and speed reading is not the answer. As Lucy told Charlie Brown: "I just completed a course in speed reading and last night I read *War and Peace* in one hour! . . . It was about Russia."

My own brother, who is severely dyslexic, having had the misfortune of receiving his schooling before much was known about learning disabilities, only learned to read well enough to get along in his trade. Recently he became a Christian, and with his newfound motivation to know God's Word he purchased tapes of the Scriptures. His wife also reads to him. He is reading better each year.

Most people, however, will find that reading the Scripture through once a year is the best way because it requires only five pages a day and offers a reachable annual goal. Believers, whatever your ability, you must regularly read and study God's Word. If you refuse, you are in effect "editing God" and will never have a fully Christian mind.

In the Resources section of this book, you will find several detailed plans for annually reading through the Bible ("M'Cheyne's Calendar for Daily Reading," "Through the Bible," and "Topical Guide to Daily Devotional Bible Reading in a Year") and also sources for obtaining the Scriptures on audiocassette ("The Bible on Audiocassette"). I would encourage you to avail yourself of these opportunities.

Christian Literature

Along with reading the Word, we ought to be reading good books. The brilliant Jewish radio talk show host Dennis Prager, a man who makes sure he is well-informed, said in a recent interview in *The Door*:

> One thing I noticed about Evangelicals is that they do not read. They do not read the Bible, they do not read the great Christian thinkers, they have never heard of Aquinas. If they're Presbyterian, they've never read the founders of Presbyterianism. I do not understand that. As a Jew, that's confusing to me. The commandment of study is so deep in Judaism that we immerse ourselves in study. God gave us a brain, aren't we to use it in His service? When I walk into an Evangelical Christian's home and see a total of 30 books, most of them best-sellers, I do not understand. I have bookcases of Christian books, and I am a Jew. Why do I have more Christian books than 98 percent of the Christians in America? That is so bizarre to me.[13]

It *is* bizarre — especially when a commitment to Christ is a commitment to believe in things that go far beyond the surface of life. Sadly, the bulk of the non-reading Christian public are men, who buy only 25 percent of all Christian books.[14]

Men, to deny ourselves the wealth of the accumulated saints of the centuries is to consciously embrace spiritual anorexia. Great Christian writing will magnify, dramatize, and illuminate life-giving wonders for us. Others have walked the paths we so want to tread. They have chronicled the pitfalls and posted warnings along the way. They have also given us descriptions of spiritual delights which will draw us onward and upward.

In preparation for speaking and writing about the subject of the mind, I mailed a questionnaire to thirty Christian leaders, including such people as Charles Colson, James Dobson, Carl F. H. Henry, J. I. Packer, Warren Wiersbe, and Calvin Miller. I received twenty-six responses. The survey asked four questions:

1) What are the five books, secular or sacred, which have influenced you the most?
2) Of the spiritual/sacred books which have influenced you, which is your favorite?
3) What is your favorite novel?
4) What is your favorite biography?

The devotional/theological books mentioned most were C. S. Lewis's *Mere Christianity*, Oswald Chambers's *My Utmost for His Highest*, John Calvin's *Institutes*, A. W. Tozer's *The Pursuit of God*, and Thomas a Kempis's *The Imitation of Christ*. The most frequently mentioned biographies were Mr. and Mrs. Howard Taylor's *Hudson Taylor's Spiritual Secret* and Elisabeth Elliot's *Shadow of the Almighty*. The favorite novels were Leo Tolstoy's *Anna Karenina* and Fyodor Dostoyevski's *The Brothers Karamazov* (which was, for example, the favorite of Charles Colson, Wayne Martindale, Harold Myra, J. I. Packer, and Eugene Peterson). These titles make a superb list from which to select if you have not done some serious Christian reading. (All the survey responses can be found in the Resources section of this book — "Personal Reading Survey.")

Also, today many books are available on audiocassette (great for listening as you drive to work or when traveling, etc.). For example, my own town's public library carries tapes of such great books as *Pride and Prejudice* by Jane Austen, *Pilgrim's Progress* by John Bunyan, *Brothers Karamazov* by Fyodor Dostoyevski, the *Diary of Anne Frank*, *Scarlet Letter* by Nathaniel Hawthorne, Homer's *Odyssey*, *Screwtape Letters* by C. S. Lewis, *Lord of the Rings* by Tolkien, *War and Peace* by Leo Tolstoy, and many others.

Men, you need to fill your mind with good stuff. I am not suggesting a manic spree (George Will, for example, is able to read two hefty books a week). But many of you would do well to commit to reading two or three good books this next year.

What amazing instruments reside in the three or four pounds between our ears, instruments with greater capacity than a thousand busy New York City switchboards. The mind is greater than all the computers put together, for it can possess the *mind of Christ* and think God's thoughts after Him, wear His heart, and do His works. What an eternal tragedy it is, then, to have this mind and have it redeemed, yet not have a Christian mind.

We must protect our minds. We must refuse to allow our culture's media to write our program. We must say no to the wastelands that invade our homes.

And we must make a conscious effort to submit to the Divine Programmer through reading His Word. There has got to be some holy sweat. ". . . train yourself to be godly. For physical training is of some value, but godliness has value for all things, holding promise for both the present life and the life to come" (1 Timothy 4:7, 8). Prayerfully commit yourself to reading and studying God's Word.

Further, read the great works of those who have gone before you.

Prayerfully make your commitments now.

Food for Thought

What does a comparison of Harry Blamires's statement ("[T]he Christian mind has succumbed to the secular drift with a degree of weakness and nervelessness unmatched in Christian history") and Proverbs 4:23 tell you? Do the things we think about really matter?

What does Philippians 4:8 say about the thought life? Are we supposed to take a Polly-anna approach to life and deny the stresses and strains of life? If not, then what is this passage teaching?

What do Matthew 5:29 and Psalm 101:2, 3 tell us about a disciplined mind? Is it really possible to live out these verses day by day? How?

What can the Word of God do to help us in this area (see Psalm 119:97-100)? Are you doing what these verses prescribe? Why or why not?

Have you ever read the Bible through in a year (or even two years or three)? Will you covenant with God to do this now, in order to become more familiar with the whole of Scripture and to better hear God's voice to you through His Word?

Name at least three or four Christian books that have made a major impact on your life. Then list at least two Christian books you have been meaning to read. By what date will you read these books?

Application/Response

What did God speak to you about most specifically, most powerfully in this chapter? Talk to Him about it right now!

Think About It!

In what ways do you know you need greater discipline of mind? What are your greatest struggles in this area — perhaps sexual lust? self-pity? dwelling on past pain? pride? worry? other? What can you do, practically and spiritually, to experience growth toward wholeness in these areas?

7

DISCIPLINE OF DEVOTION

A S MY PERSONAL understanding of the interior life has developed, I have learned that apart from the well-known Scriptural calls to prayer, there are two great human reasons we ought to pray.

The first is because of what prayer does to our *character*. Prayer is like a time exposure to God. Our souls function like photographic plates, and Christ's shining image is the light. The more we expose our lives to the white-hot sun of His righteous life (for, say, five, ten, fifteen, thirty minutes, or an hour a day), the more His image will be burned into our character — His love, His compassion, His truth, His integrity, His humility. As we have seen, this was true of General William Harrison, who maintained a disciplined devotional life for over seventy years. People say his presence brought a distinct sense of Christ.

The second corresponding reason is that prayer bends our *wills* to God's will. E. Stanley Jones, the world-renowned missionary and man of prayer, explained it like this:

> If I throw out a boathook from the boat and catch hold of the shore and pull, do I pull the shore to me, or do I pull myself to the shore? Prayer is not pulling God to my will, but the aligning of my will to the will of God.[1]

What tantalizing personal benefits are offered by time spent in the presence of God in prayer! Herein lies the spiritual desolation of our day. As Dallas Willard has said in *The Spirit of the Disciplines*, "The 'open secret' of many 'Bible-believing' churches is that a vanishing small percentage of those talking about prayer . . . are actually doing what they are talking about."[2] This is especially true among men, to our detriment and shame. As George Gallup's statistics show, men are considerably less likely to pray than women.[3]

My own experience in talking with professional clergy corresponds with this, because many will candidly admit their prayer lives are undisciplined and even minimal. Sometimes I have heard what amounts to an attempt to find dismal comfort in mutual confessions of failure — "You are sort of okay, and I guess I am too."

Why do so many men fail in personal devotions and prayer? Partially for the same reason they attend church less and read less: they are not as spiritually sensitive and open as women. Also, more men are dominated by the time-crunching production ethic of the marketplace, which makes them feel galaxies away from meditation and prayer. But most fail because they simply do not know how to go about cultivating the disciplines of the interior spiritual life.

This chapter's teaching on the devotional life, and the following chapter on prayer, will, if taken to heart, help you develop a fruitful interior life.

As we begin, there are some necessary caveats. First, one's prayer and devotional life cannot be reduced to a few simple rules. These areas of spiritual experience are far too dynamic and personal for simplistic reduction.

We must also be cautioned against imagining from the outline we are using (*meditation, confession, adoration, submission, petition*) that there is a prescribed order for devotion, for there is not and never has been. Life's rhythms sometimes demand that we launch directly, for example, into petition with "Lord, help me!" Other times will be spent almost entirely in confession, or meditation, or adoration.

As we discussed in the preceding chapter, reading God's Word is essential to developing a Christian mind. All Christians should be systematically reading through the Bible, once a year if possible, so that our minds are being perpetually programmed by the data of Scripture.

This understood, there is yet another step: *meditation* — which involves personalizing and internalizing a segment of the Word.

MEDITATION

Listening

Meditation begins with the devotional exercise of listening to the Word. Eugene Peterson points out that Psalm 40:6 contains a brilliant metaphor in the original Hebrew text which graphically teaches the necessity of listening. It literally says, "ears you have dug for me."[4] Much to our loss, no English translation preserves the metaphor, preferring to variously paraphrase it with phrases like the RSV's "thou hast given me an open ear." Nevertheless, the

Hebrew verb retains the metaphorical nugget "dug," which suggests, apart from God's work, a human head without any ears — "A blockhead. Eyes, nose and mouth, but no ears."[5]

This remarkable metaphor, "ears you have dug for me," occurs in the context of a busy religious performance which is deaf to the voice of God — "Sacrifice and offering you did not desire . . . burnt offerings and sin offerings you did not require." The problem was that the Psalmist's religious colleagues had read about how to do the rituals of sacrifice, but had missed the message. God had spoken, but they did not hear.

So what does God do? He takes a pick and shovel and mines through the sides of the "cranial granite," making openings through which His Word can pass to the mind and heart. The result is *hearing*, and the hearer responds, "Then I said, 'Here I am, I have come — it is written about me in the scroll. To do your will, O my God, is my desire; your law is within my heart'" (vv. 7, 8). The words of Scripture are not merely to be read but to be *heard*. They are meant to go to the heart!

The importance of having our ears dug open comes to us from the lips of Jesus: "He who has an ear, let him hear . . ." (Revelation 2:7, 11, 17, 29; 3:6, 13, 22). We need to read God's Word, but we must also pray that He will blast through our granite-block heads so we truly hear His Word.

Muttering

When the Psalmist speaks of meditating on the Law of God day and night (Psalm 1:2), he uses a word which means "to mutter."[6] This word was used to describe the murmurings of kings in Psalm 2:1, and for the chattering of doves in Isaiah 59:11. In fact, St. Augustine translated Psalm 1:2, "On his law he chatters day and night."[7] Meditation is intrinsically verbal. This means the Psalmist *memorized* God's Word — for one cannot continually mutter the Scripture without memorizing it, and vice versa.

Personally applied, this tells us that along with our systematic reading of the Bible, we ought to select especially meaningful segments to reverently mutter over. Sometimes it may be a single verse — Philippians 3:10, for example, the four emphases of which I like to murmur in the NASB:

> . . . that I may know Him,
> and the power of His resurrection,
> and the fellowship of His sufferings,
> being conformed to His death.

Slowly and prayerfully turning over Scripture in this manner engages the eyes, the ears, and the mouth, and drills through the granite to the heart — maximizing internalization and devotion.

Larger segments, especially classic texts, are tailor-made for meditation. The Ten Commandments, with the first four *Godward* commands, and the six *manward* injunctions following, should be regularly murmured in reverent self-examination (cf. Exodus 20:1-17 and Deuteronomy 5:1-22). There are eight Beatitudes which consecutively consider poverty of spirit, mourning over sin, gentleness, spiritual hunger, mercy, purity, peacemaking, and persecution. The Lord's Prayer begins with the foundational awareness "Our Father, who art in Heaven" and then presents three *upward* petitions and three *horizontal* petitions — a perfect pattern for prayer and meditation. There are endless possibilities, including the so-called *kenosis* passage, Philippians 2:5-11, which begins, "Your attitude should be the same as that of Christ Jesus. . . ." Other food for meditation includes Jesus' parables, the Psalms, and the epigrams of James. Both practical and esoteric passages can provide divine substance for reverent soul chatter.

The effects of meditation are supernal, bringing:

- *Revival* — "The law of the Lord is perfect, reviving the soul" (Psalm 19:7).
- *Wisdom* — "The statutes of the Lord are trustworthy, making wise the simple" (Psalm 19:7); "Oh, how I love your law! I meditate on it all day long. Your commands make me wiser than my enemies, for they are ever with me" (Psalm 119:97, 98).
- *Increases in our faith* — "Consequently, faith comes from hearing the message, and the message is heard through the word of Christ" (Romans 10:17).

We may be challenged, convicted, and exhilarated with the call to meditation. The question is, how is this to be done? The Scriptures say it should be continual, telling us we ought to meditate "day and night" (Psalm 1:2; cf. 119:97), and even while we lie awake at night (Psalm 63:6; 119:148). Ideally, we are to make meditation part of our regular devotion, giving hidden time to reverently muttering God's Word. But even our busy schedules can be punctuated with Scriptural meditation — in the car, at lunch break, or waiting for a bus. Select a choice text, write it on a card, and slip it into your pocket. Pull it out in those spare moments. Murmur it. Memorize it. Pray it. Say it. Share it.

The discipline of meditation is a must. Moses told Israel as he finished the "Song of Moses": "Take to heart all the words I have solemnly declared to you this day. . . . They are not just idle words for you — *they are your life"* (Deuteronomy 32:46, 47, italics added).

CONFESSION

There can be no ongoing devotion without confession, which can take place anytime. Ideally it ought to take place whenever we sin. But all too often we are too proud and emotionally charged to acknowledge our sin at the time we commit it — for example, when we lose our temper in an argument. But devotion is impossible if we are overloaded with guilt.

Spontaneous Confession
If we have put off admitting our sins to God, confession may need to come first in our devotional time. There is also the probability that during Scriptural meditation, or even during adoration, further hidden sins will come to light. So our moments of devotion may be filled with repeated confession. It is instructive to notice that Psalm 139, which systematically contemplates God's omnipotence and omniscience, ends with a prayer for divine investigation of the Psalmist's soul:

> Search me, O God,
> and know my heart;
> test me and know my anxious thoughts.
> See if there is any offensive way in me,
> and lead me in the way everlasting."
>
> (Psalm 139:23, 24)

Likewise, as Isaiah was worshiping he cried out in confession, "Woe to me! . . . I am ruined! For I am a man of unclean lips, and I live among a people of unclean lips, and my eyes have seen the King, the Lord Almighty" (Isaiah 6:5).

Systematic Confession
While understanding that confession should happen spontaneously, our discipline of devotion ought to involve systematic confession as well. First, we must confess what we are, the ontological reality that we truly are *sinners*. Romans 3:9-20 is the text I have found most helpful on this point, for it repeatedly affirms that we are sinners — that, in fact, our entire being is tainted with evil. It is most important that we regularly make this confession because, as regenerated men who are making some progress in spiritual growth, it is sinfully nat-

ural to falsely suppose we are rising above our condition — a delusion which testifies to our very depravity.

Second, we must confess our specific *sins*. I would suggest making a list of our sins, for the act of writing them out helps materialize this personal reality for us. C. S. Lewis said, "We must lay before him what is in us, not what ought to be within us."[8] This done, we should confess each sin by its ugly name, and then thank God for His forgiveness through the blood of His Son.

The importance of confession for the devotional life cannot be overstated. "If I had cherished sin in my heart, the Lord would not have listened" (Psalm 66:18; cf. Proverbs 28:13). Unconfessed sin makes the heavens seem like brass. But confession not only opens the heavens, it also enhances our intimacy with God, as François Fenelon urged:

> Tell [God] all that is in your heart, as one unloads one's heart to a dear friend. . . . People who have no secrets from each other never want for subjects of conversation; they do not . . . weigh their words, because there is nothing to be kept back. Neither do they seek for something to say; they talk out of the abundance of their heart — without consideration, just what they think. . . . Blessed are they who attain to such familiar, unreserved intercourse with God.[9]

ADORATION

The disciplines of devotion should culminate in sublime adoration and worship. This begins with a proper sense of awe in the presence of the God we know and serve.

Reverence

Reverence must always characterize our approach to God and is especially needed today in our flip-the-channel evangelical culture. Most Christians could use some of the terror that came to Luther, "the horror of Infinitude"[10] that smote him at the altar — for our access to the awesome God of Heaven is real!

Along with proper reverence, there must be concentration. Our minds must be fully engaged. Luther said, "To let your face blabber one thing while your heart dwells on another is just tempting God. . . . Any and every thing, if it is to be well done, demands the entire man, all his mind and faculties."[11] This is why we must give the best time of our day to devotion, when we are the freshest.

Reverence and concentration must be linked with a humble spirit which has worship as its conscious goal — *to lift God up as worthy and to ascribe great worth to Him*. "You are worthy, our Lord and God, to receive glory and honor and power, for you created all things, and by your will they were created and have their being" (Revelation 4:11; cf. 5:9-13).

Contemplation

At the very heart of adoration is contemplation. Numerous Psalms call us to contemplate God as seen in His creation. They never suggest that God is in His creation, but that His excellencies can be seen in His created works. Psalm 29, for example, ascribes glory to God through the visual medium of a great thunder and lightning storm. Psalm 19 begins with these majestic words: "The heavens declare the glory of God; the skies proclaim the work of his hands. Day after day they pour forth speech; night after night they display knowledge" (vv. 1, 2). Listen to God speak through His macrocosm, says the Psalmist! In contrast, Psalm 139 celebrates God's omniscience (vv. 1-6), omnipresence (vv. 7-12), and omnipotence (vv. 13-16) in the microcosm of the human mind and body.

Nature radiates and breathes the glory of God. The very trees do this if we take time to notice. Perhaps you have *really looked* and had an experience like that of Annie Dillard and have seen your backyard tree for what it is: full of lights, "each cell buzzing with flame," and you were "knocked breathless," and your heart went up in wonder to God.[12]

I remember fishing at Cabo San Lucas at the mouth of the Sea of Cortez, with the cloudless, windless day, the perfect sunlight dancing rhythmically on the water in platinum and blue. I recall gliding into an emerald cove surrounded by a cactus desert, donning a snorkel, and slipping over the side into a world of green and turquoise and yellow and pink — another world of slower, gentler rhythm. I also remember the sunset, with its Pacific fire, as we sat on the sand gazing at the summer stars. I was indeed seeing God through His handiwork. That same day I marveled at His animate creation: the ever-present gulls in flight, a seemingly endless sea of yellow-finned tuna and porpoise I could not see across, a striped marlin walking on its tail and crashing back into the water like a fallen horse.

Then there is the microcosm: a newborn baby, eyes and mouth wide open, arms reaching for life — the apex of God's creation. The baby's mind is an amazing computer, recording virtually everything it experiences. Its eyes pass on incredible amounts of data — first through the cornea, then through the focusing lens, where the image strikes the retina and stimulates 125 million nerve endings simultaneously. This is processed by millions of microswitches and funneled down the optic nerve, which contains one million separate insulated fibers (so there are no short circuits). When the information reaches the brain, an equally complex process begins — all of which takes place in a millisecond! Likewise, the infant's ears are so tuned to the vibrating around her that one day she will make music. What a God we have!

> *Take not, oh Lord, our literal sense Lord, in Thy great*
> *Unbroken speech our limping metaphor translate.*[13]

Through the Scriptures, theologians have discerned about twenty attributes of God (though the number is disputed), and contemplation of the attributes has been a time-honored avenue to adoration. Spending twenty consecutive days with a book like A. W. Tozer's *The Knowledge of the Holy*, which devotes three pages to each attribute — God's self-existence, God's eternity, God's infinitude, God's omnipresence, God's grace, God's holiness, to name a few — can catch one's soul up to glory.[14]

Lastly, contemplation and meditation join hands in contemplating God through His mighty acts as described in Scripture. Take the Transfiguration, for example. Read of it in Matthew 17 and Mark 9 and visualize what happened. See it from the disciples' perspective: Jesus is framed by a thousand summer stars, and His clothing has become a glowing white. Overhead are the Bear and Pleiades, and Jesus is shining like a star Himself! Or see the Transfiguration from Jesus' perspective: His glory illuminating the faces of His awestruck inner ring of disciples — His very image dancing in their wide eyes. See it. Touch it. Smell it. Taste it. Participate in the story, and fall down with Peter, James, and John in worship.

This can also be done with such events as the Incarnation, Jesus' death, and the Resurrection, or with the great saving acts of God in the Old Testament — perhaps the Israelites' march through the parted Red Sea, or the revival preaching of Jonah after being delivered from the belly of the great fish. There is much marvelous fuel for reverent meditation from Genesis 1 to Revelation 22.

Worship

The height of devotion is reached when reverence and contemplation produce passionate worship, which in turn breaks forth in thanksgiving and praise in word and song. Jonathan Edwards described his experience like this:

I had vehement longings of soul after God and Christ, and after more holiness, wherewith my heart seemed to be full, and ready to break. . . . I spent most of my time in thinking of divine things, year after year; often walking alone in the woods, and solitary places, for meditation, soliloquy, and prayer, and converse with God; and it was always my manner, at such times, to sing forth my contemplations. . . . Prayer seemed to be natural to me, as the breath by which the inward burnings of my heart had vent.[15]

As we worship we can *pray* or *read* or *sing* God's Word back to Him. The Psalms are perfect for this because they are a worship manual. For example, Psalms 146 — 150, the last five Psalms, begin and end with "hallelujah" (i.e., "praise the Lord!"). And Psalm 150 says, "praise the Lord" in every sentence.[16] (The Resources section of this book lists numerous Psalms which are great for one's worship of the Lord — "Praise Psalms Especially Appropriate for Personal Worship.")

There are some fabulous New Testament hymns as well — for example, those in Luke, beginning with Mary's Magnificat (Luke 1:46-55). There is also the Christological hymn of Colossians 1:15-18, and the Incarnational hymns in John 1 and Philippians 2, and the heavenly hymns of Revelation 4 and 5.

And, of course, there is the music of the Church. Bach's music is universally regarded as Christian meditation transposed into musical form. The hymns and spiritual songs of the Church are the richest sources of poetic praise set to music, with words by the likes of Bernard of Clairvaux, Paul Gerhardt, Charles Wesley, Isaac Watts, George Herbert, and John Donne. In addition, we could mention the beautiful Scripture songs which have risen in our day — so many conveniently in the first person. (The Resources section of this book lists numerous hymns and spiritual songs which lend themselves to the devotional life — "Hymns for Personal Adoration and Praise" and "Choruses and Scripture Songs for Personal Adoration and Praise.")

Our private devotion ought to rise in lyrical extemporaneous praise from our heart's adoration: "Lord, I love You, and I thank You for _____. Lord, glorify Your name through me. . . ." We must prayerfully read and sing Psalms and hymns and spiritual songs back to Him.

May the mind of Christ my Savior
Live in me from day to day,
By His love and power controlling
All I do and say.

—Kate B. Williamson

We taste Thee, O Thou Living Bread,
   And long to feast upon Thee still,
We drink of Thee, the Fountainhead,
   And thirst our souls from Thee to fill.

—Bernard of Clairvaux

Were the whole realm of nature mine,
   That were a present far too small;
Love so amazing, so divine,
   Demands my soul, my life, my all.

—Isaac Watts

Thou art worthy,
   Thou art worthy,
   Thou art worthy, O Lord,
To receive glory, glory and honor,
   Glory and honor and pow'r;
For Thou hast created,
   Hast all things created,
   Thou hast created all things,
And for thy pleasure they are created:
   For Thou art worthy, O Lord.

—Pauline Michael Mills

I love you, Lord
   And I lift my voice
   To worship you, oh my soul rejoice.
Take joy, my king
   In what you hear
May it be a sweet, sweet sound
   In your ear.

—Laurie Klein

Obviously the possibilities of praise are endless and exponential — a truth we will live out for all eternity.

Submission

Does adoration lead to anything else? Yes — the presentation of our bodies — our entire lives — in an ultimate act of worship. This is how Isaiah capped his great experience with God: "Here am I. Send me!" (Isaiah 6:8). Similarly, after the great Apostle Paul sings in worshipful doxology — "For from him and through him and to him are all things. To him be the glory forever! Amen" (Romans 11:36), he immediately calls us to submission: "Therefore, I urge you, brothers, in view of God's mercy, to offer your bodies as living sacrifices, holy and pleasing to God — which is your spiritual worship" (Romans 12:1).

Thomas a Kempis made this the first part of his daily worship, using the prayer of submission: "As thou wilt; what thou wilt; when thou wilt."[17]

Our devotion must culminate in a conscious yielding of every part of our personality, every ambition, every relationship, and every hope to Him. This done, we have reached the apex of personal devotion.

As I cautioned when we began, personal devotion cannot and must not be reduced to a few principles such as *meditation, confession, adoration* and *submission*. Neither can it be put in a logical straitjacket. Sometimes we may be called to confession and submission only. Other times, adoration may occupy an extended time, or our devotions will properly be confined to petition only. There will be times when *all* of it takes place in twenty minutes.

But one thing is certain — it will not happen without discipline. The reason many men never have an effective devotional life is, they never plan for it. They do not know what it is because they have never taken the time to find out. They do not pray because they do not set aside the time. Their character never rises to that of Christ's because they do not expose their lives to His pure light. Their wills stay crooked because they do not tie into Him.

The question for prayerless men is a very masculine one: Are we man enough to meditate? To confess? To adore? To submit? To sweat and endure?

Food for Thought

How much time do you generally spend in conversation with God? In your view (without using evangelical clichés), why is prayer an important part of the Christian walk?

What does the word *meditation* suggest to you? Why should you meditate on the Lord and His Word and will (compare Psalm 1:2; Revelation 2:7, 11, 17, 29; 3:6, 13, 22)?

What does devotion have to do with confession, and vice versa? Check out Psalm 139:23, 24; 66:18 in this regard.

In what ways do you identify with Isaiah's confession in Isaiah 6:5? When you are aware that God knows all about the things you think and do and say, do you feel "ruined"? Why or why not?

Are you usually in too much of a hurry to "see" God or hear His voice? What can you do to make more time for Him?

Do you find it difficult to make time to meditate, to confess, to worship, to consciously surrender to God? What barriers or distractions keep you from doing these things?

Application/Response

What did God speak to you about most specifically, most powerfully in this chapter? Talk to Him about it right now!

Think About It!

What facets of true worship do you find in the following assorted Bible passages: Psalms 146 — 150; Luke 1:46-55; Revelation 4 — 5; Isaiah 6:8; Romans 12:1? What can you do to experience these aspects of worship?

8

DISCIPLINE OF PRAYER

E. M. BOUNDS said, "When the angel of devotion has gone, the angel of prayer has lost its wings and it becomes a deformed and loveless thing."[1] Our previous study was about our devotional wings (*meditation*, *confession*, *adoration*, and *submission*). Now, wings formed and stretched in flight, we come to *petition*, the offering of our requests to God. It is my hope this study will instruct and motivate us to a soaring life of petitionary prayer which will call down God's power upon our lives and the Church.

The Scriptural setting for the classic text on petitionary prayer could scarcely be more dramatic — it is a soldier preparing for battle. His heart pounds *ka-thump, ka-thump* under his metal breastplate. As he steadies himself, he hitches up his armor belt and scuffs at the earth like a football player with his studded boots, testing his traction. He repeatedly draws his great shield across his body in anticipation of the fiery barrages to come. Reflexively he reaches up and repositions his helmet. He gingerly tests the edge of his sword and slips it back into his scabbard.

The enemy approaches. Swords pulled from their scabbards ring in chilling symphony. The warriors stand motionless, breathing in dreadful spasms.

And then the believing soldier does the most astounding thing. He falls to his knees in deep, profound, petitionary prayer — for he has obeyed his divine instructions to take up what John Bunyan referred to as "All-Prayer."[2] The Holy Scriptures themselves portray this weapon: "And pray in the Spirit on all occasions with all kinds of prayers and requests. With this in mind, be alert and always keep on praying for all the saints" (Ephesians 6:18).

We are charged with five elements necessary to fully experience the power of petitionary prayer.

IN-SPIRITED PRAYER

"And pray in the spirit . . ." begins Paul, giving us the first element of petition
— in-Spirited or Spirit-directed prayer. How does *prayer in the Spirit* occur?
Romans 8:26, 27 eloquently tells us:

> In the same way, the Spirit helps us in our weakness. We do not know what
> we ought to pray, but the Spirit himself intercedes for us with groans that
> words cannot express. And he who searches our hearts knows the mind of
> the Spirit, because the Spirit intercedes for the saints in accordance with
> God's will.

The indwelling Holy Spirit, through His superior intimate knowledge,
both prays for us and joins us in our praying, infusing His prayers into ours
so that we "pray in the Spirit." Jude 20 challenges us to cultivate and experience this wonderful Spirit-wrought phenomenon: "But you, dear friends,
build yourselves up in your most holy faith and pray in the Holy Spirit."
Praying in the Spirit is the will of God, and what God wills He empowers as
we let Him.

Two supernatural things happen here: First, the Holy Spirit tells us what
we ought to pray for. Apart from the Spirit's assistance, our prayers are limited
by our own reason and intuition. But with the Holy Spirit's help they become
informed by Heaven. As we seek the Spirit's help, He will speak to us through
His Word, which conveys His mind regarding every matter of principle. Thus,
in Spirit-directed prayer we will think God's thoughts after Him. His desires will
become our desires, His motives our motives, His ends our ends.

Further, as He shows our hearts which matters to pray for, He gives us the
absolute conviction they are God's will. Oswald Sanders, former director of
Overseas Missionary Fellowship (formerly China Inland Mission), says in this
regard:

> The very fact that God lays a burden of prayer on our hearts and keeps us
> praying is *prima facie* evidence that He purposes to grant the answer. When
> asked if he really believed that two men for whose salvation he had prayed
> for over fifty years would be converted, George Muller of Bristol replied,
> "Do you think God would have kept me praying all these years if He did
> not intend to save them?" Both men were converted, one shortly before, the
> other after Muller's death.[3]

Such confident direction in one's prayer life is not unusual. I had a similar conviction regarding my brother, who came to Christ after I had been praying for him for thirty years! When God's people truly "pray in the Spirit," they receive similar direction and conviction, not only about people, but about events and projects and even whole nations.

The second benefit of "praying in the Spirit" is that it supplies the energizing of the Holy Spirit for prayer, infusing tired, even infirm, bodies and elevating the depressed to pray with power and conviction for God's work.

Men, learn to pray in the Spirit! To help myself do this, I have written "Pray in the Spirit" at the top of my prayer list as a constant reminder to patiently wait on the Lord, asking the Spirit to give me prayers. My list contains numerous long-standing petitions for which I regularly pray, but I also want to be consciously open to the Spirit, so that as He wishes, He will regularly invade my list with His direction and energy.

Says John Bunyan:

> Prayer is a sincere, sensible, affectionate pouring out of the heart or soul to God, through Christ, in the strength and assistance of the Holy Spirit, for such things as God has promised, or according to the Word of God, for the good of the church, with submission in faith to the will of God.[4]

Let us learn to pray in-Spirited prayer using the strength and assistance of the Holy Spirit.

CONTINUAL PRAYER

The next ingredient of petitionary prayer is that it is continuous — "on all occasions." This characterized the practice of the Apostolic Church, as Acts 1:14 indicates: "They all joined together constantly in prayer, along with the women and Mary the mother of Jesus, and his brothers" (cf. 2:42). Paul told the Thessalonians to "pray continually" (1 Thessalonians 5:17), and he recommended that the Philippians "in everything, by prayer and petition, with thanksgiving, present your requests to God" (4:6).

Is continual prayer possible? Yes and no. It is, of course, impossible to carry on a running dialogue while we are working or at other times, but the prayer called for here is not so much the articulation of words as the *posture of the heart.*

Thomas Kelly explains in his *Testament of Devotion*:

> There is a way of ordering our mental life on more than one level at once. On one level we can be thinking, discussing, seeing, calculating, meeting all the demands of external affairs. But deep within, behind the scenes, at a profounder level, we may also be in prayer and adoration, song and worship, and a gentle receptiveness to divine breathings.[5]

The irrepressible medieval monk Brother Lawrence recorded his experience of continual prayer in the classic *The Practice of the Presence of God*:

> The time of business does not differ with me from the time of prayer; and in the noise and clatter of my kitchen, while several persons are at the same time calling for different things, I possess God in as great tranquility as if I were on my knees.[6]

This was also John Wesley's experience, who modestly explained it in the third person:

> [H]is heart is ever lifted up to God at all times and in all places. In this he is never hindered, much less interrupted, by any person or thing. In retirement or company, in leisure, business, or conversation, his heart is ever with the Lord. Whether he lie down or rise up, God is in all his thoughts; he walks with God continually, having the loving eye of his mind still fixed upon Him, and everywhere "seeing him that is invisible."[7]

Thus we see that a life of continual prayer is not only possible, but some actually live it out. Paul challenges us to understand that this life is not meant just for some, or for a spiritual elite, but for all of us. Continual prayer is God's will for every Christian, no exceptions. I can do it; you can do it. Business people, students, young parents — all can do it. We are to have a perpetual inner dialogue with God. We must always be looking up, even when driving to work or mowing the lawn.

VARIED PRAYER

The third aspect of the prayer life is that it is varied — "with all kinds of prayers and requests." Later Paul would similarly write to Timothy, "I urge, then, first of all, that requests, prayers, intercession and thanksgiving be made for everyone . . ." (1 Timothy 2:1). Varied prayer grows out of what we have just seen about continual prayer, because if we pray continually, the various situations we encounter will demand a variety of prayers. Think of the variety appropriate to life's situations — prayer to resist temptation, prayer for wisdom, for power, for self-restraint, for protection of others, for growth, for conviction.

Floyd Pierson, a retired Africa Inland Mission worker, was a man who literally prayed "on all occasions with all kinds of prayers and requests." So habitual was this that in his seventies, when he went to take a driver's test, he said to the examiner, "I always pray before I drive — Let's bow our heads together." The official likely wondered what kind of a ride he was in for! We can imagine him checking his seat belt and setting his perspiring hand on the door handle. Pierson passed!

Apart from the humor, there is something quite beautiful here — the unaffected witness of a vibrant inner spiritual reality which bubbles up "with all kinds of prayers and requests."

PERSISTENT PRAYER

The fourth aspect of effective prayer is persistence — "With this in mind, be alert and always keep on praying . . ."

Exodus 17 describes aged Moses standing atop a hill, arms lifted up to Heaven, interceding for Israel, which was engaged in a pitched battle with the Amalekites below. As long as his arms were extended upward, Israel prevailed, but when in weariness they began to fall, the Amalekites dominated. Poor Moses was in agony as gravity drew his hands toward destruction. But then came Aaron and Hur, who placed a stone under Moses and, standing on either side, held his hands up to God until sunset and victory came (vv. 10-13). That story graphically emphasizes that there is a mysterious efficacy to persistent prayer. This is not to suggest that God regards prayer as a meritorious work — so that when there are enough prayers, He answers. Rather, He sovereignly chooses to encourage persistence in prayer and to answer it to His everlasting glory.

In one of His prayer parables, the Lord dramatized what He wants from all believers:

> Then Jesus told his disciples a parable to show them that they should always pray and not give up. He said: "In a certain town there was a judge who neither feared God nor cared about men. And there was a widow in that town who kept coming to him with the plea, 'Grant me justice against my adver-

sary.' For some time he refused. But finally he said to himself, 'Even though
I do not fear God or care about men, yet because this widow keeps bother-
ing me, I will see that she gets justice, so that she won't eventually wear me
out with her coming!'" (Luke 18:1-5)

The cultivation of persistence was a recurring motif in Jesus' teaching on
prayer. In Gethsemane Jesus challenged His disciples when they failed to persevere by saying, "Watch and pray so that you will not fall into temptation. The
spirit is willing, but the body is weak" (Mark 14:38).

At the end of the Sermon on the Mount, Jesus enjoined His followers to
prayerful tenacity: "Ask and it will be given to you; seek and you will find;
knock and the door will be opened to you" (Matthew 7:7). The language is
unusually compelling because the three verbs ("ask . . . seek . . . knock") indicate an ascending intensity. "Ask" implies requesting assistance for a conscious
need. It also suggests humility, for the Greek word here was commonly used by
one approaching a superior. "Seek" involves asking, but adds action. The idea
is not just to express need, but to get up and look around for help. "Knock"
includes asking, plus seeking, plus persevering — for example, one who keeps
pounding on a closed door. The stacking of these verbs is powerful, and the fact
that they are present imperatives gives them even more punch. Jesus' words
actually read: "Keep on asking, and it shall be given to you; keep on seeking,
and you will find; keep on knocking, and it shall be opened to you."

Such tenacity is exactly what Paul has in mind in his call to petitionary
prayer when he says to "be alert and always keep on praying . . ."

Men, do we pray with Scriptural persistence for our families? For the
Church? Are there individuals, groups, causes, souls for which we hold up our
hands in prayer? There ought to be, for God answers persistent prayer.

INTERCESSORY PRAYER

The fifth aspect of asking prayer is *intercessory* prayer — "for all the saints."
There are many worthy petitions to make, but "saints" — believers in Jesus
Christ — are to have a large place in our prayers.

Notice that this call to pray "for all the saints" occasions Paul's request for
prayer for himself: "Pray also for me, that whenever I open my mouth, words
may be given me so that I will fearlessly make known the mystery of the gospel,
for which I am an ambassador in chains. Pray that I may declare it fearlessly,
as I should" (Eph. 6:19, 20). Paul knew what others' prayers could do for him.

Petitionary prayers for others brings grace to their lives. Few people know that the stupendous achievement of William Carey in India was fueled by his bedridden sister who prayed for him for over fifty years.

Tennyson beautifully gave verse to Paul's wisdom, saying:

If thou shouldst never see my face again,
  Pray for my soul.
More things are wrought by prayer
  Than this world dreams of.
Wherefore, let thy voice
  Rise like a fountain for me night and day.
For what are men better than sheep or goats
  That nourish a blind life within the brain
If, knowing God, they lift not hands of prayer
  Both for themselves and those who call them friend?
For so the whole round earth is every way
  Bound by gold chains about the feet of God.[8]

How beautiful is the five-fold anatomy of petitionary prayer: *In-Spirited* — prayer "in the Spirit"; *continual* — prayer "on all occasions"; *varied* — "all kinds of prayers and requests"; *persistent* — "be alert and always keep on praying"; and *intercessory* — "for all the saints." Certainly we are challenged and motivated! But the question is, how are we to pray in this way? Here we must turn to very practical advice.

THE PRACTICE OF PETITIONARY PRAYER

The Prayer List

Essential to our effective petitionary prayer is a prayer list. I say this first because of my own repeated experiences. For example, I may be praying for my mother, and as I pray for her I see our old family home at 747 Edmaru Avenue. In front is parked my gray-primered 1941 Ford. It has racing slicks on the back, a hopped-up '48 Merc engine, and on the side, custom pin-striping which reads "Swing Low, Sweet Chariot." Suddenly I am seventeen, wearing my blue suede leather jacket, sitting behind my gold steering wheel, and heading down Beach Boulevard to Huntington Beach. I can smell the ocean and cocoa butter. So much for my "prayers for Mother"!

This is why I need a prayer list. To be sure, even using a list, my mind still wanders. But when it does, I always have my list to bring me back. And when I am especially prone to distraction I can place my index finger on her name and pray with my eyes wide open — moving from name to name in this way.

Every Christian man should have a prayer list which lists, among other things, the names of his family and, if married, spouse and children. Moreover, the list ought to be detailed, featuring personal items under the names of those closest to him. I have found that small "Post-its" placed under headings help keep my list updated.

My daily prayer list carries the following headings, each with several details under it:

FAMILY, STAFF, SECRETARIES AND CUSTODIANS, ILL, GRIEVING, IMPORTANT EVENTS, PRESENT PROBLEMS, MINISTRIES, WEEKLY WORSHIP, NEW BELIEVERS, MISSIONS LIST.

In addition to my daily list, I have four other lists which I try to go through once a week.

List 1 has: ONGOING ILL, PERSONAL REQUESTS FROM OTHERS, EVANGELISM, SPIRITUAL WARFARE.

List 2 has: WORLD, USA, PERSONAL LIFE, NEEDED PERSONAL QUALITIES.

List 3 has: CHRISTIAN LEADERS, PASTORS, UPCOMING MINISTRIES AND VISION.

List 4 has: GOVERNMENT LEADERS (federal, state, and local).

Quite frankly, I could not get on at all without a prayer list, not only because it tames my wandering mind, but also because it insures that I will not neglect things that are important to me, including the many requests for personal prayer which I receive. Without a prayer list, my promises to "pray for you" would be totally empty. In addition, a prayer list is perfect for keeping track of answers to prayer.

If you do not have a prayer list, start small. Simply list the relationships and matters most important to you on a 3 x 5 card, add a few specifics under the names, and put it in your wallet for daily reference. I guarantee that if you use it, it will greatly enhance your prayer life.

"Quiet" Time

Next you need some quiet. I am well aware that *quiet* is a relative term in today's world where there is virtually no silence. Many of us never experience silence during our waking hours. We wake up to a clock radio, shave to the news, drive through noisy traffic, enter a noisy, busy office, return home listening to the rush-hour reports, "relax" in front of the TV, and drift off to sleep as the house pulsates with the *thump, thump* of the family stereo.

What is more, the occasional silence we do encounter can be distracting because it heightens other distracting noises. Trappist monk Thomas Merton tells how in the deep quietness of a monastery, a cough repeated at predictable intervals can destroy every possibility of collected thought.[9] Silence is sometimes louder than the noise you are trying to ignore! So you need to choose the situation that works best for you. It may be dominated by road noise, but if that is the atmosphere you need to concentrate, use it.

Place

Along with this you must find a place where you will not be disturbed. Early in my ministry, my office was in a twenty-five-foot trailer. My part-time secretary was on the other side of a thin plywood partition. I could hear everything! If that was not enough, the whole trailer shook when the door opened.

My solutions were many, and all off the premises — the beautiful old and always open and empty sanctuary of a neighboring church, the park, the wonderful anonymity of my car parked at a busy shopping center. Even today, though I now have a quiet office, I often go to similar places for my devotions.

Time

I also try to give my best time to prayer — which for me is never the time just before going to bed. One's last waking moments should never be given to powerful intercessory prayer (except, perhaps, for students who have a final exam in the morning).

Here Jesus' habit is instructive: "Very early in the morning, while it was still dark, Jesus got up, left the house and went off to a solitary place, where he prayed" (Mark 1:35). The early bird gets the prime time. The real question for you is, when is your best time? For some it may be at lunch or before dinner.

Posture

A certain man could not find the right posture for prayer. He tried praying on his knees, but that was not comfortable; besides, it wrinkled his slacks. He tried praying standing, but soon his legs got tired. He tried praying seated, but that did not seem reverent. Then one day as he was walking through a field, he fell headfirst into an open well. And did he ever pray!

Seriously, one's prayer posture can make a difference. While the Scriptures mention numerous postures for prayer, none is prescribed. What is important is that your posture enhance reverent attention. Sometimes I kneel, sometimes

I walk about the room, often I sit at my desk with list in hand. There are times when I lift my hands, and other times I have been on my face. Heart attitude is the key factor.

Preparation

As to preparation for prayer, honest practicality is of greatest importance. Sometimes a man needs a shower and a shave. If you are into coffee like I am, a good cup of coffee is a divine cordial. Again, it is not the physical details that are of prime importance but the condition and stance of the heart. Whatever helps you focus on the Lord, use it.

Length

Often the best prayers are short and passionate. Luther himself said: "Look to it that you do not try to do all of it, do not try to do too much, lest your spirit grow weary. Besides, a good prayer mustn't be too long. Do not draw it out. Prayer ought to be frequent and fervent."[10] A legalistic commitment to duration can kill one's prayer life.

THE DISCIPLINE OF PETITIONARY PRAYER

The practice of prayer — the *list*, the *quiet*, the *place*, the *time*, the *posture*, *preparation*, and the *length* — all suggest one thing — *discipline*.

Work

Candidly, prayer is work, not a sport. It is not something that you do if you like it, or devote your spare time to, or do only if you are good at it.[11] Prayer is the proper work of the soul which loves Christ (Ephesians 6:18):

> And pray in the Spirit
> on all occasions
> with all kinds of prayers and requests.
> With this in mind, be alert
> and always keep on praying
> for all the saints.

This is a call to work!

We must never wait until we *feel* like praying — otherwise we may never pray, unless, perhaps, we fall headfirst into an open well. The context of Paul's charge in Ephesians 6 is spiritual warfare — and that is what prayer is! Christian men face the world — and fall on their knees. Work and war, war and work — these are the words we must keep before us if we are to become men of prayer.

Measured Work

This understood, we must also understand that we must not overcommit ourselves, especially if we are just beginning. The tendency, when truly challenged, is to say, "I'm committing myself to two hours of daily prayer, I am going to read the Bible through twice this year, and I'm going to practice every day the disciplines of devotion (meditation, confession, adoration, submission) and also the discipline of petition. I'm going to have a prayer list that is second to none." That will last about three days — maybe!

Better to commit yourself to a total of fifteen minutes and maintain it — with perhaps five minutes of Bible reading, five minutes of meditation, and five minutes of disciplined prayer. A regular time of devotion and prayer will become a habit, and the habit of prayer will give wings to your spiritual life.

In this respect, Dr. J. Sidlow Baxter once shared a page from his own pastoral diary with a group of pastors who had inquired about the discipline of prayer. He began by telling how in 1928 he entered the ministry determined he would be the "most Methodist-Baptist" of pastors, a real man of prayer. However, it was not long before his increasing pastoral responsibilities and administrative duties and the subtle subterfuges of pastoral life began to crowd prayer out. Moreover, he began to get used to it, making excuses for himself.

Then one morning it all came to a head as he stood over his work-strewn desk and looked at his watch. The voice of the Spirit was calling him to pray. At the same time another velvety little voice was telling him to be practical and get his letters answered, and that he ought to face up to the fact that he was not one of the "spiritual sort" — only a few people could be like that. "That last remark," says Baxter, "hurt like a dagger blade. I could not bear to think it was true." He was horrified by his ability to rationalize away the very ground of his ministerial vitality and power.

That morning Sidlow Baxter took a good look into his heart, and found there was a part of him which did not want to pray and a part which did. The part which did not was his emotions; the part which did was his intellect and will. This analysis paved the way to victory. In Dr. Baxter's own inimitable words:

> As never before, my will and I stood face to face. I asked my will the straight question, "Will, are you ready for an hour of prayer?" Will answered, "Here I am, and I'm quite ready, if you are." So Will and I linked arms and turned

to go for our time of prayer. At once all the emotions began pulling the other way and protesting, "We are not coming." I saw Will stagger just a bit, so I asked, "Can you stick it out, Will?" and Will replied, "Yes, if you can." So Will went, and we got down to prayer, dragging those wriggling, obstreperous emotions with us. It was a struggle all the way through. At one point, when Will and I were in the middle of an earnest intercession, I suddenly found one of those traitorous emotions had snared my imagination and had run off to the golf course; and it was all I could do to drag the wicked rascal back. A bit later I found another of the emotions had sneaked away with some off-guard thoughts and was in the pulpit, two days ahead of schedule, preaching a sermon that I had not yet finished preparing!

At the end of that hour, if you had asked me, "Have you had a 'good time'?" I would have had to reply, "No, it has been a wearying wrestle with contrary emotions and a truant imagination from beginning to end." What is more, that battle with the emotions continued for between two and three weeks, and if you had asked me at the end of that period, "Have you had a 'good time' in your daily praying?" I would have had to confess, "No, at times it has seemed as though the heavens were brass, and God too distant to hear, and the Lord Jesus strangely aloof, and prayer accomplished nothing."

Yet something *was* happening. For one thing, Will and I really taught the emotions that we were completely independent of them. Also, one morning, about two weeks after the contest began, just when Will and I were going for another time of prayer, I overheard one of the emotions whisper to the other, "Come on, you guys, it is no use wasting any more time resisting: they'll go just the same." That morning, for the first time, even though the emotions were still suddenly uncooperative, they were at least quiescent, which allowed Will and me to get on with prayer undistractedly.

Then, another couple of weeks later, what do you think happened? During one of our prayer times, when Will and I were no more thinking of the emotions than of the man in the moon, one of the most vigorous of the emotions unexpectedly sprang up and shouted, "Hallelujah!" at which all the other emotions exclaimed, "Amen!" And for the first time the whole of my being — intellect, will, and emotions — was united in one coordinated prayer-operation.[12]

Food for Thought

Why is the image of warfare an appropriate one for a consideration of the discipline of prayer (see Ephesians 6:18)? Apply this to your own victories and defeats regarding prayer.

What do Romans 8:26, 27 and Jude 20 say to you about the Holy Spirit and prayer? Why are the truths here important to you personally?

Review the picture of prayer portrayed in the story of Moses in Exodus 17. Practically speaking, what are some things we can do to help one another persist in prayer? Be as specific as you can.

What does Paul ask prayer for in Ephesians 6:19, 20? Do you want other Christians to pray for you in this area? Why or why not? What does action on your part have to do with prayer along these lines?

Do you find it difficult to find enough time and a quiet place away from interruptions for your prayer times? Why? Is it because your life is too busy, or are there conflicting loyalties you prefer to ignore?

What can you do practically to pray more frequently and to be better prepared for prayer times when they come?

Application/Response

What did God speak to you about most specifically, most powerfully in this chapter? Talk to Him about it right now!

Think About It!

Make a list of those individuals for whom you want to pray regularly, then establish a time when you will pray for several people on the list often (at least three times a week). And when you pray, ask for specific answers, so you will see them as they arrive.

9

DISCIPLINE OF WORSHIP

T HE FEATURE ARTICLE of the October 1978 issue of *Harper's Magazine*, entitled "Trendier Than Thou," reported that Kilmer Myers, then Episcopal Bishop of California, had welcomed Bay Area transcendentalists to the Gothic splendor of Grace Cathedral for nature festivals and pagan ceremonies. The article went on to report:

> During one nature ceremony in the cathedral, a decidedly ecumenical audience watched reverently as the poet Allen Ginsberg, wearing a deer mask, joined others similarly garbed to ordain Senators Alan Cranston and John Tunney as godfathers of animals (Cranston of the Tule elk and Tunney of the California brown bear) . . . while movie projectors simultaneously cast images of buffalo herds and other endangered species on the walls and ceilings, to the accompaniment of rock music.[1]

As we would expect, many Episcopal priests protested what they rightly termed "a profane employment of their sacred house of worship." Regardless, Bishop Myers wholeheartedly participated in the druidic ceremonies, offering prayers for a "renaissance of reverence for life in America."[2] To borrow T. S. Eliot's phrase, there has been "Murder in the Cathedral" — in this case the death of the reverent worship of God in truth and spirit.

To some, troubles for the great religious traditions may seem far removed. But the truth is, similar troubles are common in the more independent, evangelical traditions. A friend of mine one Sunday morning visited a church where, to his amazement, the worship prelude was the theme from the movie *The Sting*, entitled (significantly, I think) "The Entertainer." The congregation was preparing for divine worship while cinematic images, not of buffalo herds, but of Paul Newman and Robert Redford in 1920s garb hovered in their consciousness!

And that was just the prelude, for what followed was an off-the-wall service that made no attempt at worship, the "high point" being the announcements when the pastor (inspired no doubt by the rousing prelude) stood unbeknownst behind the unfortunate person doing announcements making "horns" behind his head with his forked fingers and making faces for the congregation. This buffoonery took place in a self-proclaimed "Bible-believing church" which ostensibly worships the holy Triune God of the Bible. "Murder in the Chapel"?

Sadly, stories like these are not uncommon in today's secularized, man-centered culture. Many Christians have never thought through the meaning and importance of worship. It is not an overstatement to say that our pleasure-centered culture has produced many who work at their play and play at their worship.

Why this confusion and tragic failure regarding worship? The answer lies in another question: Why do we worship — is it for God or for man? The unspoken but increasingly common assumption of today's Christendom is that worship is primarily for *us* — to meet our needs. Such worship services are entertainment-focused, and the worshipers are uncommitted spectators who are silently grading the performance. From this perspective preaching becomes a homiletics of consensus — preaching to felt needs — man's conscious agenda instead of God's. Such preaching is always topical and never textual. Biblical information is minimized, and the sermons are short and full of stories. Anything and everything that is suspected of making the marginal attender uncomfortable is removed from the service, whether it be a registration card or a "mere" creed. Taken to the nth degree, this philosophy instills a tragic self-centeredness. That is, everything is judged by how it affects man. This terribly corrupts one's theology.

The telltale sign of this kind of thinking is the common post-worship question, What did you think of the service today? The real questions ought to be, What did God think of it and of those who worshiped? and What did I give to God? It is so easy to forget that in going to worship our main concern should be to "worship in spirit and in truth" (John 4:24) — not to receive a lift for ourselves.

Therefore, it is important that we understand, in distinction to the popular view that worship is for us, that worship begins not with man as its focus, but God. Worship must be orchestrated and conducted with the vision before us of an august, awesome, holy, transcendent God who is to be pleased and, above all, glorified by our worship. Everything in our corporate worship should flow from this understanding.

What about our needs then? When we worship and adore God in our singing and prayer and listening to the Word, His *shalom* will well in our souls so that we will leave with a glad sense of personal blessing — a great lift. But this is a byproduct, not a goal, a further evidence of the generous grace of God.

REASONS FOR GOD-CENTERED WORSHIP

Divine Priority
In considering the rationale for God-centered worship, we must begin with the realization that worship is the number one priority of the Church. Jesus' famous statement in John 4:23 that the Father *seeks* worshipers is unparalleled, for nowhere in the entire corpus of Holy Scripture do we read of God's seeking anything else from a child of God.[3] *God desires worship above all else.*

Thus, every man who calls himself a Christian must understand that worship is the ultimate priority of his life. Worship is what God wants from you and from me. Jesus hallowed and substantiated this in His chiding of busy, frenetic Martha, who was so critical of her sister's sitting at Jesus' feet: "Martha, Martha . . . you are worried and upset about many things, but only one thing is needed. Mary has chosen what is better, and it will not be taken away from her" (Luke 10:41, 42).

A look at the massive emphasis on worship in the Old Testament reveals God's mind on worship's priority. Exodus devotes twenty-five chapters to the construction of the Tabernacle, the locus of divine worship. Leviticus amounts to a twenty-seven chapter liturgical manual. And the Psalms are a spectacular 150-chapter worship hymnal. Divine worship has always been the occupation and sustenance, the priority, of the believing soul.

Divine Presence
The other reason we ought to worship is the promise of God's presence. We all know God is everywhere — He is omnipresent — and that He has promised us, "Never will I leave you; never will I forsake you" (Hebrews 13:5). Nevertheless, He has given the Church the unique promise that "[W]here two or three come together in my name, there am I with them" (Matthew 18:20) — which means that His presence is with us in a very special way when we assemble to focus on Him.

Dr. A. J. Gordon, founder of Gordon College and Gordon-Conwell Divinity School, had a dream which heightened this Scriptural reality. One Saturday night Dr. Gordon, worn-out from working on Sunday's sermon, fell asleep and began to dream. He dreamt he was in the pulpit when a stranger came in and sat down.

Gordon saw everything around the man with surreal clarity, even the pew number. But he could not see the man's face. He did remember, however, that the face wore a serious look, as of a person who had great sorrow — and that it gave him the most respectful attention. As he preached, he could not take his eyes off the man. The man held his gaze rather than Gordon his.

The service over, Dr. Gordon tried to reach him through the crowded aisle, but the man was gone. Approaching the man who had sat beside the stranger, he asked who he was. Then came the laconic reply, "It was Jesus of Nazareth." Gordon chastised him for letting Jesus go, but the man replied nonchalantly, "Oh, do not be troubled. He has been here today, and no doubt will come again."

Gordon goes on to record his shock and subsequent self-examination, and then concludes,

> One thought . . . lingered in my mind with something of comfort and more of awe. "*He has been here today, and no doubt will come again*"; and mentally repeating these words as one regretfully meditating on a vanished vision, I awoke and it was a dream. No, it was not a dream. It was a vision of the deepest reality, a miniature of an actual ministry.

The impact on A. J. Gordon was historic. In fact, he says the new sense of Christ's presence brought great blessing to Clarendon Street Church, which ultimately resulted in the establishment of a Bible training school, destined to become Gordon College.[4]

Think what such an awareness of Christ's presence would do to corporate worship of the confessing Church if we would just let the truth sink in. One thing is for sure: murder would cease in cathedral and chapel alike!

Men, when we meet for corporate worship, *Christ is in our midst*. He walks among the glowing lampstands of His churches (Revelation 1:20). He treads the aisles of our churches and sits beside us. He searches for those who worship in spirit and truth. He desires our praise.

This being the highest priority, we must answer truthfully: do we worship as He desires?

DOING GOD-CENTERED WORSHIP

If I have learned anything in leading worship after twenty-five years in the ministry, I have learned that worship does not just "happen." Worship requires careful preparation on the part of ministers and congregations.

I have experienced both sides of this, and I know Sunday morning can be the worst time of the week. It is probably true that couples, especially those with young children, have more fights on Sunday morning than on any other day of the week. Sometimes by the time we get to church, worship is an impossibility — unless, perhaps, the sermon is on repentance!

Preparation

The answer to the problem begins with Saturday preparation. (Any men who interpret the following as women's work are wrong. Both husband and wife should share responsibility for the practical and spiritual preparations for the Lord's Day.) It is advisable that young families have their clothing clean and laid out on Saturday night, and even that the breakfast be decided upon. The whereabouts of Bibles and lessons should be known, and even better, ought to be collected and ready. There should be an agreed-upon time to get up which leaves plenty of time to get ready for church. Going to bed at a reasonable hour is also a good idea. Spiritually, prayer about the Lord's Day is essential — prayer for the service, the music, the pastors, one's family, and oneself.[5]

The Puritans understood this well. As one of their great preachers, George Swinnock, quaintly expressed it:

> Prepare to meet thy God, O Christian! Betake thyself to thy chamber on the Saturday night. . . . The oven of thine heart thus baked, as it were, overnight, would be easily heated the next morning; the fire so well raked up when thou wentest to bed, would be the sooner kindled when thou shouldst rise. If thou wouldst thus leave thy heart with God on the Saturday night, thou shouldst find it with him in the Lord's Day morning.[6]

On Sunday everyone needs to get up on time, eat at a set hour, and leave plenty early, ideally after a short time of family prayer asking that God will be glorified and speak to each family member. If you do this, Sunday worship will ascend to new heights.

Expectancy

Next you ought to come expecting to uniquely meet God in corporate worship. Congregational worship makes possible an intensity of devotion which does not as readily come in individual worship. On the tragic level, a mob tends to descend to a much deeper level of cruelty than individuals by themselves. It is also understood that the appreciation and enjoyment of an informed group of music lovers at a symphony is more intense than that of a single listener at home. This holds true for worship as well, because corporate worship provides a context where passion is joyously elevated and God's Word comes with unique power. Martin Luther spoke of this when he confided, "At home in my own house there is no warmth or vigor in me, but in the church when the multitude is gathered together, a fire is kindled in my heart and it breaks its way through."[7] We must come with great expectation — for we will experience just what we expect.

In Truth

Jesus tells us in John 4:24 that we must "worship in spirit and in truth." Worshiping "in truth" means that we come informed by the objective revelation of God's Word about the great God we serve and the precepts He has spoken. In this sense our worship is governed by what we know and believe of God. The better informed we are, the better we can worship. If we know and have taken to heart passages like Genesis 1, Psalm 139, Psalm 23, the Book of Job, John 7, John 17, Romans 1 — 3, Revelation 19 — to name a few, the better equipped we will be to worship "in truth."

This knowledge of God through his Word ought to heighten our expectations and instill healthy fear and reverence. As Annie Dillard wrote:

> On the whole, I do not find Christians, outside of the Catacombs, sufficiently sensible of conditions. Does anyone have the foggiest idea what sort of power we so blithely invoke? Or as I suspect, does no one believe a word of it? . . . It is madness to wear ladies' straw hats and velvet hats to church; we should all be wearing crash helmets. Ushers should issue life preservers and signal flares; they should lash us to our pews. For the sleeping god may wake someday and take offense, or the waking god may draw us out to where we can never return.[8]

Men, we need to fill ourselves with God's truth so our worship will be electrified with proper reality!

In Spirit

Besides worshiping in stupendous truth, we worship "in spirit." Notice the small "s," referring to our human spirits, the inner person. True worship flows from the inside out. Worship is not an external activity, but is of necessity first internal. Jesus warned hypocrites with the words of Isaiah: "'These people honor me with their lips, but their hearts are far from me. They worship me in vain'" (Mark 7:6, 7, quoting Isaiah 29:13).

Thus true worship must spring from within a man's spirit, from the spontaneous affections of the heart — as it did so regularly from the heart of David. Psalm 130, a Psalm of Ascents, expresses the anticipation of one worshiping in spirit:

> I wait for the Lord, my soul waits,
> and in his word I put my hope.
> My soul waits for the Lord
> more than watchmen wait for the morning,
> more than watchmen wait for the morning.
>
> (Psalm 130:5, 6)

THE DISCIPLINE OF WORSHIP

It is the Lord's Day. You have come to church to worship God "in spirit and in truth." You are in church to give him worth — *worth-ship*, as the English word properly means. What now? Here again the word which is the theme of this book comes to center stage — *discipline*.

It is of great significance that one of the two most prominent words denoting worship in the New Testament is the word *latreuo*, which means "to work or serve." This tells us implicitly that worship involves work — disciplined work. It is from this word that *liturgy* is derived, for liturgy is one's work in worship.

All churches have liturgies, even those which would call themselves "non-liturgical." In fact, having no liturgy is a liturgy! Relaxed charismatic services may be as liturgical in their format as a high-church service — and in some cases more rigid. My purpose is not to recommend one liturgy over another, though, of course, I have my opinion. The point I wish to make is that whatever your liturgy may be, you must work at it with all you have, for worship is work. There must be some holy sweat if you are to please and glorify God.

Using a typical order of service from my church as an example, I will be very specific (and admittedly idealistic). Do not be put off because your service is different, for to properly worship, the same worth-ship ethic applies.

Prelude

You have arrived early (admittedly this is impossible in many churches — if there is an earlier service, for example), and you have the bulletin in hand. You pray silently, read the morning's Scripture text, pray for the sermon, look up the hymns in prayerful thought, and perhaps end by praying for the choir and the participants in the service. You have begun properly. You are working at worship.

Announcements
If these are at the beginning of the service, they are less intrusive than in the middle of worship.

The Call to Worship and Invocation
The call, properly done, is a call from God who is inviting us corporately into His presence. We listen to God's words with reverent, prayerful anticipation. As the call ends, we are led in an invocation which invites God to meet us and calls us to submit ourselves in worship, for His glory.

The Apostles' Creed
This Creed, scholars believe, dates from before A.D. 250 and is the oldest creedal affirmation to attain universal acceptance. The purpose of the Creed is to make a Trinitarian confession and to affirm our solidarity with the universal Church of the ages. To do this properly the Creed must never be recited, but confessed. That is, one's heart and mind must work together to genuinely affirm authentic belief.

The "Gloria Patri"
The "*Gloria Patri*" ("Doxology") is meant to draw us upward in music for the purpose for which we have come — to give glory to God. It should be sung with our whole heart.

Hymns
Surveys have shown that about 50 percent of any worship service is music, whether the service be formal or informal. Vocal praise to God in this way requires work. It is easy to let your mind wander so that you are mouthing the words with no comprehension — like the little boy who thought the gospel refrain "Gladly the cross I'd bear" was about a bear with crossed eyes! The antidote to this common peril is to realize that God is our audience and to sing to Him, thus fulfilling Paul's determination, "I will sing with my spirit, but I will also sing with my mind" (1 Corinthians 14:15).

What a glory to God when a hundred or two hundred or a thousand are all truly singing to God with their minds and spirits in the sublime labor of praise. Saint Augustine rightly said, "A Christian should be an alleluia from head to foot."[9]

The Resources section of this book includes lists of Christian songs and choruses appropriate for adoration and praise ("Hymns for Personal Adoration and Praise" and "Choruses and Scripture Songs for Personal Adoration and Praise"), and also a list of praise Psalms which are outstanding tools for worship ("Praise Psalms Especially Appropriate for Personal Worship"). These can be used at home in one's own worship times, as well as in corporate worship.

The Anthem

Church choirs have their precedent in the huge choirs of voices and instruments in the Old Testament. No less than thirty-five of the Old Testament Psalms have the superscription "For the director of music." Others were sung according to recommended tunes such as "The Hind of the Dawn," tunes no doubt well-known to many in Israel.[10]

Choirs offer music in a way that is beyond the average person's capacity. It is the congregation's way of offering its best to God and is an especially beautiful gift for Him.

Silence and Congregational Prayer

Americans seem to be obsessed with the need for unending sound. Some consider silence in worship a breach of etiquette. They want no dead spots — "Pastor, I think it would be better if the organ played."

But silence slows the frantic pace and gives time for reflection and individual dialogue with God. It bows to Habakkuk's call: "[T]he Lord is in his holy temple; let all the earth be silent before him" (2:20).

When the congregational prayer begins, all minds must engage in unison with silent or verbal agreements — "Yes, Lord" — "May it be" — "Amen." I personally think liturgical traditions ending prayers with a congregational "Amen!" are very much in accord with Scripture.

There is also the matter of the Lord's Prayer. If it is used by the congregation, it must never be merely "said" but must be prayed with all our heart. Worshipers would do well to remember that when the Lord gave the Church this great prayer, He first warned against mindless "babbling" (Matthew 6:7).

Tithes and Offerings

Giving ought to be an act of conscious worship, rather than a reflexive religious act. The giver, as he gives of his substance, ought to first give *himself* to God (cf. Romans 12:1; 2 Corinthians 8:5).

Scripture

The reading of Scripture is purely the sharing of God's Word, while it remains to be seen whether the sermon that follows is. When Ezra read the Law all Israel stood "from daybreak till noon" as he read (Nehemiah 8:3), and we should stand in solidarity with such respect for God's Word, symbolizing our submission to it. It is imperative that we do this with ears to hear.

Sermon

Admittedly the hardest work in a worship service may be listening to the sermon. Here the minister should have done his work, but the congregation has its work to do as well. Richard Baxter, in his "Directions for Profitably Hearing the Word Preached," has said:

> Make it your work with diligence to apply the word as you are hearing it. . . . Cast not all upon the minister, as those that will go no further than they are carried as by force. . . . You have work to do as well as the preacher, and should all the time be as busy as he . . . you must open your mouths, and digest it, for another cannot digest it for you . . . therefore be all the while at work, and abhor an idle heart in hearing, as well as an idle minister.[11]

Keep your Bible open, and follow the textual argument. Look up the references mentioned. Take notes. Identify the theme. List the subpoints and applications. Ask God to help you see exactly where He wants you to apply the Scriptures being preached to your life.

There is no getting around it: worship requires *discipline*. We are to worship God "in spirit and in truth," and this is impossible without discipline. We must discipline ourselves to know God's truth so we can worship Him in truth. We must discipline our human spirits, so that authentic affections pour in spirit from our hearts to God. We must discipline ourselves in preparation for corporate worship, and that does not begin with the thirty seconds after we have breathlessly sat down.

On Saturday

I have asked Christ to make me sensitive tomorrow to needs of people in the body who are hurting.

I have solved the "Sunday clothes hassle" by making sure that what I will wear is ready today.

I have spent time in confession so all will be right between myself and my Lord when we meet tomorrow.

I have determined to get to bed early so I will be refreshed and ready for church tomorrow.

I have planned on sustaining the delight of this time with Christ and his people by guarding against Sunday afternoon infringements.

On Sunday

I have gotten up in plenty of time so I will not feel rushed.

I have programmed my morning so I will not just arrive at church on time, but get there early.

I have eaten a good breakfast, so an empty stomach will not detract from my worship.

I have my Bible in hand plus a pen and paper for taking notes.

I have left for church with a great sense of expectancy because I know Christ will be there.[12]

Finally we must also understand that the discipline of worship is the way to bounding *gladness* in worship. As Eugene Peterson has so well said: "Worship is an *act* which develops feelings for God, not a *feeling* for God which is expressed in an act of worship."[13]

Let us discipline ourselves for the purpose of worship!

Food for Thought

Which is more important—a *habit* of worship or a *heart* of worship? Which do you experience most frequently? Why? If change is needed, how will you go about working with God to effect that change?

John 4:23 tells us God is *seeking* worshipers. Is He being selfish? Why or why not? Why does God want us to worship Him?

What does God's presence have to do with our worshiping Him (see Hebrews 13:5; Matthew 18:20)? Generally, when you are worshiping God, whether by yourself or with a group of believers, do you find the divine presence encouraging or intimidating?

What more do you (and your family) need to do to be spiritually prepared for Sunday morning worship at your church? Make a list, share it with the others in your household, and work together at putting it to work.

In your own words, what does it mean to worship God "in spirit and in truth"? How does your experiencing this or not experiencing this affect your Christian walk?

What type of worship is identified in Romans 12:1? How long has it been since you've done what this verse says to do?

Application/Response

What did God speak to you about most specifically, most powerfully in this chapter? Talk to Him about it right now!

Think About It!

Make a list of your ten favorite passages about the character or promises of God. Then make those passages, plus appropriate Christian songs (whether traditional or contemporary), the basis for a worship service to be celebrated with others in your family or with a Bible study group or even with your entire church.

CHARACTER

10

DISCIPLINE OF INTEGRITY

*T*HE DAY AMERICA *Told the Truth*, a new book based on an extensive opinion survey which guaranteed the anonymity of the participants, reveals an alarming crisis of integrity in America.

Only 13 percent of Americans see all Ten Commandments as binding on us today. Ninety-one percent lie regularly — at home and at work. In answer to the question, "Whom have you regularly lied to?" the statistics included 86 percent to parents and 75 percent to friends. A third of AIDS carriers admit to not having told their lovers. Most workers admit to goofing off for an average of seven hours — almost one whole day — a week, and half admit that they regularly call in sick when they are perfectly well.

The survey also posed the question, "What are you willing to do for $10 million?" Twenty-five percent would abandon their families, 23 percent would become a prostitute for a week, and 7 percent would kill a stranger.[1] Think of it! In a gathering of 100 Americans, there are seven who would consider killing you if the price was right. In 1,000 there are seventy!

Even casual observers can see the demise of integrity in the whole range of our culture — with its Watergates, Irangates, Savingsgates, Pearlygates — the much chronicled dalliances of prominent Senators — congressmen perjuring themselves — the artful embellishment of academic records — and even the war records of recent Presidents.[2] The straightforward poem/prayer of Fred Holloman, chaplain of the Kansas Senate, comes as no surprise:

Omniscient Father:
Help us to know who is telling
the truth. One side tells us one
thing, and the other just the opposite.
And if neither side is telling the truth, we would like to know that, too.

And if each side is telling half the truth,
give us the wisdom to put the right halves
together.
In Jesus' name, Amen.

Truth and integrity have not only proven elusive for many in leadership, but likewise for our future leaders, some of whom are literally schooling themselves in deception. Magazines such as the *New York Times Book Review* and *Rolling Stone* carry ads with such captions as "Term Paper Blues?" and list a toll-free hot line to "Research Assistance" in West Los Angeles: "Our 306 page catalogue contains detailed descriptions of 14,278 research papers, a virtual library of information at your finger tips. Footnote and bibliographic pages are included at no extra cost. Ordering is as easy as picking up your phone. Let this valuable educational aid serve you throughout your college years."[3] They should also add: "Here is your chance to cheapen your education and establish a fraudulent character for life."

Today in American business there is epidemic ethical decline. In 1983 the *Wall Street Journal* asked George Gallup to conduct a now-famous survey among business executives. The study revealed a shocking disparity between top executives and the general population. Eighty percent of the executives confessed to driving while drunk, as compared to 33 percent of the general public. Seventy-eight percent admitted using the company phone for personal long-distance calls. Thirty-five percent had cheated on their income tax reports. And 75 percent had stolen work supplies for personal use, as compared to 40 percent of the general populace.[4] The sad truth is, a resident of Beverly Hills as compared with a resident of the impoverished South Bronx is more likely to have used illegal drugs, have committed a crime, or had an extramarital affair.[5]

These are damning statistics for the upscale life, but such numbers by no means let the general populace off the hook. In a paper presented at a symposium on employee theft, sponsored by the American Psychological Association, the authors pointed out that inventory shortages cost department stores and specialty chains $8 *billion* every year. Of that, 10 percent is attributed to clerical error, 30 percent to shoplifting, and a whopping 60 percent — or sixteen million dollars a day — to theft by employees. "Phone theft," employees stealing phone service from their companies, is costing industry so much that call accounting has become one of the fastest growing parts of the telecommunications industry.[6]

Significantly the bulk of the blame for declining ethics resides with men, as the authors of *The Day America Told the Truth* are quick to point out:

Our current ethics at work are low, but they'd be a lot lower were it not for the great number of women who've entered the work force in recent years.

When we compared the answers given by the two sexes, we confirmed that women in this country simply behave more ethically than men.

On every question we probed, American women in the workplace held to a higher moral standard than men did. . . .

Less than half as many women as men believe that the only way to get ahead is to cheat, and not as many believe in politics rather than work as the way to success. . . .

In addition, women are much less willing to compromise their values to get ahead and somewhat more willing to quit as a matter of principle if they learn that their company is engaging in illegal activities. . . .

If valuable company property is stolen, the thief will be a man six times in seven.[7]

The truth is, American culture is in big trouble. The colossal slide of integrity (especially masculine ethics) has grim spiritual, domestic, and political implications which threaten the survival of life as we know it.

But for the Christian, the most chilling fact is this: *there is little statistical difference between the ethical practices of the religious and the nonreligious.* Doug Sherman and William Hendricks, in their book *Keeping Your Ethical Edge Sharp*, note Gallup's statistics that 43 percent of non-church attenders admit to pilfering work supplies, compared to 37 percent of attenders. Seventeen percent of the unchurched use the company phone for long-distance personal calls, but 13 percent of those who attend worship do likewise.

But is this true of *real* Christians? we may ask. Sherman and Hendricks answer yes. The general ethical conduct of Christians varies only slightly from non-Christians, with grand exceptions, of course.[8]

Sadly, Christians are *almost* as likely as non-Christians to:

- Falsify their income tax returns.
- Commit plagiarism (teachers especially know this).
- Bribe to obtain a building permit — "That's the way business is done."
- Ignore construction specs.
- Illegally copy a computer program.
- Steal time.

- Commit phone theft.
- Exaggerate a product.
- Tell people what they want to hear.
- Selectively obey the laws.

Many reasons can be cited for this. A popular culprit is the subjectivism and moral relativism of our day. With people like Justice Harlan giving the doctrinaire statement "[O]ne man's vulgarity is another's lyric"[9] — with the man in the street appealing to the supreme court of self, "My opinion is as good as yours!" — ethics and integrity suffer.

When a cultural icon such as Ernest Hemingway (who still arbitrates literary style) was an inveterate liar who lied about everything, including his childhood, his athletic prowess, his military exploits, his liaisons, so that he was, as one of his wives called him, "the biggest liar since Munchausen"[10] — how can we expect our culture to be otherwise? If our gods be mendacious frauds, how can we escape?

But the main reason for the integrity crisis is that we humans are fundamentally dishonest. We are congenital liars. Right smack in the middle of the Apostle Paul's string of observations on the depravity of man in Romans 3, we read, "Their throats are open graves; their tongues practice deceit" (v. 13). No one had to instruct us in the art of dishonesty. Even once we are regenerated, if we do not discipline ourselves under the Lordship of Christ, we return to deceit like a duck to water.

Our situation is exacerbated by the subtle seas of deception which surge back and forth over our culture through its media, so much so that we scarcely know where reality is. Many Christian men traffic in delusion. Some who lack integrity do not even know it.

GOD ON INTEGRITY

Ananias and Sapphira (Acts 5) knew they were deceiving the church when they sold some property and agreed to act as if they were giving all when they were only giving part. But the story does not give the impression that they thought what they were doing lacked integrity. After all, they were doing something good and generous.

If it happened today, Ananias would wait until the organ was playing "I Surrender All" and then humbly come forward, laying his check at Peter's feet, mumbling, "I wish I had more to give, Peter, but this is all I have."

Imagine the scene in the Early Church: Ananias' heart was thumping rapidly under the thrill of his public display, but Peter was not smiling. Somehow he knew!

> "Ananias, how is it that Satan has so filled your heart that you have lied to the Holy Spirit and have kept for yourself some of the money you received for the land? Didn't it belong to you before it was sold? And after it was sold, wasn't the money at your disposal? What made you think of doing such a thing? You have not lied to men but to God." (Acts 5:3, 4)

Poor Ananias. His racing heart stopped, and he could not breathe. Peter's grim visage gave way to darkness as Ananias' life ended, and the young men came and carried Ananias out — as they later did his dead widow.

The story of Ananias and Sapphira shocks us because they suffered death for such a "small" infraction. So they misrepresented the percentage they gave of their profits — why death? After all, *they did give* — which is more than many people do!

The answer is, the Church cannot prosper with deception among its members — and God wanted to make this clear for all time. Deception wounds the Body of Christ — makes it dysfunctional — and is a *sin against God*! This is why Peter cried to Ananias and Sapphira at the moment of their deaths, "You have not lied to men but to God" (Acts 5:4).

Integrity is one of the greatest needs of the Church today. The Church needs people who not only refrain from blatant lying, but are free from hypocrisy. Paul says, in fact, that honesty is necessary for growth in the Church: "Instead, speaking the truth in love, we will in all things grow up into him who is the Head, that is, Christ" (Ephesians 4:15). Literally, the divine medium for authentic church growth is *truthing in love* — speaking and doing truth to one another.

The Church's great need for integrity is directly linked to the needs of our lost world, for the world longs for liberation from dishonesty. Sure, it cultivates and promotes deception, but deep down inside many people long to escape the pretense. A substantial number of people outside the four walls of the Church will eagerly embrace the faith of believers who model the honesty and integrity for which they long.

Helmut Thielicke, the great German theologian and pastor who maintained his integrity all through Hitler's Third Reich, said: "The avoidance of one small fib . . . may be a stronger confession of faith than a whole 'Christian philosophy' championed in lengthy, forceful discussion."[11]

A truthful spirit is a great evangelistic tool. I have known people who were magnetized to Christ because they saw this quality in a church or individual. Integrity will be for some a tantalizing cool drink in the secular desert of delusion.

Men, the experience of Ananias and Sapphira tells us that our integrity matters to God. We need to declare with Job, "[T]ill I die, I will not deny my integrity" (Job 27:5).

THE SHAPE OF INTEGRITY

It is essential that we understand that the Biblical idea of integrity has the root idea of completeness, that a person of integrity is whole.[12] The derivation of our English word *integrity* from the Latin emphasizes the same quality because *integritas* means "wholeness," "entireness," "completeness."[13]

Integrity characterizes the entire person, not just part of him. He is righteous and honest through and through. He is not only that inside, but also in outer action. Psalm 15 celebrates the completeness of the man of integrity:

> Lord, who may dwell in your sanctuary?
> Who may live on your holy hill?
> He whose walk is blameless
> and who does what is righteous,
> who speaks the truth from his heart
> and has no slander on his tongue,
> who does his neighbor no wrong
> and casts no slur on his fellow man,
> who despises a vile man
> but honors those who fear the Lord,
> who keeps his oath
> even when it hurts,
> who lends his money without usury
> and does not accept a bribe against the innocent.
> He who does these things
> will never be shaken.

Surveys indicate that usually people lie to cover up something they did wrong.[14] Take, for example, the employee who has negligently jammed the copy machine, then slyly covers himself by calling out, "OK, who jammed the machine?"

The second most frequent reason for lying is to keep things pleasant emotionally. Have you avoided expressing the truth for the sake of peace?

This does not mean we have license to tell everyone what we think no matter what — a spiritual mandate to always speak our minds. Rather, we are never to deceive others by omission, or by using unclear talk to save face or avoid offending another. We are to be "speaking the truth in love" (Ephesians 4:15). Integrity demands that all speech be *intentionally* true. Such speech gives pleasure to God — "The Lord detests lying lips, but he delights in men who are truthful" (Proverbs 12:22).

Next, a man of integrity never cheats or defrauds another, never steals. Proverbs tells us: "Differing weights and differing measures — the Lord detests them both" (20:10). "The Lord abhors dishonest scales, but accurate weights are his delight" (11:1). "Food gained by fraud tastes sweet to a man, but he ends up with a mouth full of gravel" (20:17).

There are so many ways to casually steal which the consensus regards as justified: taking office supplies from work, long lunches, extravagant meals, accepting gifts from customers, ignoring copyright laws, claiming improper deductions. But the man of integrity avoids all such temptations, to God's glory.

The man of God keeps his word. He never promises to do something he does not intend to do. And he follows through — he does not conveniently "forget" what he has promised. One is never "put on" by the man of integrity. Faithfulness, one of the fruits of the Spirit (Galatians 5:22), is his trademark. Even when he discovers that keeping his word is not to his benefit, he does so, for as the Psalmist says, the man of integrity "keeps his oath even when it hurts" (15:4). This man, the Scripture says, is unique: "Many a man claims to have unfailing love, but a faithful man who can find?" (Proverbs 20:6). Integrity is a rare beauty.

Last, a man of integrity is a man of principle. We must understand that being a man of principle means more than having principles. It means having the courage to stand up for your convictions when it costs you. At present my daughter and son-in-law, Brian and Holly Hoch, and their three children have been looking for housing in Vienna, Austria for four months, largely because housing is scarce, and because the owners of the few they have found want them to sign a document which falsely states they are paying less for the apartment than they would really be paying. My daughter and her family are at this point victims of their integrity — an enviable victimization.

THE BENEFITS OF INTEGRITY

Integrity can cost you a relationship, reputation, promotion, job, even your life. But integrity also has its benefits.

Character

There can be no doubt that integrity is its own reward, for it produces character, and notwithstanding divine intervention, character determines the course of one's life here on earth. Even more, it will glorify God for eternity by His grace.

Conscience

Closely aligned with this is the parallel benefit of a clear conscience. This is a prime benefit, because if you have a clear conscience you will be able to stand firmly in the storms that swirl around you. If your heart does not condemn you, but affirms you, you can be a tower of strength. "The man of integrity walks securely" (Proverbs 10:9).

Intimacy

But the benefits of integrity go even farther, because integrity of soul assures a deep intimacy with God. God desires truth in the inward parts (Psalm 51:6), and when it is there He rejoices in the fellowship with that heart. A transparent, honest soul is a haven for the Spirit of God.

Elevation

There are also outward benefits of integrity, for integrity elevates the lives of believers. Integrity encourages more integrity, ethical conduct spawns further ethical conduct, honesty leads to honesty, character produces character! "The righteous man leads a blameless life," says Solomon; "blessed are his children after him" (Proverbs 20:7).

Evangelism

Lastly, as before, we mention the evangelistic magnetism of integrity. The following ad appeared in *The East African Standard* in Nairobi:

> ALL DEBTS TO BE PAID
> I ALLAN HARANGUI ALIAS WANIEK HARANGUI, of P. O. Box
> 40380, Nairobi, have dedicated services to the Lord Jesus Christ. I must
> put right all my wrongs. If I owe you any debt or damage personally or
> any of the companies I have been director or partner i.e.
> GUARANTEED SERVICES LTD.

WATERPUMPS ELECTRICAL
AND GENERAL CO. SALES AND SERVICES
Please contact me or my advocates J. K. Kibicho and Company,
Advocates, P.O. Box 73137, Nairobi for a settlement. No amount will be
disputed.
GOD AND HIS SON JESUS CHRIST BE GLORIFIED.

For a golden moment all of the great city of Nairobi took note that Jesus
Christ had made an ethical difference in a man's life. And no doubt souls were
turned to Christ as a result. Integrity and evangelism are a potent combination.

We can hardly overstate the importance of integrity to a generation oi
believers which is so much like the world in its ethical conduct. The world is
dying for us to have integrity! Its enviable benefits of *character, a clear conscience,* deep *intimacy with God,* the *elevation of others,* and the *winning of
the lost* all powerfully argue its importance.

And the stilled hearts of Ananias and Sapphira declare its urgency.

THE DISCIPLINE OF INTEGRITY

The urgency and importance of integrity suggests one thing to the serious heart
— the necessity of dicipline. God wants us to be men of principle. G. K.
Chesterton said, "Morality, like art, consists in drawing a line somewhere."[15]
We must let God's Word draw the line, not culture. The elevated ethics of Holy
Scripture must be kept at all costs, even though culture thinks them quaint and
impossible. And we must discipline ourselves through the power of the Holy
Spirit to maintain them.

Here UPI correspondent Wesley Pippert offers wise advice:

> One of the most effective disciplines I know is not to do something that first
> time — for repetition will come far easier. . . . Not doing something for the
> first time is a tremendous bulwark against not doing it later. As moral
> philosopher Sissela Bok has said in her book, *Lying* (New York: Pantheon,
> 1978, p. 28), "It is easy to tell a lie but hard to tell only one." Discipline will
> help us avoid the guilt that we often experience by dabbling in things we
> shouldn't. An important fruit of discipline is integrity. Few things are more
> important than whether one has a good reputation, a "good name." Not all
> people are gregarious or outgoing. Not all people are sought after or love-
> able. But everyone can have integrity. Integrity flows more out of a disci-
> plined character than a daring personality.[16]

We must discipline ourselves to be truthful in all that we say. The Scriptures' intent is not to rule out having fun with our friends, indulging in playful exaggeration, or even telling fanciful tales. But God's Word does call us to be honest through and through, to never lie or equivocate to save face or to stay in the good graces of others.

We must never be careless about the truth. We must measure our words. If we deceive we must immediately admit it, because deception can become a habit. William James, in his classic *Principles of Psychology*, put it this way:

> Could the young but realize how soon they will become mere walking bundles of habits, they would give more heed to their conduct while in the plastic state. We are spinning our own fates, good or evil, and never to be undone. Every smallest stroke or virtue or vice leaves its ever so little scar. The drunken Rip Van Winkle, in Jefferson's play, excuses himself for every fresh dereliction by saying "I won't count this time!" Well! He may not count it, but it is being counted nonetheless. Down among his nerve cells and fibers the molecules are counting it, registering and storing it up to be used against him when the next temptation comes. Nothing we ever do is, in strict scientific literalness, wiped out. Of course, this has its good side as well as its bad one.[17]

We must discipline ourselves to tell the truth, for truth can become a habit — something we do without thinking.

Habitual honesty — integrity — must be the goal in all our dealings. We must discipline ourselves not to succumb to the so-called "small things": the occasional phone theft, or time stealing, or misappropriating the office supplies, or indulging ourselves in the largesse of an expense account, or estimating mileage to our favor, or twisting the truth ever so slightly.

If this discipline becomes habitual, the "big things" will take care of themselves.

Sow an act,
   and you reap a habit.
Sow a habit
   and you reap a character.
Sow a character
   and you reap a destiny for yourself
   your family
   your church
   your world.[18]

Food for Thought

In what ways do you see a drought of truth and integrity in your culture? What are the effects, practically and specifically, in the nation, the family, the workplace, the church? How do these results affect you personally?

Review the story of Ananias and Sapphira in Acts 5. Do you think their punishment was too severe . . . too lenient? (Be honest!) What does this early-church account teach you today?

Do you agree with Helmut Thielicke's statement, "The avoidance of one small fib . . . may be a stronger confession of faith than a whole 'Christian philosophy' championed in lengthy, forceful discussion." What small fibs do you sometimes find yourself telling? What can you do practically to stop doing this?

Do you share Job's determination on this matter ("[T]ill I die, I will not deny my integrity," Job 27:5)? Why or why not?

Considering the connection between integrity and wholeness, what is really at stake in the twentieth-century quest for wholeness and integrated health (physical, emotional, mental, spiritual)? What does it mean to you to be "whole"? Are you willing to pay God's price for integrity?

Which benefits of integrity mean the most to you personally? What are you willing to do to make these traits real in your life? What part does God play in this?

Application/Response

What did God speak to you about most specifically, most powerfully in this chapter? Talk to Him about it right now!

Think About It!

Read through Psalm 15, making a list of every mentioned character trait or personal action that relates to integrity and its companions, truth and honesty. Then go back through the list and indicate how you are doing on each point (poor, fair, varies, consistently obedient, etc.). Now pray for God's help in living out all this.

11

DISCIPLINE OF TONGUE

IN 1899 FOUR reporters from Denver, Colorado, met by chance on a Saturday night in a Denver railroad station. Al Stevens, Jack Tournay, John Lewis, and Hal Wilshire worked for the four Denver papers: the *Post*, the *Times*, the *Republican* and the *Rocky Mountain News*.

Each had the unenviable task of finding a scoop for the Sunday edition. They hoped to spot a visiting celebrity arriving that evening by train.

However, none showed up, so the reporters wondered what on earth they would do. As they discussed options in a nearby saloon, Al suggested they make up a story. The other three laughed — at first. But before long they were all agreed — they would come up with such a whopper that no one would question it and their respective editors would congratulate them on their find.

A phony local story would be too obvious, so they decided to write about someplace far away. They agreed on China. "What if we say that some American engineers, on their way to China, told us they are bidding on a major job: the Chinese government is planning to demolish the Great Wall?"

Harold was not sure the story would be believable. Why would the Chinese ever tear down the Great Wall of China? "As a sign of international goodwill, to invite foreign trade."

By 11 P.M. the four reporters had worked out the details, and the next day all four Denver newspapers carried the story — on the front page. The *Times* headline that Sunday read: "Great Chinese Wall Doomed! Peking Seeks World Trade!"

Of course, the story was a ridiculous tall tale made up by four opportunistic newsmen in a hotel bar. But amazingly their story was taken seriously and soon ran in newspapers in the Eastern U.S. and even abroad.

When the citizens of China heard that the Americans were sending a demolition crew to dismantle the Great Wall, most were indignant, even enraged. Particularly angry were members of a secret society made up of Chinese patriots already against any kind of foreign intervention. Moved to action by the news story, they attacked the foreign embassies in Peking and murdered hundreds of missionaries from abroad.

In the next two months twelve thousand troops from six countries, working together, invaded China to protect their countrymen. The bloodshed of that time, born out of a journalistic hoax fabricated in a saloon in Denver, was the time of violence known ever since as the Boxer Rebellion.[1]

What power the written or spoken word has! Nations have risen and nations have fallen to the tongue. Lives have been elevated and lives have been cast down by human speech. Goodness has flowed like a sweet river from our mouths, and so has the cesspool. The tiny tongue is a mighty force indeed.

INTRINSIC POWER

James, the Lord's brother, understood this as well as any man in history, and through the use of graphic analogies he has given us the most penetrating exposition of the tongue anywhere in literature, sacred or secular: "When we put bits into the mouths of horses to make them obey us, we can turn the whole animal. Or take ships as an example. Although they are so large and are driven by strong winds, they are steered by a very small rudder wherever the pilot wants to go. Likewise the tongue is a small part of the body, but it makes great boasts" (James 3:3-5).

The horse is an incredibly powerful animal. Take 550 pounds (as much as a puffing Olympic heavyweight lifter can hoist overhead), set it on a horse's back, and it will barely snort as it stands breathing easily under the burden. The same horse, unburdened, can sprint a quarter-mile in about twenty-five seconds. A horse is half a ton of raw power! Yet, place a bridle and bit in its mouth and a 100-pound woman on its back who knows what she is doing and the animal can literally be made to dance.

James observed the same phenomenon in ancient ships, as ships small and large were steered by an amazingly small rudder. Today it is still the same, whether it be an acrobatic ski boat or the USS Enterprise. He who controls the rudder controls the ship.

So it is with the mighty tongue, that "movable muscular structure attached to the floor of the mouth" (Webster's Unabridged Dictionary). "[T]he tongue is a small part of the body, but it makes great boasts," says James (v. 5). Or as

Phillips has helpfully paraphrased it, "the human tongue is physically small, but what tremendous effects it can boast of." Though it weighs only two ounces, it can legitimately boast of its disproportionate power to determine human destiny. The lives of Adolf Hitler and Winston Churchill bear eloquent testimony to the dark and bright sides of the tongue's power. The Führer on one side of the Channel harangued a vast multitude with his hypnotic cadences. On the other side, the Prime Minister's brilliant, measured utterances pulled a faltering nation together for its "finest hour."

But we need not look to the drama of nations to see the truth of James' words. Our own lives are evidence enough. Never doubt the power of the tiny tongue — and never underestimate it.

DESTRUCTIVE POWER

James' principal concern is with the destructive power of the tongue, and this produces a most provocative statement: "Consider what a great forest is set on fire by a small spark. The tongue also is a fire, a world of evil among the parts of the body. It corrupts the whole person, sets the whole course of his life on fire, and is itself set on fire by hell" (vv. 5, 6).

The tongue has awesome potential for harm, as the forest fire analogy suggests. At 9:00 one Sunday evening, October 8, 1871, poor Mrs. O'Leary's cow kicked over the lantern as she was being milked, starting the great Chicago Fire. That disaster blackened three and one half miles of the city, destroying over 17,000 buildings before it was checked by gunpowder explosions on the south line of the fire. The fire lasted two days and cost over 250 lives.

But ironically that was not the greatest inferno in the Midwest that year. Historians tell us that on the same day that dry autumn a spark ignited a raging fire in the North Woods of Wisconsin, a blaze which burned for an entire month, taking more lives than the Chicago Fire. A veritable firestorm destroyed billions of yards of precious timber — all from one spark!

The tongue has that scope of inflammatory power in human relationships, and James is saying that those who misuse the tongue are guilty of spiritual arson. A mere spark from an ill-spoken word can produce a firestorm that annihilates everyone it touches. Furthermore, because the tongue is a "world of evil," it contains and conveys all the world system's wickedness. It is party to every evil there is and actively intrudes its evil into our lives.

What is the effect of the tongue's cosmic wickedness? "It corrupts the whole person, sets the whole course of his life on fire" (v. 6). "[C]ourse of life" is literally "the wheel of our genesis," "genesis" referring to our human life or existence.[2] What an apt description of human experience! About nine-tenths of the flames we experience in our lives come from the tongue.

Having grabbed our imaginations with his graphic language, James adds the final touch: "and is itself set on fire by hell." Here the language means *continually* set on fire. James used the same word for Hell that his brother Jesus used — "*Gehenna*" — derived from the perpetually burning garbage dump outside Jerusalem, a place of fire and filth where, as Jesus said, "their worm does not die, and the fire is not quenched" (Mark 9:48).

Can anyone miss the point? The uncontrolled tongue has a direct pipeline to Hell! Fueled by Hell, it burns our lives with its filthy fires. But it is also, as Calvin says, an ". . . instrument for catching, encouraging, and increasing the fires of hell."[3]

Taking James' words seriously, we recognize that the tongue has more destructive power than a hydrogen bomb, for the bomb's power is physical and temporal, whereas the tongue is spiritual and eternal. Walter Wangerin, in his collection of short stories *Ragman and Other Cries of Faith*, turns to Nature for a chilling metaphor of the tongue's power. He explains that a female spider is often a widow for embarrassing reasons — she regularly eats those who come her way. Lonely suitors and visitors alike quickly become corpses, and her dining room is a morgue. A visiting fly, having become captive, will appear to be whole, but the spider has drunk his insides so that he has become his own hollow casket. Not a pleasant thought, especially if you have a touch of arachnaphobia, as I do!

The reason for this macabre procedure is that she has no stomach and so is incapable of digesting anything within her. Through tiny punctures she injects her digestive juices into a fly so that his insides are broken down and turned into warm soup. "This soup she swills," says Wangerin, "even as most of us swill souls of one another after having cooked them in various enzymes: guilt, humiliations, subjectivities, cruel love — there are a number of fine, acidic mixes. And some among us are so skilled with the hypodermic word that our dear ones continue to sit up and to smile, quite as though they were still alive."[4]

This is a gruesome but effective metaphor to describe the destructive power of evilly intended words. Words do not dissolve mere organs and nerves but souls! This world is populated by walking human caskets because countless lives have been dissolved and sucked empty by another's words.

VERBAL CYANIDE

Significantly, James does not tell us how the tongue's destructive power is manifested in human speech. He knows that the spiritual mind, informed by the Scriptures, will have no problem in making the connections.

Gossip

The tongue's destructive power in gossip leads the list, of course. A physician in a Midwestern city was a victim of a disgruntled patient who tried to ruin him professionally through rumor, and almost did. Several years later the gossiper had a change of heart and wrote the doctor asking his forgiveness, and he forgave her. But there was no way she could erase the story, nor could he. As Solomon wisely observed, "The words of a gossip are like choice morsels; they go down into a man's inmost parts" (Proverbs 18:8). Gossip is greedily picked up and stored away by the hearers like tasty tidbits. Vigorous denial would only bring more suspicion — "He protests too much!" The damage was done. Hereafter the innocent doctor would always look into certain eyes and wonder if they had heard the story — and if they believed it.

Gossip often veils itself in acceptable conventions such as "Have you heard . . . ?" or "Did you know . . . ?" or "They tell me . . ." or "Keep this to yourself, but. . . ." or "I do not believe it is true, but I heard that . . ." or "I wouldn't tell you, except that I know it will go no further." Of course, the most infamous such rationalization in Christian circles is, "I am telling you this so you can pray." This seems so pious, but the heart that feeds on hearing evil reports is a tool of Hell, and it leaves flaming fires in its wake. Oh, the heartache that comes from the tongue.

Innuendo

A cousin of gossip is innuendo. Consider the ship's first mate who after a drunken binge was written up by the captain on the ship's log: "mate drunk today." The mate's revenge? Some months later he surreptitiously wrote on his own entry, "captain sober today." So it goes with the word unsaid, the awkward silence, the raised eyebrows, the quizzical look — all freighted with the misery of Hell.

Flattery

Gossip involves saying behind a person's back what you would never say to his or her face. Flattery means saying to a person's face what you would never say behind his or her back. The Scriptures warn us repeatedly against flatterers, for they are destructive people who carry a legion of unwholesome motives:

"Whoever flatters his neighbor is spreading a net for his feet" (Proverbs 29:5). "A lying tongue hates those it hurts, and a flattering mouth works ruin" (Proverbs 26:28). "May the Lord cut off all flattering lips and every boastful tongue that says, 'We will triumph with our tongues . . .'" (Psalm 12:3, 4).

Criticism

Fault-finding seems endemic to the Christian Church. Perhaps this is because a taste of righteousness can be easily perverted into an overweening sense of self-righteousness and judgmentalism. Once while John Wesley was preaching, he noticed a lady in the audience who was known for her critical attitude. All through the service she sat and stared at his new tie. When the meeting ended, she came up to him and said very sharply, "Mr. Wesley, the strings on your tie are much too long. It's an offense to me!" He asked if any of the ladies present happened to have a pair of scissors in their purse. When the scissors were handed to him, he gave them to his critic and asked her to trim the streamers to her liking. After she clipped them off near the collar, he said, "Are you sure they're all right now?" "Yes, that's much better." "Then let me have those shears a moment," said Wesley. "I'm sure you wouldn't mind if I also gave you a bit of correction. I must tell you, madam, that your tongue is an offense to me — it's too long! Please stick it out . . . I'd like to take some off." On another occasion someone said to Wesley, "My talent is to speak my mind." Wesley replied, "That's one talent God wouldn't care a bit if you buried!" This is good advice for all Christians.

Diminishment

In a subsequent context James gives the command, "Do not speak against one another, brethren" (4:11, NASB) — literally, "Do not speak down on one another, brothers." James forbids *any speech* (whether true or false) which runs down another person.

Certainly no Christian should ever be a party to slander — making false charges against another's reputation. Yet some do. But even more penetrating is the challenge to refrain from any speech which intends to run down someone else, even if it is totally true. Personally I can think of few commands that go against commonly accepted conventions more than this, for most people think it is okay to convey negative information if it is true. We understand that lying is immoral. But is passing along damaging truth immoral? It seems almost a moral responsibility! By such reasoning, criticism behind another's back is thought to be all right as long as it is based on fact. Likewise, denigrating gossip (of course it is never called gossip!) is seen as okay if the information is true. Thus many believers use truth as a license to righteously diminish others' reputations.

Related to this, some reject running down another behind his back, but believe it is okay if done face to face. These persons are driven by a "moral" compulsion to make others aware of their shortcomings. Fault-finding is, to them, a spiritual gift — a license to conduct spiritual search-and-destroy missions.

What people like this do not know is that most people are painfully aware of their own faults — and would so like to overcome them — and are trying very hard to do so. Then someone mercilessly assaults them believing they are doing their spiritual duty — and, oh, the hurt!

This destructive speaking down against others can also manifest itself in the subtle art of minimizing another's virtues and accomplishments. After being with such people, your mental abilities, athletic accomplishments, musical skills, and domestic virtues seem not to be quite as good as they were a few minutes earlier. Some of this feeling came perhaps from their words about your Steinway — "what a nice little piano" — or from surprised exclamations about what you did not know. It was also the tone of the voice, the cast of the eye, and the surgical silences.

There are many sinful reasons why brothers in Christ talk down one another. Revenge over some slight, real or imagined, may be the motivation of "Christian" slander. Others imagine that their spirituality and sensitivity equips them to pull others from their pedestals and unmask their hypocrisies. Gideon once righteously cried, "A sword for the Lord and for Gideon!" (Judges 7:20), and we may do the same, but in our case it is too often a sword of self-righteousness.

Talking down others may also come from the need to elevate oneself — like the Pharisee who thanked God he was not like other sinners "or even like this tax collector" (Luke 18:11). We thus enjoy the dubious elevation of walking on the bruised heads of others.

Sometimes this diminishing of others simply comes from too much empty talk. People do not have much to talk about, so they fuel the fires of conversation with the flesh of others. The abilities and motivations of the Body of Christ to run itself down could fill a library.

We are all skillful in rationalizing such talk, but God's Word still speaks: "Brothers, do not speak against one another."

Verbal cyanide comes in many forms. *Gossip, innuendo, flattery, criticism, diminishment* are only a few of the venoms with which Christians inject each

other. And the results are universal: toxic gastric juices brew a Devil's feast —
the swill of souls.

WORTHLESS RELIGION

James' words are consistently surgical. But none are so penetrating as these: "If
anyone considers himself religious and yet does not keep a tight rein on his
tongue, he deceives himself and his religion is worthless" (1:26). An exercise in
futility!

This is a spiritually terrifying statement, to say the least, for it cuts like a
hot knife through warm butter, dissecting the cant and piety of the self-satis-
fied religious. An out-of-control tongue suggests bogus religion, no matter how
well one's devotion is carried out. The true test of a man's spirituality is not
his ability to speak, as we are apt to think, but rather his ability to bridle his
tongue.

The Lord Jesus Himself explained this in no uncertain terms in a heated
exchange with the Pharisees: "Make a tree good and its fruit will be good, or
make a tree bad and its fruit will be bad, for a tree is recognized by its fruit. You
brood of vipers, how can you who are evil say anything good? For out of the
overflow of the heart the mouth speaks" (Matthew 12:33, 34). *The tongue will
inevitably reveal what is on the inside.* This is especially true under stress, when
the tongue is compulsively revealing.

A preacher with hammer in hand, doing some work on a church workday,
noticed that one of the men seemed to be following him around. Finally the
preacher asked why. The man answered, "I just want to hear what you say
when you hit your thumb." The curious parishioner understood that would be
the existential moment of truth. The same could be said of the domestic stresses
of the home, where the mouth unfailingly trumpets one's essence.

James does not mean that those who *sometimes* fall into this sin have a
worthless religion, for all are guilty at times. Rather, he is saying that if anyone's tongue is *habitually* unbridled, though his church attendance be impec-
cable, his Bible knowledge envied, his prayers many, his tithes exemplary, and
though he "considers himself religious . . . he deceives himself and his religion
is worthless."

The ever practical James has cut through all the religious decorum, but it
is not butter that glistens under his knife, but the marrow of our souls. True
religion controls the tongue.

Men, how is your religion? How is mine?

- Do you talk too much?
- Do you pass along choice morsels for others to gleefully take in?
- Do you say to people's faces what you would never say behind their backs?
- Do you have the "gift" of a sharp tongue?
- Are people elevated or diminished through your words?

> *"The boneless tongue, so small and weak,*
> *Can crush and kill," declares the Greek,*
> *"The tongue destroys a greater horde,"*
> *The Turk asserts, "than does the sword."*
> *The Persian proverb wisely saith,*
> *"A lengthy tongue — an early death!"*
> *Or sometimes takes this form instead,*
> *"Do not let your tongue cut off your head."*
> *"The tongue can speak a word whose speed,"*
> *Say the Chinese, "outstrips the steed."*
> *The Arab sages said in part,*
> *"The tongue's great storehouse is the heart."*
> *From Hebrew was the maxim sprung,*
> *"Thy feet should slip, but ne'er the tongue."*
> *The sacred writer crowns the whole,*
> *"Who keeps the tongue doth keep his soul."*[5]

THE DISCIPLINED TONGUE

The tongue, so tiny, is immensely powerful. Four reporters, good old boys, having a few beers in a Denver bar in 1899, provided the specious spark that ignited the infamous Boxer Rebellion. The tongue is indeed mightier than generals and their armies. It can fuel our lives so they become fiery furnaces, or it can cool our lives with the soothing wind of the Spirit. It can be forged by Hell, or it can be a tool of Heaven.

Offered to God on the altar, the tongue has awesome power for good. It can proclaim the life-changing message of *salvation* : "And how can they hear without someone preaching to them? And how can they preach unless they are sent? As it is written, 'How beautiful are the feet of those who bring good news!'" (Romans 10:14, 15). It has power for *sanctification* as we share God's Word: "Sanctify them by the truth; your word is truth" (John 17:17). It has power for *healing*: "For when we came into Macedonia, this body of ours had no rest, but we were harassed at every turn — conflicts on the outside, fears within. But God, who comforts the downcast, comforted us by the coming of Titus, and not only by his coming but also by the comfort you had given him. He told us about your longing for me, your deep sorrow, your ardent concern for me, so that my joy was greater than ever" (2 Corinthians 7:5-7). It has power for *worship*: "Through Jesus, therefore, let us continually offer to God a sacrifice of praise — the fruit of lips that confess his name" (Hebrews 13:15).

Men, it is up to us. No sweat, no sanctification!

First, *we must ask God to cauterize our lips*, confessing as Isaiah did, "Woe to me! . . . I am ruined! For I am a man of unclean lips, and I live among a people of unclean lips, and my eyes have seen the King, the Lord Almighty" (Isaiah 6:5). Then we need to submit to the cleansing touch: "Then I heard the voice of the Lord saying, 'Whom shall I send? And who will go for us?' And I said, 'Here am I. Send me'" (v. 8). Isaiah's outline as a spiritual exercise, performed with all one's heart, will work wonders in our lives. Let us all do this today!

Second, hand-in-hand with the first step, there must be *an ongoing prayerfulness* regarding the use of our tongues — regular, detailed prayer. This, coupled with the first step, will work a spiritual miracle.

Third, we must resolve to *discipline ourselves* regarding the use of the tongue, making solemn resolutions such as the following:

- To perpetually and lovingly speak the truth in love (Ephesians 4:15).
- To refrain from being party to or a conduit for gossip (Proverbs 16:28; 17:9; 26:20).
- To refrain from insincere flattery (Proverbs 26:28).
- To refrain from running down another (James 4:11).
- To refrain from degrading humor (Ephesians 5:4).
- To refrain from sarcasm (Proverbs 26:24, 25).
- To memorize Scriptures that teach the proper use of the tongue. (See the resource materials at the end of this book [page 275, Section G, "Selected Proverbs Regarding the Tongue"] for a list of Proverbs which provide instruction on the tongue.)

Men, discipline your tongue for the purpose of godliness!

"Who keeps the tongue doth keep his soul."

Food for Thought

"Lives have been elevated and lives have been cast down by human speech. Goodness has flowed like a sweet river from our mouths, and so has the cesspool." In what ways have the words of others helped you . . . hurt you?

Which image for the tongue in James 3 speaks most pointedly to you? How have you tried to tame your tongue? Did it work? How has God helped you in this area?

Do you personally find it tempting to indulge in gossip? (Beware of calling this by some more benign name.) Why do you enjoy talking behind someone's back? How do you feel afterwards? What kind of talk should replace the gossip?

Do you ever find yourself expressing sinful flattery? What do you hope to gain? What kind of talk should replace the flattery?

What exhortation concerning our words do we find in James 4:11? Again, identify your motives for such talk and the proper replacement(s).

Is it possible to even sin during prayer (see Luke 18:11)? Do you ever do this? Why? How do you see yourself . . . others . . . God at such a time?

Application/Response

What did God speak to you about most specifically, most powerfully in this chapter? Talk to Him about it right now!

Think About It!

Jot down a brief thought about the tongue from each of the following passages, then summarize them all in a short paragraph: 2 Corinthians 7:5-7; Isaiah 6:1-8; Ephesians 4:15; Proverbs 16:28; 17:9; 26:20; 26:24, 25; 26:28

12

DISCIPLINE OF WORK

S TUDS TERKEL OPENS his widely-acclaimed book *Working: People Talk About What They Do All Day and How They Feel About What They Do* with these words:

> This book, being about work, is by its very nature, about violence — to the spirit as well as to the body. It is about ulcers as well as accidents. About shouting matches as well as fist fights. About nervous breakdowns as well as kicking the dog around. It is, above all (or beneath all), about daily humiliations.[1]

Millions of people regard their work as something they must bear, a living indignity. Their feelings are not without precedent. Herman Melville felt much the same: "They talk of dignity of work, bosh. The dignity is in the leisure."

A dark cloud of dissatisfaction blankets today's work force. Only one-tenth of American workers say they are satisfied with their jobs.[2] For the overwhelming majority, work is dull and meaningless. This pervasive discontent has spawned the paradoxical problems of laziness on the one hand and overwork on the other. Patterson and Kim in *The Day America Told the Truth* tell us that only one in four employees gives his or her best effort on the job, and that about 20 percent of the average worker's time is wasted, thus producing, in effect, a four-day work week.[3]

But though sloth is epidemic, so is overwork. Moonlighting is a way of life for a substantial part of our work force. This was given classic illustration when the workers at a rubber manufacturing plant in Akron, Ohio, were given six-hour workdays — and over half of them took on a second full- or part-time job![4]

The managerial counterpart to workers' moonlighting is the workaholism of those who sublimate everything — family, leisure, friends, church — to career. The depths to which careerism can go is chronicled by Dr. Douglas LaBier, senior fellow of the Project on Technology, Work and Character in Washington, D.C., who relates the "extreme but not uncommon expression" of a man who told him that he feared dying, not because of death, but because it would end his career.[5]

This mind-set has produced an unending list of shallow folk-religion epigrams which tout the requisite qualities of successful careers: *discipline* — "Creativity is 2 percent inspiration and 98 percent perspiration"; *goals* — "If you aim at nothing, you'll hit it every time"; *savvy* — "Success in life comes not from holding a good hand, but from playing a poor hand well"; *perseverance* — "Tough times never last, but tough people do"; *vision* — "Some men dream dreams and ask, Why? I dream dreams and ask, Why not?"; *self-confidence* — "Believe in God, and you are halfway there; believe in yourself, and you are three-quarters there."[6] The careerists who espouse the hubris of these credos wrongly think themselves heirs of the Protestant work ethic, but they are anything but that, as we shall see.

This delusion takes on personally tragic dimensions, because surveys have indicated that the work ethics of Christians and non-Christians are virtually identical. "At church they swear allegiance to values informed by creeds and Scriptures. But at work they bow to idols of expedience and career success. Moral camouflage has become *de rigueur* in the workplace."[7] The plain truth is, many Christian men miserably fail in their work ethics either because of sloth or overwork or, ironically, both.

What we need is a work ethic which is informed by God's Word and religiously lived out in the workplace and the Church. The reason this is so important is that most of us spend eight to ten hours of our sixteen waking hours at work five or six days a week. So how we work not only reveals who we are, but determines what we are.

The Christian discipline of work must be observed *de rigueur* wherever God has placed us.

WHAT THE BIBLE SAYS ABOUT WORK

The Scriptural/Christian doctrine of work has an exalted origin because it is closely related to the doctrines of the creative energy of God and the image of God in man. We meet God the Creator as a worker in Genesis 1:1 — 2:2. In fact, that entire section is a log of God's work, ending with the statement that upon completion "[He] rested from all the work of creating that he had done" (2:2). As Milton expressed it:

> *The planets in their stations listening stood,*
>   *While the bright pomp ascended jubilant.*
> *"Open, ye everlasting gates," they sung;*
>   *"Open, ye heavens, your living doors; let in*
> *The great Creator, from his work return'd*
>   *Magnificent, his six days' work, a World.*
>   —*Paradise Lost*, VII.563

God's being a worker endows all legitimate work with an intrinsic dignity.

The additional teaching of Genesis 1 is that "God created man in his own image" (1:27). We are compelled to understand from this that the image of God in man means man is to be a worker. The way we work will reveal how much we have allowed the image of God to develop in us. There is immense dignity in work and in being workers.

Men, you must set this on your hearts: *Your work matters to God!*

A further observation of great importance is that work was given to man *before* the Fall, before sin, before imperfection: "Now the Lord God had planted a garden in the east, in Eden" (Genesis 2:8); "The Lord God took the man and put him in the Garden of Eden to work it and take care of it" (2:15). From this we come to the inescapable conclusion that work is good, despite the modern thinking that it is evil and dehumanizing. David Ben-Gurion, pioneer leader of the modern state of Israel, gave this memorable expression of the innate nobility of work:

> We do not consider manual work as a curse, or a bitter necessity, not even as a means of making a living. We consider it as a high human function. As a basis of human life. The most dignified thing in the life of a human being and which ought to be free, creative. Men ought to be proud of it.[8]

Work Under a Curse

So we see that God is a worker and that man, created in God's image, is a worker and that work is good. But then come the Fall and the Curse:

> "Cursed is the ground because of you; through painful toil you will eat of it all the days of your life. It will produce thorns and thistles for you, and

you will eat the plants of the field. By the sweat of your brow you will eat your food until you return to the ground, since from it you were taken; for dust you are and to dust you will return." (Genesis 3:17-19)

The Curse made nature uncooperative, so that work became painful toil and man had to sweat for a living. Today our working conditions vary. Some sweat more than others. We may be in a better position than some. But the norm for the world is "painful toil."

Even more, the normal experience of mankind in his labor is a malaise of futility. The writer of Ecclesiastes gave this universal expression as he bemoaned his plight from the perspective of one who leaves God out of his life. In 2:4-10 he described his professional success in acquiring vineyards and gardens and parks and slaves and flocks and treasures. He was greater than all his contemporaries. He was denied nothing his eyes desired. But he concluded in verse 11, "Yet when I surveyed all that my hands had done and what I had toiled to achieve, everything was meaningless, a chasing after the wind; nothing was gained under the sun." And he reiterates in verse 17, "So I hated life, because the work that is done under the sun was grievous to me. All of it is meaningless, a chasing after the wind."

Men, this is as far as work will take you apart from God. You will engage in it because, though fallen, you are in the image of God and because work is part of the natural order, and it will produce its benefits and satisfactions — but it will also be toil, and its joys will be ephemeral. Studs Terkel has revealed what has always been true under the sun when God is left out.

Work Redeemed
There is a Christian view of work which makes God the center of the equation. To be sure, God does not remove the curse and its painful, sweaty toil, but He does replace the meaninglessness.

Those who have been saved by faith fall heir to this grand declaration: "For we are God's workmanship, created in Christ Jesus to do good works, which God prepared in advance for us to do" (Ephesians 2:10). Being His workmanship, we are, as F. F. Bruce translates it, "his work of art, his masterpiece."[9] We are the pinnacle of God's creation because, above every other created thing (even angels!), we are made in His image. This has mind-boggling possibilities. Beyond this, we have been regenerated — "created in Christ Jesus" — thus undergoing an even greater second creation. As Paul says in 2 Corinthians 5:17, "[I]f anyone is in Christ, he is a new creation." God's most stupendous creation is man made alive in Christ. To quote Jonathan Edwards, the "spiritual life which is reached in the work of conversion, is a far greater and more glorious effect than mere being and life."[10] As subjects of Christ's two creations, we are His ultimate workmanship!

As His masterworks, we have been "created in Christ Jesus to do good works, which God prepared in advance for us to do." Each of us has an eternally designed work assignment which includes the *task*, the *ability*, and a *place* to serve. Whatever the task to which He has called you, you will be equipped for it as surely as a bird is made for flight. And in doing the works He has called you to do, you will be both more and more His workmanship and more and more your true self.

The practical implications of this are stupendous. There is no secular/sacred distinction, for all honest work done for the Lord is sacred. Historians agree that Luther's understanding of this revolutionized his life, and indeed the world of his day. He wrote: "Your work is a very sacred matter. God delights in it, and through it He wants to bestow His blessings on you. This praise of work should be inscribed on all tools, on the forehead and the faces that sweat from toiling."[11] There are no first-class and second-class Christians because of their varying jobs. All work is sacramental in nature, be it checking groceries, selling futures, cleaning teeth, driving a street sweeper, teaching, or painting trim.

Everything we do ought to be done to the glory of God. Listen to God's call to serve Him:

So whether you eat or drink or whatever you do, do it all for the glory of God. (1 Corinthians 10:31)

And whatever you do, whether in word or deed, do it all in the name of the Lord Jesus, giving thanks to God the Father through him. (Colossians 3:17)

Whatever you do, work at it with all your heart, as working for the Lord, not for men, since you know that you will receive an inheritance from the Lord as a reward. It is the Lord Christ you are serving. (Colossians 3:23, 24)

You may feel you are in a "nothing job." Because of the Curse, your job may involve painful toil and yield little job satisfaction. But you can glorify God where you are by your heart attitude. You may feel your occupation is not holy, but it is if you see it so and do it for God's glory. You are God's masterpiece, created in Christ Jesus to do good works which God planned in advance for you. Men, everything about your work must be directed toward Him — your attitudes, your integrity, your intensity, and your skill.

THE DISCIPLINE OF WORK

The disciplines of work are *practical* disciplines. The Scriptures are very explicit here.

Energy

Both the Old and New Testaments are crystal-clear on the necessity of energetic work as opposed to laziness. Proverbs mocks the false wisdom of the lazy:

> Do you see a man wise in his own eyes?
> There is more hope for a fool than for him.
> The sluggard says, "There is a lion in the road,
> a fierce lion roaming the streets!"
> As a door turns on its hinges,
> so a sluggard turns on his bed.
> The sluggard buries his hand in the dish;
> he is too lazy to bring it back to his mouth.
> The sluggard is wiser in his own eyes
> than seven men who answer discreetly.
>
> (Proverbs 26:12-16; cf. 6:6-11)

The New Testament epistles likewise disparage all laziness — sort of a spiritual ultra slim-fast for sluggards. Evidently the Thessalonian church had some "brothers" who ostensibly lived "by faith" while they sponged off the church — Christian parasites, we might say. For such, Paul gave explicit advice: "In the name of the Lord Jesus Christ, we command you, brothers, to keep away from every brother who is idle and does not live according to the teaching you received from us" (2 Thessalonians 3:6) — "For even when we were with you, we gave you this rule: 'If a man will not work, he shall not eat'" (v. 10).

In our Lord's Parable of the Talents the master tells the servant who had done nothing with his talent, "You wicked, lazy servant!" (Matthew 25:26). No one has ever been both faithful to God and lazy! It is impossible. But perhaps the most withering epithet comes from Paul: "If anyone does not provide for his relatives, and especially for his immediate family, he has denied the faith and is worse than an unbeliever" (1 Timothy 5:8). There is no escaping it — godliness is associated with hard work. You cannot be lazy and be a godly employee (or employer for that matter).

This said, it must be understood that the Scriptures do not commend the workaholism that comes from pursuing wealth and a career instead of God's glory. In this respect it should be noted that the hard-working Puritans were zealous in enforcing Sabbath laws without which employers would have made people work seven days a week.

The bottom line for us, men, is: Are we truly hard-working? And if so, are we doing it for God or merely for self?

Enthusiasm

A second, and parallel, aspect of the Christian work ethic is enthusiasm. "Whatever you do," Paul told the Colossians, "work at it with all your heart, as working for the Lord, not for men" (Colossians 3:23). To the Romans Paul admonished, "Never be lacking in zeal, but keep your spiritual fervor, serving the Lord" (Romans 12:11).

It is natural — actually quite easy — to be enthusiastic if your work is prominent, but less natural the more hidden it is, as the conductor of a great symphony orchestra once revealed when asked which was the most difficult instrument to play. "Second violin," he answered. "We can get plenty of first violinists. But to get someone who will play second violin with enthusiasm — that is a problem!"

And so it is. But actually, doing one's work with enthusiasm, even if hidden, plays for an audience far greater than that of the most famous symphony orchestras or world champion sports teams! If we could but really see this, our enthusiasm would never flag.

Wholeheartedness

A third aspect of the Christian work ethic, very close to energy and enthusiasm, but nevertheless bearing a distinctive and important nuance, is wholeheartedness:

> Slaves, obey your earthly masters with respect and fear, and with sincerity of heart, just as you would obey Christ. Obey them not only to win their favor when their eye is on you, but like slaves of Christ, doing the will of God from your heart. Serve wholeheartedly, as if you were serving the Lord, not men, because you know that the Lord will reward everyone for whatever good he does, whether he is slave or free. (Ephesians 6:5-8)

If you have ever observed a gym class doing push-ups, you will understand the sense of this verse. The coach orders everyone down and begins to intone "up-down, up-down," and all are following until he looks to the right, because in that moment the half on the left go on "hold," until his gaze begins to move back to the left, whereupon they begin to do proper push-ups again, and those on the right go on "hold." There are employees who are all action when the boss is around, but otherwise loll around the watercooler. Out of his eye there is no energy, no enthusiasm, no heart.

The cheerful wholeheartedness recommended here comes, as before, when one's work is done for the Lord. Men, we are to work as we did as boys when we knew our father was watching, because He is — always!

Excellence

Lastly, our work must be done with an eye to excellence. Dorothy Sayers said that the Church in our time

> has forgotten that the secular vocation is sacred. Forgotten that a building must be good architecture before it can be a good church; that a painting must be well painted before it can be a good sacred picture; that work must be good work before it can call itself God's work.[12]

Work that is truly Christian is work well done.

Genesis 1 logs God's commitment to excellence when it says, "God saw all that he had made, and it was very good" (v. 31). Christians should always do good work. Christians ought to be the *best* workers wherever they are. They ought to have the *best* attitude, the *best* integrity, and be the *best* in dependability.

If what the pollsters tell us is true — that there is little difference in the work ethics of Christians and non-Christians — we have cause for alarm. If there is no difference, then large numbers of God's children have succumbed to the extremes of laziness and overwork which characterize today's work force. It also means that vast numbers of Christian lives are spiritually dysfunctional, for it is impossible to dedicate over half of one's waking hours (some 80- to 100,000 hours in an average lifetime) to a sub-Biblical work ethic and *not* suffer immense spiritual trauma.

We must recover the Biblical truth — the Reformation truth — that our vocation, be it ever so humble, is a divine calling and thus be liberated to do it for the glory of God. This alone will take the Church out into the world.

Men, if you sense you are deficient, you need to do three things.

First, take an honest assessment of your life, using the Scriptures as a standard as you answer the questions:

- Do I do my work for the glory of God?
- Do I honestly work hard?
- Do I work with enthusiasm?
- Do I work wholeheartedly?
- Do I do excellent work?

Second, after honest evaluation confess your sins.

And, thirdly, commit your work life to the glory of God alone.

Will you do this now?

Food for Thought

How do you feel about Hughes' statement that "many Christian men miserably fail in their work ethics either because of sloth or overwork or, ironically, both"? How does your work ethic match up with your beliefs? Explain.

What do we learn in Genesis 1:1 — 2:2 about the example God sets as a worker? How should what you see there be applied to your working life?

What does Genesis 3:17-19 tell us about the current nature of work? (Compare 2:4-11, 17.) Does this mean it is useless to seek fulfillment or usefulness or success in our business, family, and church labors? If not, why not?

What work do we read about in Ephesians 2:10? What is the origin of this work? Its purpose? What must you do to experience this work in your life?

Do you agree with Martin Luther that "Your work is a very sacred matter"? What can you do to remind yourself that your work matters to God?

What is the relation between a healthy work ethic and wholeheartedness (see Ephesians 6:5-8)?

Application/Response

What did God speak to you about most specifically, most powerfully in this chapter? Talk to Him about it right now!

Think About It!

Read Colossians 3:15-17, 22-25, then list as many applications as you can for your work life. Then honestly put a check beside every application you have not been putting into practice. Confess this to God, and ask for His help in doing better.

13

DISCIPLINE OF PERSEVERANCE

URING MY STUDENT YEARS, when I was working a swing shift in a factory in Los Angeles, I became friends with a law student who played tennis named Larry King (not to be confused with the CNN talk show host), and Larry and I talked a lot of tennis during breaks. Soon we began to exchange a little tennis "trash" as to who was the best, which after some weeks eventuated into a casual "we'll find out" tennis match. The game was fairly casual until Larry's wife, the famous Billy Jean King, showed up and began to do a little of her own talking. She was not impressed. Predictably our shots became crisper, and we began to sweat more — all, of course, with a conscious male "who cares!" casualness. Wimbledon champion Billy Jean's presence definitely elevated our game.

Golfers, think what would happen to your concentration if Tiger Woods joined your foursome! Or imagine the adrenaline rush if while shooting some hoops, Michael Jordan appeared saying, "Mind if I join you?" Every ounce of "wanna be" in our mortal bodies would suddenly be on the court! The presence of pros, Hall of Famers, is immensely elevating.

On a transcending spiritual level the truth also applies. In fact, the author of Hebrews draws an awesome picture of heavenly observers in an attempt to motivate and instruct a faltering church to persevere. The scene is a great coliseum. The occasion is a footrace, a distance event. The contestants include the author and the members of his flock and, by mutual faith, us. The "cloud of witnesses" (12:1) that fills the stadium are the great spiritual athletes of the past, Hall of Faith members — every one a Gold Medal winner. They are not live witnesses of the event, but "witnesses" by the fact that their past lives bear testimony to monumental, persevering faith that, like Abel's, "still speaks, even though he is dead" (11:4).[1] Everywhere you look in the vast arena, there is a kind face nodding encouragement, saying, "I did it, and so can you. You can do it. You have my life to help you do it!" Abraham strokes his long beard and smiles. Sarah winks and gives a royal wave. Moses settles back to watch.

Your heart is pumping rapidly. You are afraid, and yet with all your being you want to do well. But how? Hebrews 12 answers eloquently with a discipline that can be summarized in four succeeding commands to *Divest!* — *Run!* — *Focus!* — and *Consider!*

DIVEST!

The call to divestment is clearly spelled out in the opening line: "Therefore, since we are surrounded by such a great cloud of witnesses, let us throw off everything that hinders and the sin that so easily entangles" (v. 1a). The divestment here refers to the radical stripping off of your clothing before a race, as was the Greek custom of the day. The writer orders a double divestment — first, of all hindrances, and second, of sin.

The sin that we are especially commanded to throw off is described as "the sin that so easily entangles" us — that is, the specific sin(s) unique to us as individuals and to which we so easily fall — "besetting sin" as the older translations have it. There are certain sins that easily beset us and then envelop us, though they may not entice others. There are some sins that have no trouble wiggling in through our eyes, ears, touch, taste, and thought — simply because of who we are.[2] Likewise, there are sins that have little appeal to us but irresistibly engulf others. Sensuality may be the Achilles heel for many men, but not all. Another man who has gained victory over such sins might be beset by jealousy.

Among the most clinging of the besetting sins are:

- Jealousy — a soul that actually aches when another does well.
- Pessimism — a despairing negativism that perpetually sours everything.
- Lust — for others, for more things, for position.
- Pride — the self-absorbed sin that plants you in the center of all things.
- Anger — a Vulcan heart that belches fire.
- Lying — a sin that tinges your most intimate relationships with deceit.

Besetting sins are the sins that attract and hold us with the promise of pleasure, including even some "pleasures" that bring no happiness or enjoyment but only disappointment and more despair. Their terrifying pathology has been seen in nature billions of times over. A fly lights on a leaf to taste the sweetness that grows there. Instantly three crimson-tipped, fingerlike hairs bend over and touch the fly's wings, holding it firm in a sticky grasp. The fly struggles mightily to get free, but the more it struggles, the more hopelessly it is coated with adhesive. Soon the fly relaxes, but to its fly-mind "things could be worse," because it extends its tongue and feasts on the sweetness while it is held even more firmly by still more sticky tentacles — just as happens when we swill our besetting sins. When the captive is entirely at the plant's mercy, the edges of the leaf fold inward, forming a closed fist. Two hours later the fly is an empty sucked skin, and the hungry fist unfolds its delectable mouth for another easy entanglement. That is a truly terrifying allegory.

The scriptural command calls for extreme actions. If we are to finish well in the faith, we must strip our souls naked of "everything that hinders and the sin that so easily entangles" us. The benevolent, knowing faces of those who have run the race before us beckon us to do so. The eternal fact is, you'll never run the race that is set before you if you do not put off your clinging sins. What are *your* besetting sins? Will you name them before God? He knows them perfectly. Why not do that now?

Going deeper, the question is: What "hinders" you? Literally, *what is the weight that hinders you?* Most likely, it is not a sin. It might be something that is good — good for others, but bad for you — a place, a habit, a pleasure, a hobby, an event, an entertainment. If this otherwise good thing pulls you down, you must strip it away. For example, there may be an apparently harmless place (a forest, a store, an apartment, a city) that, because of your past sins, still lures you downward. You must toss aside such a place and forgot it.

This is radical talk. But it's a matter of life! It has to do with finishing — and finishing well.

RUN!

Properly divested, with every hindrance cast aside, there remains one great thing to do — and that is to run: "and let us run with perseverance the race marked out for us" (v. 1b). Persevering grit is an awesome, beautiful thing. Writer and sometimes marathoner Art Carey described in a memorable piece for the *Philadelphia Inquirer* his experience of "hitting the wall" and then going on to finish the Boston Marathon. We pick up his story near the end:

> By now, the rigors of having run nearly twenty miles are beginning to tell. My stride has shortened. My legs are tight. My breathing is shallow and fast.

My joints are becoming raw and worn. My neck aches from all the jolts that have ricocheted up my spine. Half-dollar-size blisters sting the soles of my feet. I'm beginning to feel queasy and light-headed. I want to stop running. I have "hit the wall." Now the real battle begins. Up the first of many long inclines I start to climb . . . "Heartbreak Hill" — the last, the longest and the steepest, a half-mile struggle against gravity designed to finish off the faint and faltering. . . . The last four miles are seemingly endless. . . . Finally, the distinctive profile of the Prudential Building looms on the horizon. I begin to step up my pace. . . . I can see the yellow stripe 50 yards ahead. I run faster, pumping my arms, pushing off my toes, defying clutching leg cramps to mount a glorious, last-gasp kick . . . cheers and clapping . . . 10 yards . . . finish line . . . an explosion of euphoria . . . I am clocked in at two hours, 50 minutes and 49 seconds. *My place*: 1,176. I find the figures difficult to believe, but if they are accurate, then I have run the best marathon of my life. While times and places are important, and breaking a personal record is thrilling (especially as you grow older), the real joy of the Boston Marathon is just finishing . . . doing what you have set out to do.[3]

Persevering grit possesses a terrible beauty, but it is eternally beautiful when devoted to the real-life spiritual race that is marked out for us. The sense of biblical "perseverance" is *patient fortitude,* patiently "gutting it out."

We each have a specific race mapped out for us; the course for each runner is unique. Its uniqueness is determined by God, who charts it factoring in who you and I are right now as to our giftedness, background, responsibilities, age, health — and most of all who we are in Christ. Your race is like no one else's. It is marked out for you where you are as a student, a single, a parent.

Some races are relatively straight; some are all turns. Some seem all uphill; some are a flat hiking path. They are not equal. All races are long, but some are longer. But the glory is, each of us (no exceptions!) can finish the race "marked out for us." I may not be able to run your course, and you may find mine impossible, but I can finish my race and you yours. Both of us can finish well if we choose and if we rely on Him who is our strength and our guide. We can experience the same exhilaration the Apostle Paul did as he neared the finish line: "I have fought the good fight, I have finished the race, I have kept the faith" (2 Timothy 4:7). Depending upon God, there is no doubt that we can finish "the race marked out for us" — and finish it with satisfaction. Whoever you are and wherever you are, you can do it!

Perseverance has nothing to do with giftedness, but everything to do with your heart. In 1981 Bill Broadhurst entered the Pepsi Challenge 10,000-meter race in Omaha, Nebraska. Surgery ten years earlier for an aneurysm in the brain had left him paralyzed on his left side. But on that misty July morning, he stood with 1,200 lithe men and women at the starting line. The gun sounded, and the crowd surged ahead. Bill threw his stiff left leg forward and pivoted on it as his foot hit the ground. His slow plop-plop-plop rhythm seemed to mock him as the pack raced into the distance. Sweat rolled down his face, and pain pierced his ankle, but he kept going. Some of the runners completed the race in about thirty minutes, but two hours and twenty-nine minutes later Bill reached the finish line.

A man approached from a small group of remaining bystanders. Though exhausted, Bill recognized him from pictures in the newspaper. It was Bill Rodgers, the famous marathon runner, who then draped *his* newly won medal around Bill's neck. Bill Broadhurst's finish was as glorious as that of the world's greatest though he finished last because he ran with perseverance. Biblical perseverance that refuses to be deflected, overcomes obstacles and delays, and is not stopped by discouragement within nor opposition without is available to us all.

It is quite within the reach of every one of us to manifest positive, conquering perseverance — putting one heavy foot in front of the other until we reach the glorious end. The race is not for sprinters who flame out after 100 or 200 or 400 meters. It is for faithful plodders — people like you and me. Fast or slow, strong or weak, we must all persevere.

FOCUS!

If we have stripped ourselves bare of all besetting sins and every hindrance and have begun to run with perseverance our race — the race that God has marked out for us — we are then given the focus that guarantees our finishing well. That focus, of course, is Jesus: "Let us fix our eyes on Jesus, the author and perfecter of our faith" (v. 2a).

Focus on Jesus
The writer is very intentional in commanding us to focus on Jesus, rather than using His title Christ or Jesus Christ. We are to focus on Jesus the *incarnate* Son of God as He lived as a *man* here on earth. Jesus was the runner without parallel. Every obstacle was thrown in His way, but He never stumbled once — and He finished going away.

He became "the author and perfecter of our faith" by the way He lived. His life authored (literally, *pioneered*) faith. There never was a millisecond that He did not trust the Father, resting everything in Him. So great was His trust that He lived on every word that came from the mouth of God (cf. Matthew 4:4). And He continues to be "the author and perfecter of our faith" by what He does in us. He bestows the gift of faith (cf. Ephesians 2:8-9; Matthew 11:27) and then perfects it in His children (cf. Hebrews 11).

Since we need faith to run the race, we must "fix our eyes on Jesus, the author and perfecter of our faith." That is, as the Greek literally indicates, *we must deliberately lift our eyes from other distracting things and focus with utter concentration on Him — and continue doing so.*[4] We must not look away even for an instant. Such focus is indispensable to a life of faith and to finishing the race.

On August 7, 1954, during the British Empire Games in Vancouver, Canada, the greatest mile-run matchup ever took place. It was touted as the "miracle mile" because Roger Bannister and John Landy were the only two sub-four-minute milers in the world. Bannister had been the first man ever to run a four-minute mile. Both runners were in peak condition.

Roger Bannister, M.D., who is today Sir Roger Bannister and master of an Oxford college, strategized that he would relax during the third lap and save everything for his finishing drive. But as they began that third lap, John Landy poured it on, stretching his already substantial lead. Immediately Bannister adjusted his strategy, increasing his pace and gaining on Landy. The lead was quickly cut in half, and at the bell for the final lap they were even. Landy began running even faster, and Bannister followed suit. Both men were flying. Bannister felt he was going to lose if Landy did not slow down.

Then came the famous moment (replayed thousands of times in print and celluloid) as at the last stride before the home stretch the crowds roared. Landy could not hear Bannister's footfall and looked back — a fatal lapse of concentration. Bannister launched his attack and won the "miracle mile" that day by five yards.

Those who look away from Christ — the end and goal of our race — will not finish well. And this was exactly what was happening to some treading the stormy waters mounting around the early church. They had begun to take their eyes off Christ and to fix them instead on the hardships challenging them. Some had begun to look elsewhere for answers.

Focus on His Focus

Along with focusing on Jesus, we must focus on His focus — "who for the *joy* set before him endured the cross, scorning its shame" (v. 2b, emphasis added). Jesus' focus on the coming joy of his resurrection, ascension, and enthronement at God's right hand, plus the joys of redeeming a people for Himself, strengthened Him to do two things: First, to endure the terrible agony of the cross with an "intensity, and with a unity of perception, which none of us can possibly fathom . . . because His soul was so absolutely in His power . . . so utterly surrendered, so simply subjected to the suffering" (John Henry Newman).[5] The agony that Jesus endured on the cross was worse for Him precisely because He was God. Second, He scorned the shame of the cross. That is, He thought nothing of the shame — He dismissed it with contempt as nothing. Jesus did all this because He fully knew the bounding, dancing, endless joy that awaited Him.

Now here's the wonder: *Jesus' joy is our joy!* His joy is the joy set before us! How can this be? The answer is that we are one with Him. Christ is *in* us, and we are *in* Him (2 Corinthians 5:17). Where Christ is, we are! God has already seated us in Christ in the heavenly places, so "that in the coming ages he might show the incomparable riches of his grace, expressed in his kindness to us in Christ Jesus" (Ephesians 2:7). We are "heirs of God and co-heirs with Christ, if indeed we share in his sufferings in order that we may also share in his glory" (Romans 8:17). His boundless, dancing, endless joy will be ours!

To doubt this is to doubt God's holy Word. If we will focus on the joy that Christ has set before us, we will endure the sufferings of this world and will dismiss any shame incurred in His name as nothing. And we will run the race to His glory.

CONSIDER!

In capping his famous challenge to "run with perseverance the race marked out for us," the writer restates the command to focus on Jesus in fitting terms of the athlete: "Consider him who endured such opposition from sinful men, so that you will not grow weary and lose heart" (v. 3). The phrase "grow weary and lose heart" was sports lingo in the ancient world used to describe a runner's exhausted collapse.[6]

Therefore, the way for the Christian to avoid spiritual collapse is to consider Christ and the opposition He faced from the likes of sinners like Caiaphas, Herod, and Pilate. Consider how He faced them with confidence, meekness, and strength. No one must miss the overarching message of this passage: We are to be totally absorbed with Jesus. He is to fill our skies like the morning sunrise. He is to be our high noon and our sunset.

Whether we have been or are athletes or not, we have a race to run in this hostile world, whether we're nine or nineteen or ninety. We are surrounded by a great cloud of lives whose examples call for our best — *patriarchs* like Abraham, Isaac, and Jacob; *prophets* like Moses, Elijah, and Daniel; the inner circle of *apostles* like Peter, James, and John; *martyrs* like Stephen, Cranmer, and Elliot; great *preachers* like Luther, Calvin, Wesley, and Spurgeon; exemplary *missionaries* like Carey, Taylor, and Carmichael; our departed *family and friends*; and on and on. Their kind faces invite us to finish well. Their memories whisper, "You can do it! Don't lose heart. The end will come before you know it. Hang sweet and tough."

So the discipline of perseverance confronts us to:

- *Divest.* We must throw off every besetting sin, those sins whose crimson-tipped fingers so easily entangle us. Our besetting sins are unique to us. They may not tempt others, but they slay us as we swill their seeming sweetness. Probing deeper, we must cast off everything that hinders us — even the good things. If we don't, we'll never run as we ought. Are you willing to do some radical divesting? That is the question.

- *Run.* Then we must run our own race, the race God has marked out for us. Your race is not my race, and my race is not yours. You can finish your race. It is God's will. And He will give you the grit to persevere as you run. So run, my brother, run!

- *Focus.* We must focus on Jesus. There must be no distracted glances. Jesus must cover the sky. He must be our center. And we must focus on His focus and His joy because it is our joy. His joy set before us will give us the power to endure, even despising the world's disdain.

- *Consider.* So we are to consider Him. Our life is to be spent considering how He lived.

We are to run like Jesus did, completely divested. We are to run with Him. We are to run toward Him. We are to fix our eyes on Him. We are to focus on His focus. He is to be our perpetual consideration.

He has a race for us to run. And we can do it as we lean on Him.

Food for Thought

What entanglements (besetting sins) and hindrances (legitimate things that are pulling you down) do you need to cast aside and leave behind? Be specific. Why is it so hard to do this?

What is the race that God has mapped out for you like — straight, twisting, flat, hilly? Why or why not are you able to persevere in that race? What has been your greatest victory so far?

Do you think that at the end of your life you will be able to say, "I have fought the good fight, I have finished the race, I have kept the faith"? Why or why not? What would it take to be able to say that? What can you do today to lead to that result?

What does it really mean to "fix our eyes on Jesus"? Is His joy your joy? Why or why not?

Are you ever like John Landy — looking back and so having a wrong focus and running the risk of failing to finish the race well? What sorts of things do you look back at? How can you avoid this or get the right focus back when it happens?

Does the list of witnesses that Hughes lists encourage you or discourage you? Do you think "I really identify with Peter — I have great intentions but I find it so easy to give in" or "Abraham, Daniel, Luther? I'll never have that kind of courage"? How can the examples of the godly who have gone before us help us in our walk?

Application/Response

What did God speak to you about most specifically, most powerfully in this chapter? Talk to Him about it right now!

Think About It!

Read Hebrews 12:1-3 again. Note every detail given about Christ, then praise Him for all of it. Then list the responsibilities God gives you in those verses, and pray to Him about how well (or poorly) you are doing with each.

MINISTRY

14

DISCIPLINE OF CHURCH

ASTUTE OBSERVERS ARE becoming increasingly aware that the doctrine of the Church has become progressively weakened and in some cases abandoned by American evangelicals. Robert W. Patterson, associate to the executive director of the National Association of Evangelicals, voiced his concern in the March 1991 issue of *Christianity Today*:

> When President Dwight Eisenhower became a Christian, he made a public profession of faith in Christ, was baptized, and was extended the right hand of fellowship at the National Presbyterian Church in Washington, D.C., the second Sunday after his inauguration in 1953. Had the former President expressed interest in becoming a Christian a generation later under more consciously evangelical auspices, he might never have been challenged to identify with the body of Christ through baptism and church membership. A personal relationship with Jesus, he would have been told, is all that really matters.[1]

Of course, we must wholeheartedly agree that without a saving relationship with Jesus Christ all is lost. But we must not mistakenly reason that one's relationship with Christ minimizes the importance of His Church. Yet this is precisely what multitudes of evangelicals assume and act out.

Church attendance is infected with a malaise of conditional loyalty which has produced an army of ecclesiastical hitchhikers. The hitchhiker's thumb says, "You buy the car, pay for repairs and upkeep and insurance, fill the car with gas — and I'll ride with you. But if you have an accident, you are on your own! And I'll probably sue." So it is with the credo of so many of today's church attenders: "You go to the meetings and serve on the boards and committees, you grapple with the issues and do the work of the church and pay the bills —

and I'll come along for the ride. But if things do not suit me, I'll criticize and complain and probably bail out — my thumb is always out for a better ride."

This putative loyalty is fueled by a consumer ethos — a "McChristian" mentality — which picks and chooses here and there to fill one's ecclesiastical shopping list. There are hitchhikers who attend one church for the preaching, send their children to a second church for its dynamic youth program, and go to a third church's small group. Church hitchhikers have a telling vocabulary: "I go to" or "I attend," but never "I belong to" or "I am a member." Pollster George Barna supports this, saying: "[T]he average adult thinks that belonging to a church is good for other people, but represents unnecessary bondage and baggage for himself."[2]

So today, at the end of the twentieth century, we have a phenomenon unthinkable in any other century: churchless Christians. There is a vast herd of professed Christians who exist as nomadic hitchhikers without accountability, without discipline, without discipleship, living apart from the regular benefits of the ordinances. To borrow from Cyprian's idea,[3] they have God as their Father, but reject the Church as mother and as a result are incomplete and stunted. The tragedy is compounded because statistics indicate that men are far less committed to the Church than women[4] — inevitably producing a shriveled leadership.

As to why the Church has fallen on such hard times, historians tell us that an overemphasis on the "invisible" Body of Christ by evangelical leaders produced an implicit disregard for the visible Church. However, membership in an invisible Church without participation in its local expression is never contemplated in the New Testament.[5]

Another reason for the de-churching of many Christians is the historic individualism of evangelical Christianity and the grass-roots American impulse against authority. The natural inclination is to think that one needs only an individual relationship with Christ and needs no other authority. Such thinking produces Christian Lone Rangers who demonstrate their authenticity by riding not to church, but out to the badlands, reference Bible in hand, to do battle single-handedly with the outlaw world.

Such a cavalier disregard for the doctrine of the Church is eccentric, to say the least. It disregards not only Scripture, but the consensus of the doctors of the Church. St. Augustine in his *Enchiridion* holds up the visible Church saying: "[F]or outside the church they [*one's sins*] have no remission. For it is the Church in particular which has received the earnest, the Holy Spirit, apart from whom no sins receive remission"[6] (italics added). Augustine could not conceive of one being regenerated yet consciously separate from the visible Church. "The deserter of the Church," he said, "cannot be in Christ, since he is not among Christ's members."[7]

Martin Luther similarly stated, "Outside this Christian Church there is no salvation or forgiveness of sins, but everlasting death and damnation; even though there may be a magnificent appearance of holiness. . . ."[8]

John Calvin echoed Cyprian's thought that the evidence of having God as your Father is having the Church as your mother. In fact, he subtitled chapter 1 of book 4 of his *Institutes* "The True Church with Which as Mother of All the Godly We Must Keep Unity."[9] And in his commentary on Ephesians he wrote, "The Church is the common mother of all the godly, which bears, nourishes, and governs in the Lord both kings and commoners; and this is done by the ministry. Those who neglect or despise this order want to be wiser than Christ. Woe to their pride!"[10]

The Swiss *Second Helvetic Confession* put the idea even more forcefully:

> For as there was no salvation outside Noah's ark when the world perished in the flood; so we believe that there is no certain salvation outside Christ, who offers himself to be enjoyed by the elect in the Church; and hence we teach that those who wish to live ought not to be separated from the true Church of Christ. (Chapter 27)[11]

Finally, the *Westminster Confession* refers to "The visible church . . . out of which there is no ordinary possibility of salvation" (Chapter 25.2).[12]

So we conclude that church hitchhikers, ecclesiastical wanderers, spiritual Lone Rangers, Christians who disdain membership, are aberrations in the history of the Christian Church and are in grievous error.

THE DOCTRINE OF THE CHURCH

So many today need to be blasted from their delusions by an understanding of the great doctrine of the Church. There is no text that will ignite one's soul more than Hebrews 12:22-24, which describes the seven stupendous meetings which the Christian experiences in the Church:

> But you have come to Mount Zion, to the heavenly Jerusalem, the city of the living God. You have come to thousands upon thousands of angels in joyful assembly, to the church of the firstborn, whose names are written in

heaven. You have come to God, the judge of all men, to the spirits of righteous men made perfect, to Jesus the mediator of a new covenant, and to the sprinkled blood that speaks a better word than the blood of Abel.

First, we come to the *city of God* — "But you have come to Mount Zion, to the heavenly Jerusalem, the city of the living God." Mount Zion was the location of the Jebusite stronghold which David captured and made the religious center of his kingdom by bringing to it the golden Ark of God's presence. When Solomon built the Temple and installed the Ark, Zion/Jerusalem became synonymous with the earthly dwelling-place of God. In Christ we have come to its heavenly counterpart, the spiritual Jerusalem from above. In one sense it is still to come, but at the same time we have already arrived there in spirit. Christians are *now* citizens of the heavenly city and enjoy its privileges.

Second, as the Church we meet *angels* — "You have come to thousands upon thousands of angels in joyful assembly." Moses tells us that "myriads of holy ones" attended the giving of the Law (Deuteronomy 33:2), and from Daniel we hear that "Thousands upon thousands attended him [the Ancient of Days — God]; ten thousand times ten thousand stood before him" (Daniel 7:10). David said, "The chariots of God are tens of thousands and thousands of thousands" (Psalm 68:17). In the Church we come to these dizzying thousands of angels, all of whom are in joyful celebration. They are everywhere — mighty flaming spirits, "ministering spirits sent to serve those who will inherit salvation" (Hebrews 1:14), passing in and out of our lives, moving around us and over us, just as they did to Jacob of old.

Third, we come to *fellow believers* — "to the church of the firstborn, whose names are written in heaven." Jesus was the firstborn *par excellence*, and by virtue of our union with Him we are firstborn. All the rights of inheritance go to the firstborn — to us, "co-heirs with Christ" (Romans 8:17). In the Church we do more than come into each other's presence — we share membership together.

Fourth, we come to *God*— "You have come to God, the judge of all men." We come in awe because He is the Judge — but we do not come in craven dread, because His Son has borne the judgment for us. This is our highest delight — to gather before our God!

Fifth, we come to the heavenly *Church Triumphant* — "to the spirit of righteous men made perfect." Though they are in Heaven, we share a solidarity with those who have gone before. The same spiritual life courses through us as through them. We share the same secrets and joys as Abraham and Moses and David and Paul.

Sixth, we have come to *Jesus* — "to Jesus the mediator of a new covenant." It is through Jesus that the promises come to us. He is the source and dispenser of all for which we hope. He is in us, and we are in Him.

Seventh, we come to forgiveness because of *sprinkled blood* — "and to the sprinkled blood that speaks a better word than the blood of Abel." Abel's warm blood cried condemnation and judgment from the ground, but Christ's blood shouts that we are forgiven and have peace with God. *Hallelujah!*

Brothers, the Scriptures tell us that in the Church "you have come" (*right now!*) to these seven sublime realities: 1) to the *city of God*, 2) to *myriads of angels*, 3) to *fellow believers*, 4) to *God*, 5) to the *Church Triumphant*, 6) to *Jesus*, and 7) to *forgiveness*! If this does not create a wellspring of thanksgiving in your hearts and a longing for fellowship in the visible Church, nothing will!

John Bunyan once told of falling into despondency which lasted for several days and desperately seeking a word from God to meet his need — and then this same grand text came to him. Bunyan wrote:

> But that night was a good night to me; I have had but few better; I longed for the company of some of God's people, that I might have imparted unto them what God had showed me. Christ was a precious Christ to my soul that night; I could scarce lie in my bed for joy, and peace, and triumph through Christ.[13]

Savior, if of Zion's city,
I through grace a member am,
Let the world deride or pity,
I will glory in Thy name.

—John Newton, 1779

The dazzling images of the Church assault us again and again in the New Testament in an effort to raise our thinking to the proper height. As the Church, actually we are Christ's *Body* (Ephesians 1:22, 23). He is the Head, and as members of His Body we have at the same time a profound unity, diversity, and mutuality. We are a *temple* (Ephesians 2:19-22). He is the cornerstone, and we are living stones (1 Peter 2:5) — forming a living place of worship. We are the *bride* (Ephesians 5:25-33). And Christ, our groom, loves us with a holy love which will bring us to the Marriage Feast of the Lamb. We are his *sheep*, and He is the nurturing shepherd (John 10:14-16, 25-30). He is the vine, and we are the *branches*. We are organically in Him, drawing all our sustenance for life from Him (John 15:5ff.).

What should the truth that we are the Church mean to us? It should fill us with wonder and thanksgiving. We ought to sing, "I am His body, His temple, His bride, His sheep, His branch. I have come to His city — to angels — to brothers and sisters — to God Himself — to the Church glorified — to Jesus — to forgiveness through Christ's blood."

This doctrine also tells us that the Church will outlive the world. Harry Blamires wrote:

> The world is like a great express train hurtling towards disaster — perhaps towards total destruction. And in this truly desperate situation certain passengers are running up and down the corridors announcing to each other that the Church is in great danger! The irony of it would be laughable if it were not so searing. Why, most of the Church's members have already got out at stations *en route*. And we ourselves shall be getting out soon anyway. And if the crash comes and the world is burnt to ashes, then the only thing that will survive the disaster will of course be the Church.[14]

Personally, the doctrine of the Church ought to tell us that we are part of the grandest institution the universe has ever known, and that we are tragically diminished by non-participation in Christ's Body. Correspondingly, the Church is diminished by our nonparticipation as well. *You and I need the Church!* The Scriptures are most explicit regarding this: "Let us not give up meeting together, as some are in the habit of doing, but let us encourage one another — and all the more as you see the Day approaching" (Hebrews 10:25).

This straightforward exhortation ought to be enough in itself. But there are several other powerful reasons for faithful participation in the Church, not the least of which is that, as Cyprian argued, we all need a mother. The Church has certainly been that to me. It was the womb which warmed my soul till it was ready for birth when my pastor, Verl Lindley, led me to Christ. I was lovingly nurtured by the Church through my youth sponsors, Howard and Ruby Busse. The Church gave me the milk of the Word through the strong teaching of my College Department teacher, Robert Seelye. She saw me through hard times through the prayers of spiritual mothers like Roselva Taylor. She was the womb and cradle for my wife too. When our children came along, the Church stood with us as we dedicated our children to God. She has also been the mother of my best friends.

I owe so much to Christ's Church: my life, my character, my worldview, my calling, my vision, my peace, my hope — everything. *I believe in the Church!*

Understanding, then, that we need the mothering of the Church, we must also understand that we will never benefit as we should from it apart from commitment to her Head. The entire Christian life is about commitment — first and above all to Christ, but also to the Church, to family, to marriage, to friendship, to ministry. None of these will ever flourish apart from commitment.

For example, marriage can never produce the security, satisfaction, and growth that it promises unless there is commitment. This is why today's provisional live-in arrangements are coming up short. Commitment through good and bad times is what makes a marriage grow and brings the greatest fulfillment.

Men, on the most elementary level, you do not have to go to church to be a Christian. You do not have to go home to be married either. But in both cases if you do not, you will have a very poor relationship.

Among the growth-inducing benefits of commitment to the Church are:

- *Worship* — having your soul swept up to God in the unique elevating power of corporate worship.
- *Hearing the Word* — so that your soul can feed on its proper food, bringing health to your whole being.
- *Attendance at the Lord's Table* — so that you are refreshed as you thank God for the atoning work of Christ.

> *We taste Thee, O Thou living Bread,*
> *And long to feast upon Thee still;*
> *We drink of Thee, the Fountainhead,*
> *And thirst our souls from Thee to fill.*
>
> --Bernard of Clairvaux

- *Discipleship* — as one is committed to the Church through its ups and downs, an appropriate deepening takes place which the uncommitted heart can never know.
- *Vision and mission* — as one remains committed, a supernatural vision for life takes hold which results in mission.

Men, you need the Church because the Scriptures say you do, because you need a mother, and because without commitment to her you will not grow.

THE DISCIPLINE OF CHURCH

If the grand and great doctrine of the Church tells us anything, it tells us that whoever you are and however busy you may be (whether U.S. President, chairman of the Joint Chiefs of Staff, a Fortune 500 business executive, or leader of a parachurch organization), *the Church must be at the very center of your life.* Church hitchhiking is an aberration! And so is mild commitment.

Men, honestly, are you a hitchhiker, kind of a "free agent" looking for a tentative place on the roster, here for a season, there for another? If so, you will never attain to your full spiritual manhood, nor will your family reach its spiritual maturity.

Men, at the end of the twentieth century both the Church and the lost world need men who practice the *discipline of Church.*

The Discipline of Regular Attendance
As part of this matter, you need to commit yourself to regularly attend the worship services of your church. Your schedule ought to bow to your commitment. When you travel, you ought to attempt to schedule yourself to be back for church, and if that is impossible, attend elsewhere while you are on the road.

The Discipline of Membership
If you are not a church member, you need to covenant before God to find a good church, join it, and commit yourself to supporting her and submitting to her discipline.

The Discipline of Giving
Your financial support of a local church should take precedence over your parachurch commitments. This should be regular and systematic (10 percent is a good starting-point).

The Discipline of Participation
Your time, talents, expertise, and creativity must be poured into your church, to the glory of God.

The Discipline of Love and Prayer
Timothy Dwight, heir to the Puritans and the greatest president of Yale University, penned these beautiful words:

I love Thy Church, O God!
Her walls before Thee stand.
Dear as the apple of Thine eye.
And graven on Thy hand.
For her my tears shall fall;
For her my prayers ascend;
To her my cares and toils be giv'n,
Till toils and cares shall end.

Food for Thought

Why is the idea of *church* so unpopular today? Why aren't more people interested in attending a good church?

According to Hebrews 12:22-24, what spiritual treasures are found in the church? Put these in your own words, then thank God for each one of them.

What does the image of the church as Christ's *body* suggest to you (Ephesians 1:22, 23)? His *temple* (Ephesians 2:19-22)? His *bride* (Ephesians 5:25-33)?

What do our attitudes toward church and toward Christ have to do with each another? If the latter is misguided, will the former do any good?

Why are you tempted to do what Hebrews 10:25 says not to do? What spiritual blessings might you miss out on by staying away from Christian gatherings?

"On the most elementary level, you do not have to go to church to be a Christian. You do not have to go home to be married either. But in both cases if you do not, you will have a very poor relationship." True or not true? How do regular attendance and participation strengthen your relationship with God . . . with family members . . . with other believers? Be specific.

Application/Response

What did God speak to you about most specifically, most powerfully in this chapter? Talk to Him about it right now!

Think About It!

List as many strengths and weaknesses as you see in your church. Now write down the ways you personally are contributing to each of these, and also specific ways you can be part of changing the weaknesses.

15

DISCIPLINE OF LEADERSHIP

L EADERSHIP," SAYS WARREN Bennis, the poet-philosopher-scholar of organizational life, "is a word on everyone's lips. The young attack it and police seek it. Experts claim it and artists spurn it, while scholars want it . . . bureaucrats pretend they have it, politicians wish they did. Everybody agrees that there is less of it than there used to be."[1]

This pessimistic consensus and longing for leadership extends to the Church, which many today feel suffers from an alarming lack of leadership when compared to history as recent as the decades between the forties and seventies (decades which produced leaders of the stature of Harold John Ockenga, Billy Graham, Carl F. H. Henry and Francis Schaeffer, as well as dynamic local church and layleaders).[2]

Is there really less leadership than there used to be? It appears so, but objective analysis is difficult. Statistics do indicate this, however: male leadership in the Church is on the decline as women outnumber men, for men comprise only 41 percent of adult church attenders, and some smaller churches cannot find even one man to fill the office of elder. More and more men are content to let others shoulder the heavy responsibilities while they go along for the ride. It is certainly true that leadership is more difficult today due to the sheer complexity of life and the size of today's institutions, and because of the contemporary confusion as to what leadership is. Secular analysis has produced more than 350 definitions of leadership. "Leadership is like the Abominable Snowman," writes Bennis, "whose footprints are everywhere but [he is] nowhere to be seen."[3]

But none of this excuses today's Church — or today's Christian man. Unlike our culture, the Bible provides clear instruction regarding leadership through the lives of its great leaders and through specific teaching regarding the character, qualifications, and commitment of spiritual leaders. In addition to this, amidst our culture's confusion about leadership there are some astute analysts who have pinpointed the essentials of leadership and are providing information which has immense benefit for the general culture, including the Church. As we tackle the topic of the discipline of leadership, we will draw from both sources, with the greatest reliance being upon God's Word.

PREPARATION FOR SPIRITUAL LEADERSHIP

The "textbook" for learning the qualities essential for spiritual leadership comes from the mentions of Joshua in the Pentateuch, wherein the Holy Spirit has recorded seven unique experiences which endowed Joshua with qualities necessary to succeed Moses as the leader of God's people. We will consider these experiences in the order that they appear in Scripture — each one successively building a surprisingly comprehensive portrait of godly leadership.

Prayer

The first mention of Joshua comes in Exodus 17:8, 9 after the Amalekites' attack upon the stragglers at Israel's rear: "Moses said to Joshua, 'Choose some of our men and go out to fight the Amalekites. Tomorrow I will stand on top of the hill with the staff of God in my hands.'"

Moses, then in his eighties, took the rod of God with which he had parted the Red Sea and ascended a nearby hill. Joshua, in his fighting prime, took charge of the army below. In the ensuing battle, when Moses lifted his hands in intercessory prayer, Israel prevailed. But as Moses wearied and began to lower his arms, the tide of battle turned to the Amalekites. Then again, as Moses mustered all his power and elevated his hands, the advantage returned to Israel. Israel's fate ebbed and flowed with Moses' aged hands. Soon Aaron and Hur were called to assist Moses, seating him on a stone and standing at his sides to hold his hands Heavenward. When sunset came, Moses' hands were still reaching upward to God, and Israel had carried the day.

The lessons for Joshua were clearly manifest. He learned that the real power was not in his sword, but in God. The victory undoubtedly tempted him to forget that. He was an instant hero, and that night all the campfires sang the name of Joshua. But forever fixed in Joshua's mind was the image of Aaron and Hur coming to Moses' side and lifting his hands up to God.

No one attains true spiritual leadership who thinks his power is his own or that past victories are due to his own genius. The overriding lesson Joshua learned that day was that the backbone of any work done for God is prayer. E. M. Bounds said of those who have had effective spiritual leadership, "They are not leaders because of brilliancy . . . but because, by the power of prayer, they could command the power of God." [4]

How contrary this is to conventional thinking on leadership. The first thing the world (and all too often the Church!) considers is a leader's magnetism and elan — does he have the charisma to magnetize people? But the Holy Spirit places prayer first.

Vision

The next mention of Joshua in Scripture comes in Exodus 24, in the midst of the account which describes Moses' ascent of Mount Sinai to receive the Law. That chapter tells us that Moses, Aaron, Nadab, Abihu, and seventy elders of Israel (of whom Joshua was one) were called up the mountain. After climbing some distance and seeing a far-off vision of God's glory, the seventy remained behind, and Joshua and Moses went further up (v. 13). Here Joshua was with Moses six days when the glorious cloud covered Sinai (v. 16). But on the seventh day Moses went on alone, leaving Joshua alone on Sinai for forty days (v. 18).

The Sinai experience left its mark on Joshua. His initial vision of God majestically standing over a pavement of sapphire (v. 10), and his subsequent forty days of solitary meditation — while Moses, up in the glowing, thundering cloud on Sinai, received the Law — branded his heart with a deep sense of God's glory, holiness, and power.

The Christian leader's vision of God makes all the difference in his life. There is a grand visionary chain which links the great leaders in God's Word.

Consider Moses amidst the thunderings and lightnings of Sinai as God hides him in the cleft of a rock and makes His glory pass by him (Exodus 33:21-23).

Joshua not only sat below Moses on Sinai viewing God's glory, but later, on the eve of the battle for Jericho, he met God — "the captain of the Lord's host" — as a warrior in full battle dress, his sword bare and gleaming in the moonlight — and Joshua worshiped (Joshua 5:13-15, NASB).

Young David's vision of God grew so great as he shepherded under the stars and contemplated God's vastness that when he saw Goliath challenging leaderless Israel he cried, "Who is this uncircumcised Philistine that he should defy the armies of the living God?" (1 Samuel 17:26) and charged headlong into battle.

Isaiah "saw the Lord seated on a throne, high and exalted, and the train of his robe filled the temple," and this immense vision launched him into spectacular leadership and service — "Here am I. Send me!" (Isaiah 6:1, 8).

Peter, James, and John saw Jesus transfigured, so that His glory shone as the sun — and they went forward as key leaders in the apostolic Church (Mark 9:2-8).

Paul, who was not a part of the original apostolic band, became the missionary leader of the Church, fueled by being caught up to the third heaven and hearing and seeing things he could not describe (2 Corinthians 12:1-6).

An immense, growing vision of God is the *sine qua non*, the grand distinction, the continental divide of spiritual leadership. It is said that Robert Dick Wilson, the celebrated Old Testament scholar who served at Princeton Seminary at the beginning of this century, upon hearing that an alumnus was returning to preach would slip into the back of Miller Chapel and listen only once saying, "When my boys come back, I come to see if they are big godders or little godders and then I know what their ministry will be."[5] One's vision of God, his *visio Dei*, is everything!

But at the same time do not be put off or sell your leadership potential short because you have had no beatific vision. You do not need such a vision because you have two great books of vision, the book of Scripture which repeatedly reveals God's glory — and the book of creation, which continuously witnesses to God's greatness. Take, for example, the stars — "Day after day they pour forth speech; night after night they display knowledge. There is no speech or language where their voice is not heard" (Psalm 19:2, 3). The massive vision is always before you — if you will just look. Read the great Bible passages to enlarge your vision of God's greatness. Look up at the stars and around at creation. Pray for a growing revelation of God's vastness and for the grace to believe what you read and see.

Devotion

We find another aspect of Joshua's preparation for leadership in Exodus 33, where we glimpse his growing devotion to God. He was serving in the Tabernacle with Moses while the pillar of the cloud towered above the tent. Verse 11 tells us: "The Lord would speak to Moses face to face, as a man speaks with his friend. Then Moses would return to the camp, but his young aide Joshua son of Nun did not leave the tent." Though he was not privileged, like Moses, to speak with God face to face, Joshua was so overcome by God's presence that he would not leave the Tabernacle! There is such passion in this picture. "Lord, You are so wonderful, I cannot leave this room. I beg You, let me stay."

Joshua's New Testament counterpart is Mary of Bethany, who would not leave the room where Jesus was as she sat enraptured at His feet despite her sister's scolding. And she was so right! As we have it from the lips of our Lord, "Mary has chosen what is better, and it will not be taken away from her" (Luke 10:42). It was this same Mary who poured a year's fortune on Jesus and wiped His feet with her hair and of whom Jesus said, "She has done a beautiful thing to me" (Mark 14:6).

True spiritual leadership is born for devotion and demands to be closeted with God. We cannot name one great leader in the Church who has not made personal worship a top priority. Such were the lives of Luther, Bunyan, Edwards, Wesley, Müller, Lloyd-Jones, and every other truly spiritual leader. There is no spiritual leadership apart from passionate devotion.

One hundred years ago the great C. J. Vaughn said, "If I wished to humble anyone, I should question him about his prayers. I know nothing to compare with the topic for its sorrowful confessions."[6] Men, leaders, how would you answer such a question?

Magnanimity

The next mention of Joshua in Scripture is not as flattering as the previous appearance. Numbers 11 tells us that when Joshua was serving as assistant to Moses, he received disconcerting news. Some elders named Eldad and Medad were prophesying (preaching) in the camp of Israel. To Joshua this was an affront to Moses' spiritual leadership, for Moses was Israel's prophet *par excellence*. Alarmed, and jealous for Moses, Joshua immediately went to him, blurting out, "Moses, my lord, stop them!," fully expecting Moses to take action. But to Joshua's great surprise, Moses replied, "Are you jealous for my sake? I wish that all the Lord's people were prophets and that the Lord would put his Spirit on them!" (Numbers 11:28, 29).

This was a watershed experience for Joshua. Had he not been checked here by Moses' magnanimous response, his "selfless" jealousy for Moses' honor could have eventually made him a narrow, petty man, unfit for leadership. As it turned out, the lesson was well learned, and Joshua never again displayed such smallness. He became a magnanimous leader who lived only for God's glory.

Unfortunately, church leaders have not always appropriated this lesson. John Claypool said in his 1979 Yale Lectures on Preaching that while in seminary he experienced jealous jockeying for position, and that life in the parish ministry had not been much different. His tragic comments came after attending national conventions of church leaders where most of the conversation in the hotel rooms either were full of envy for a leader who was doing well or scarcely concealed delight over the failure of another.[7]

Truly spiritual leadership knows none of this, as the example of the great Charles Simeon eloquently shows. Simeon, who pastored Holy Trinity in Cambridge at the beginning of the nineteenth century, is credited with establishing the evangelical wing of the Church of England through his immense leadership exhibited in his powerful personality, his great preaching which filled twenty-one influential volumes, and his personal discipleship of some of the Church's greatest missionaries and leaders. Such a man could have been tempted to resent others who might displace him — as, for example, when his health broke and he had to spend eight months away recuperating and his curate, Thomason, stepped in to preach. Thomason surprised everyone with a preaching ability that rivaled Simeon's. And what was the great man's response? Rejoicing! In fact, as his biography says, he referenced John 3:30 ("He must become greater; I must become less") and told a friend, "Now I see why I have been laid aside. I bless God for it."[8] True spiritual leadership knows nothing of a self-promoting spirit.

Apropos to this truth is the fact that Joshua's regular designation, used several times in the Pentateuch, is Joshua the "servant of Moses." Sometimes "servant" can be rendered "page," "aide," "lieutenant," or "minister," but the title always carries the idea of subservience. Significantly, Joshua remained Moses' servant until his leader died. Though second violin is a difficult instrument to master (much harder than first chair!), Joshua played it well. In fact, he was a virtuoso second fiddle.

Magnanimous spiritual leaders like Joshua can be number two, number three, four, five . . . Jesus, the ultimate Joshua, showed us how: "For who is greater, the one who is at the table or the one who serves? Is it not the one who is at the table? But I am among you as one who serves" (Luke 22:27).

Those who qualify for spiritual leadership are big-hearted, supportive Joshuas to each other and to all those around.

Faith

We next see Joshua's name in connection with the famous incident of spying out the land in Numbers 13, 14. Moses commissioned twelve spies (one from each tribe) to reconnoiter the Promised Land as a prelude to conquest. Caleb and Joshua were representatives of their respective tribes (13:6, 8). After forty days of covert inspection, the scouts returned. All agreed that the land was bountiful (13:23, 24).

However, ten of the spies said it could not be conquered because the cities were well-fortified and some of the people were giants (vv. 28, 29). Caleb and Joshua countered by saying almost literally that victory would be a "piece of cake." The Hebrew of 14:9 literally says, "Do not fear the people of the land, for our bread they are" — "Do not worry, it is a piece of bread!"

All Israel had to do, the two men insisted, was move in (13:30; 14:9). But the rest of Israel sided with the majority report, and even tried to stone Joshua and Caleb (14:1-10). As a result the people came under God's judgment and would spend forty years wandering in the desert (one year for each of the forty days of spying out the land) until all had become corpses except Joshua and Caleb.

For Joshua, the lesson was quite clear: the majority is not always right. In fact, it is very often wrong. The men God uses have always stood against the flow — Luther, Knox, Fox, Wilberforce, Booth, Carey, Bonhoeffer. How we need to remember this. Ours is a day when truth is determined by consensus, when justice is struck by a five-four vote, when "everybody is doing it" has become the pervasive rationale for behavior, when Jefferson's fear of the tyranny of the majority is a reality. Spiritual leaders do not necessarily go along with the majority opinion.

Joshua and Caleb stood alone, a common characteristic among good leaders. But the prominent leadership quality we see in their solitary stand is a great faith. They simply believed in the glorious God Joshua glimpsed from afar on Sinai. There was no way they could share the "grasshopper" complex of the other spies, for how could they feel thus when they truly believed in such a great God. Without exception, great spiritual leaders have a faith that towers above their contemporaries. The grammar of their lives is "By faith, by faith, by faith . . ." (see Hebrews 11).

Significantly, it was at this time that Moses changed Joshua's original name Hoshea ("salvation") to Joshua ("Jehovah is salvation") (Numbers 13:16). This is a high leadership name, for *Jesus* is the Greek form of Joshua. "[Y]ou are to give him the name Jesus," said the angel, "because he will save his people from their sins" (Matthew 1:21).

The Spirit

After the forty years of wandering, it came about on the plains of Moab that, according to Numbers 26:65, "not one of them was left except Caleb son of

Jephunneth and Joshua son of Nun." It was time for Joshua's commissioning:
"So the Lord said to Moses, 'Take Joshua the son of Nun, a man in whom is
the Spirit, and lay your hand on him; and have him stand before Eleazar the
priest and before all the congregation; and commission him in their sight'"
(Numbers 27:18,19, NASB). Notice that the Spirit, capital S — that is, the Holy
Spirit — was upon and in Joshua. He had the indispensable qualification for
all spiritual leadership. J. Oswald Sanders says: "Spiritual leadership is not a
matter of superior spiritual power, and it can never be self-generated. There is
no such thing as a self-made spiritual leader."[9] The New Testament agrees:

> "Brothers, choose seven men from among you who are known to be full of
> the Spirit and wisdom. We will turn this responsibility over to them and will
> give our attention to prayer and the ministry of the word." . . . They chose
> Stephen, a man full of faith and of the Holy Spirit. . . . (Acts 6:3, 5)

There is no spiritual leadership apart from the fullness of the Holy Spirit.
Therefore, it follows that if we aspire to leadership in the Church, we must be
full of the Holy Spirit. Practically, this means that we must continually confess
our sins, keep ourselves in God's Word, and continually submit to God, asking
the Spirit to fill us. The telltale sign of this will be that we effervesce Christ
(Ephesians 5:17-20). As we walk and serve in the Spirit, the Spirit will ordain
us to specific tasks in the Church, and these will be tasks of leadership at all lev-
els, be it waiting tables or heralding the gospel.

Expendability

There is one more mention of Joshua — in the final chapter of the Pentateuch,
Deuteronomy 34, where his preparation for leadership is completed with the
death of Moses.

> Then Moses climbed Mount Nebo from the plains of Moab to the top of
> Pisgah, across from Jericho. There the Lord showed him the whole land —
> from Gilead to Dan, all of Naphtali, the territory of Ephraim and Manasseh,
> all the land of Judah as far as the western sea, the Negev and the whole
> region from the Valley of Jericho, the City of Palms, as far as Zoar. Then
> the Lord said to him, "This is the land I promised on oath to Abraham, Isaac
> and Jacob when I said, 'I will give it to your descendants.' I have let you see
> it with your eyes, but you will not cross over into it." And Moses the ser-
> vant of the Lord died there in Moab, as the Lord had said. He buried him
> in Moab, in the valley opposite Beth Peor, but to this day no one knows

where his grave is. Moses was a hundred and twenty years old when he died, yet his eyes were not weak nor his strength gone. The Israelites grieved for Moses in the plains of Moab thirty days, until the time of weeping and mourning was over. Now Joshua son of Nun was filled with the spirit of wisdom because Moses had laid his hands on him. So the Israelites listened to him and did what the Lord had commanded Moses. Since then no prophet has risen in Israel like Moses, whom the Lord knew face to face, who did all those miraculous signs and wonders the Lord sent him to do in Egypt — to Pharaoh and to all his officials and to his whole land. For no one has ever shown the mighty power or performed the awesome deeds that Moses did in the sight of all Israel. (vv. 1-12)

Moses was the greatest spiritual leader Israel ever had — far greater than Joshua. The transition from Moses to Joshua was like going from poetry to prose. Yet, God did not need Moses. *Even Moses was expendable!*

What a truth for all leaders to grasp. God does not need us. He has used donkeys to proclaim His Word! He is perfectly capable of carrying out His plans without our leadership. But wonder of wonders, joy of joys, He has chosen to use us. We must take our call to leadership seriously. We must glory in the work, but never in ourselves.

It goes without saying that leadership *per se* involves many more elements beyond the seven qualities instilled in Joshua. But one thing is sure: leadership must have a dream, a *vision*, a mental image, a precise goal of what is to be accomplished. Vision is the currency of leadership. A vision or dream must grab the leader, and when it does, it will pull others along. The challenge of leadership is so great today because modern man is dreamless.

Next, a leader must not only have a dream, he must be able to *communicate* it. This is true with artists, educators, military leaders, fast-food franchisers. A great leader communicates with clarity, whether by speech, metaphor, diagram or model.

Good leaders then *delegate and orchestrate*. They surround themselves with competent people. They build consensus. And they elevate the people with whom they work.

Good leaders lead by *demonstration*. They pull people along with them instead of pushing them. General Eisenhower used to demonstrate the art of leadership in a simple but forceful way. He would place a single piece of string on a table and say, "Pull it and it follows wherever you want it to go; push it and it goes nowhere."

Good leaders are *determined*. Ray Kroc of McDonald's fame displayed this elaborately framed statement composed by Calvin Coolidge:

Nothing in the world can take the place of persistence.
Talent will not;
     nothing is more common than unsuccessful men with great talent.
Genius will not;
     unrewarded genius is almost a proverb.
Education will not;
     the world is full of educated derelicts.
Persistence, determination alone are omnipotent.

Men, if we wish to be good leaders we must recognize and embrace this conventional wisdom: *vision, communication, delegation and organization, demonstration*, and *determination*. We laud and commend all this, but we must practice it as well.

But there is far more beyond this in our call to spiritual leadership, for the seven characteristics instilled in Joshua through his leadership training have no exact parallel in any management manual in the world — especially as they are presented in Scriptural bouquet. What is more, if they are embraced as disciplines of spiritual leadership, their collective energy will provide the animus for wisely living out conventional leadership wisdom. Put another way, the transcending wisdom of spiritual leadership will energize and elevate other types wisdom we have received — thus producing dynamic leadership.

Mature male leadership is rare in the Church. Are you part of the problem or part of the answer? Be honest with yourself and God.

Men, Joshua's preparation for leadership tells us that if we sincerely want to improve our leadership capacities there are some things we must sweat for:

- The commitment to and practice of intercessory *prayer*.
- The pursuit of a great and growing *vision* of God.
- A growing *worship of and devotion to God*.
- A big-hearted *magnanimity* that thrills at the elevation of others.
- A *faith* that transcends the doubts of others.
- A liberating understanding and embracing of one's *expendability*.

The example of Joshua's preparation calls for our perspiration — holy sweat.

Rise up, O men of God!
The Church for you doth wait,
Her strength unequal to her task;
Rise up, and make her great!

—William P. Merrill

Food for Thought

What is the relationship between *leadership*, whether at home or at work or in church, and *prayer*? Be honest, and be specific.

"There is no spiritual leadership apart from passionate devotion." Do you agree or disagree? How does this play out in your life?

In what ways does jealousy hold you back either from being a leader or from being a more effective leader? What leaders do you wrongfully envy? What specifically do you covet in their life or ministry or work?

In what ways does God want you to take a greater stand of faith? Regarding what issues or problems? Why aren't you doing this?

What leadership character traits of Stephen are mentioned in Acts 6:3, 5? Are these evident in your life as a father or boss or church leader? What can you do to allow God to develop these in you more fully?

What does the principle of expendability mean for leadership? Apply this to your own leadership roles. In view of this, what steps should you be taking?

Application/Response

What did God speak to you about most specifically, most powerfully in this chapter? Talk to Him about it right now!

Think About It!

Review the life of Joshua as described in the Scripture passages quoted in this chapter. List the aspects of his work that mean something to you, then identify why those aspects touched you. Also list those principles that are currently weak in your performance as a leader and what you will do to grow stronger in those areas.

16

DISCIPLINE OF GIVING

I N 1923 A VERY significant meeting was held at the Edgewater Beach Hotel
in Chicago. Attending that famous gathering were nine of the world's most
successful financiers. The president of the largest independent steel company, the president of the largest utility company, the president of the largest
gas company, the greatest wheat speculator, the president of the New York
Stock Exchange, a member of the President's Cabinet, the greatest bear on Wall
Street, the head of the world's greatest monopoly, and finally the president of
the Bank of International Settlements were all present. A high-powered group
if there ever was one. These men were supreme masters of the finance world!

Twenty-five years later, in 1948, the picture was much different. Charles
Schwab had died bankrupt after living on borrowed money for the last five
years of his life. Samuel Insull had died a fugitive from justice, penniless in a
foreign land. Howard Hopson was insane. Arthur Critten died abroad, insol-
vent. Richard Whitney had just been released from Sing Sing. Albert Fall was
pardoned from prison so he could die at home. Jesse Livermore died a suicide,
as did Leon Fraser and Ivar Kreuger. All these men, masters of finance, were
mastered by wealth!

The extraordinary sameness of the hellish gravity of their famous lives is a
divine warning, for God set the ghosts of these financial giants as spectral, mid-
century witnesses to a nation about to run amok in materialism. Today their
ghosts have faded, and a new gallery of forlorn spirits is assembling, with names
like Ivan Boesky and Michael Milken.

Yet few take serious notice. Perhaps it is because most, especially if they are
Christians, do not aspire to be the head of the world's greatest monopoly or to
the vulgar display of the lifestyles of the rich and famous. Instead they are quite
content to cultivate a less encumbering level of wealth — not realizing that the

dangers for themselves are the same as for the super rich: a growing delusion that this world is everything, that someday they will be content, that "providing for one's family" means being able to give them more and better, that relationships will be enriched by wealth, that wealth will make them better people.

Clearly, the abiding reality is that wealth presents substantial dangers for all, and especially for today's increasingly prosperous Christian population. But what can we do to escape the power of materialism? Step out of the competitive world? Abandon Wall Street? Avoid the professions? Join a commune? Some think so, despite Christ's firm admonitions against isolation.

Actually, however, there is a better way, taught repeatedly in God's Word. In fact, Scripture presents it as a grace — *the grace of giving*.

The most explicit teaching on this subject is 2 Corinthians 8, where the Apostle Paul deftly instructs the Corinthian church regarding giving by citing the beautiful example of the Macedonian church's giving. He begins: "And now, brothers, we want you to know about the grace [meaning the grace of giving] that God has given the Macedonian churches" (v. 1). For Paul, giving is so much a grace that he uses the Greek word five times in this short text: verse 1, "the grace" (*charin*); verse 4, "the privilege" (*charas*); verse 6, "this act of grace" (*charin*); verse 7, "this grace of giving" (*chariti*); and verse 9, "the grace" (*charin*). Giving is a matter of grace from beginning to end, as we shall see.

GRACE GIVING IN ISRAEL'S HISTORY

To adequately grasp Paul's dynamic teaching of grace giving, we need to recall earlier Biblical instruction to Israel. There is some confusion today about what it was that God actually required from his people in the Old Testament. Most think it was something like 10 percent, which is a woeful misconception. Actually there were multiple mandatory giving requirements in Israel which came to considerably more.

The Lord's Tithe
The foundational tithe was termed the Lord's tithe (or the Levites' tithe, Numbers 18:21-29, because it went to support their priestly ministry). Leviticus 27:30 says: "A tithe of everything from the land, whether grain from the soil or fruit from the trees, belongs to the Lord; it is holy to the Lord." This meant that a tithe (10 percent) of all the people's produce and animals was given to the Levites. No Israelite had any option about this. A man who did not pay it

was robbing God. Malachi 3:8 refers to this, saying, "'Will a man rob God? Yet you rob me. But you ask, "How do we rob you?" In tithes and offerings.'"

The Festival Tithe

In addition to this initial 10 percent, there was a second tithe, commonly called the festival tithe. According to Deuteronomy 12:10, 11, 17, 18, this tithe took effect when Israel conquered the Promised Land because another 10 percent had to be given for an annual celebration — feasting with one's family, friends, and servants. Whereas the purpose of the Lord's tithe was to perpetuate ministry, the festival tithe was to build religious celebration and mutual community in God's people. The two tithes together comprised a substantial economic bite — a mandatory 20 percent.

The Poor Tithe

But there was still more, for Deuteronomy 14:28, 29 commands a third tithe, a poor tithe:

> At the end of every three years, bring all the tithes of that year's produce and store it in your towns, so that the Levites (who have no allotment or inheritance of their own) and the aliens, the fatherless and the widows who live in your towns may come and eat and be satisfied, and so that the Lord your God may bless you in all the work of your hands.

This provided for the social welfare of those who could not provide for themselves. Since the tithe was 10 percent every three years, it comes to 3.3 percent per annum, thus bringing the total to over 23 percent per year.

These three mandatory tithes funded the priesthood, a national feast, and aided the poor. Enough! we might think. But Leviticus 19:9, 10 commanded even more, for the people were also charged to refrain from harvesting the corners of their fields or picking all the grapes from their vineyards, so as to leave gleanings for the poor. In addition to this, there were other taxes from time to time, such as a tax of a third of a shekel they later had to pay for the materials used in Temple offerings (Nehemiah 10:32, 33). The bottom line was this: God's people were required to give a minimum of 25 percent a year.

Grace Giving

One might think that 25 percent was certainly the limit. But it was at this point that heart giving took over — *"grace giving"* or nonrequired offerings. There were *firstfruits offerings* in which an Israelite, out of love for God, brought the firstfruits of his crop or livestock to God (Numbers 18:11-13). The beautiful thing about this was that he did so when he had not yet harvested the rest of the crop and did not know what he would ultimately reap. He gave the best to God, trusting He would bring in the rest. It was faith giving and was totally voluntary.

There were also *freewill offerings*, offerings God called for when He commanded Moses to build the Tabernacle: "Tell the Israelites to bring me an offering. You are to receive the offering for me from each man whose heart prompts him to give" (Exodus 25:1, 2). Nothing was specified except that it be voluntary and from the heart. Here the people's response was so great that Moses had to tell them to stop giving (Exodus 36:2-7).

Giving from a heart overflowing with God's grace, whether the giving be mandatory or voluntary, has always been the ideal for God's people — before and after the coming of Christ. When a heart overflows in grace giving, a substantial amount of one's income goes to God.[1]

GRACE GIVING IN THE NEW TESTAMENT

As we noted, Paul began his discussion of grace giving by holding high the example of the impoverished Macedonians' astounding giving: "And now, brothers, we want you to know about the grace that God has given the Macedonian churches. Out of the most severe trial, their overflowing joy and their extreme poverty welled up in rich generosity" (2 Corinthians 8:1, 2).

The word used for "their extreme poverty" is the word from which we derive the English word *bathysphere* — a Jacques Cousteau word for the ship used to probe the *bathos*, the depth of the ocean. The great Greek scholar Alfred Plummer translates this, "their down-to-depth poverty."[2] The Macedonians were at the bottom, they were truly poor.

Today we fancy ourselves poor if we have to think twice before going out to dinner. The "American way" today is the credit card — buying things you do not need with money you do not have to impress people you do not like. But it was not so with the Macedonian Christians.

Not only were they dirt poor, they were under "the most severe trial" (v. 2). The literal sense is, they were being squeezed by the difficulties of their life. The surrounding culture rejected them and kept squeezing them harder and harder because of their devotion to Christ. They were in an unrelenting pressure cooker. Their situation was impossible: grinding poverty and severe trials. But out of it came incredible grace, and their extreme poverty and severe trials mixed with overflowing joy which "welled up in rich generosity." This was the grace of giving.

This is truly amazing. But if this taxes one's credulity, listen to Paul's further description in verses 3 and 4: "For I testify that they gave as much as they were able, and even beyond their ability. Entirely on their own, they urgently pleaded with us for the privilege of sharing in this service to the saints." They gave "beyond [literally, "contrary to"] their ability." St. Chrysostom marveled at this, saying, "They did the begging not Paul." "Come on, Paul. Have a heart! Do not limit us!"

The *grace of giving* has nothing to do with being well off. It is not dictated by ability. It is a willingness to give. Giving is viewed as a privilege. It is joyously enthusiastic and pleads for the opportunity to give more.

What else produces such giving? Paul gives the answer in verse 5 as he relates the vertical and horizontal angles of the Macedonians' commitment: "And they did not do as we expected, but they gave themselves first to the Lord and then to us in keeping with God's will." Their remarkable giving was the result of their first giving themselves to God. It is so simple: when all one has is given to God, giving to others becomes the natural reflex of the soul.

It is easy to surrender part when we have already given the whole. This was shown in the life of a young Norwegian named Peter Torjesen when at the age of seventeen his heart was so stirred by a challenge to missionary giving that he opened his wallet and poured all his money into the offering. As an afterthought he also included a scrap of paper on which he wrote "*Og mit liv*" ("And my life").[3] Significantly, young Torjesen went on to lead a fruitful life as a missionary in China.

The Macedonians did things the right way: they gave their hearts to God, then they gave themselves to their fellow believers, which in turn resulted in their giving what they had to the work of Christ. This is where grace giving must begin — giving ourselves completely to God. Grace giving cannot exist without this (cf. Romans 12:1).

THE INFLUENCE OF GRACE GIVING

The shining example of the Macedonians' giving was held high by the apostle so as to convict and motivate the Corinthian church. Now Paul left no doubt as to what he hoped would happen: "So we urged Titus . . . to bring also to completion this act of grace on your part. But just as you excel in everything —

in faith, in speech, in knowledge, in complete earnestness and in your love for us — see that you also excel in this grace of giving" (vv. 6, 7).

The Corinthians were a gifted group who excelled in many commendable things other than giving. But Paul knew that despite all their excellences they would never become what they could and should be until they learned the grace of giving. The abiding spiritual fact is, there is no way to grow into spiritual maturity without committing one's giving to the Lord. *God can have our money and not have our hearts, but He cannot have our hearts without having all our money.* Jesus said, "For where your treasure is, there your heart will be also" (Matthew 6:21).

The spectres of the fallen Wall Street giants are not the only ones to announce the dangers of money. The entire New Testament is full of repeated warnings, many of which are from the lips of Jesus Himself, who informed His listeners more often about money than about Heaven and Hell, sexual immorality, or violence. After the rich young ruler turned away sorrowing because Jesus told him to sell all, Jesus told the disciples, "It is easier for a camel to go through the eye of a needle than for a rich man to enter the kingdom of God" (Mark 10:25) — His point being that it is impossible for a man who trusts in riches to get into Heaven. Thankfully, He added a final line: "With man this [being saved, v. 26] is impossible, but not with God; all things are possible with God" (v. 27).

Indeed, Jesus consistently presented wealth, if we depend on it rather than on God, as a spiritual handicap. At the end of the Sermon on the Mount He recommended: "Do not store up for yourselves treasures on earth, where moth and rust destroy, and where thieves break in and steal. But store up for yourselves treasures in heaven, where moth and rust do not destroy, and where thieves do not break in and steal" (Matthew 6:19, 20). A little later He warned, "No one can serve two masters. Either he will hate the one and love the other, or he will be devoted to the one and despise the other. You cannot serve both God and Money" (Matthew 6:24).

And to a man grabbing for an inheritance Christ shouted, "Watch out! Be on your guard against all kinds of greed: a man's life does not consist in the abundance of his possessions" (Luke 12:15). Then He related the story of the rich man who built bigger barns only to die that very night, ending His parable with a solemn pronouncement: "This is how it will be with anyone who stores up things for himself but is not rich toward God" (v. 21).

Men, the "rich toward God" are those who give not only themselves, but also their riches — thus laying up their treasures in Heaven. The key to liberation from the power of materialism is not an exodus from culture — abandoning Wall Street or leaving the wealth of the nation to others — but the *grace of giving*.

Grace giving goes beyond a mere tithe, but rather gives till it hurts. Grace giving affects one's lifestyle. There are things one cannot have and things foregone when one indulges in grace giving. As C. S. Lewis remarked:

> [I]f our expenditure on comforts, luxuries, amusements , etc., is up to the standard common among those with the same income as our own, we are probably giving away too little. If our charities do not at all pinch or hamper us, I should say they are too small. There ought to be things we should like to do and cannot do because our charitable expenditure excludes them.[4]

Givers for God disarm the power of money. They invite God's grace to flow through them.

It is possible you have reached a sticking point in your spiritual development and are perplexed. After all, you are attending church regularly, you enjoy the fellowship of Christians, you even read your Bible and pray regularly. The problem may be that you are not giving — that God simply does not have that part of you. If so, what you need is the grace of giving: *firstfruits giving* which gives to God one's best up-front, trusting that He will provide the rest; joyous *freewill giving* such as the Israelites experienced when Moses had to say "stop!"; the *grace giving* of the Macedonians whose liberality overflowed as they begged for the opportunity to give more.

The apostle has made his point convincingly, but he caps it with a supreme illustration: "For you know the grace of our Lord Jesus Christ, that though he was rich, yet for your sakes he became poor, so that you through his poverty might become rich" (v. 9). Though Jesus could put His finger on every star, He emptied Himself and became a poor earthly servant for us. That is Heaven's "stewardship" program, and it is the pattern for us. The Corinthians were not clubbed into giving by fear or some gimmicky financial appeal. Rather, it was the ultimate example of giving — "the grace of our Lord Jesus Christ" — that produced the grace of giving in their lives. It was simply because of Jesus.

THE DISCIPLINE OF GIVING

We must understand that God's grace in our lives demands discipline. This is why the great apostle of grace says, "discipline yourself for the purpose of godliness" (1 Timothy 4:7, NASB). And in this matter of the grace of giving, there must be the discipline of giving as well.

Mental Discipline

Before there are any outward disciplines of giving, there must be a disciplined understanding of giving.

First, you must bear in mind that giving is not a meritorious work which will enhance your position before God. Similarly, giving will not make you better than other Christians.

Second, you need to understand that while giving will not gain favor with God, giving does bring blessing! Jesus said: "Give, and it will be given to you. A good measure, pressed down, shaken together and running over, will be poured into your lap. For with the measure you use, it will be measured to you" (Luke 6:38). Correspondingly, Paul wrote: "Remember this: Whoever sows sparingly will also reap sparingly, and whoever sows generously will also reap generously" (2 Corinthians 9:6).

Admittedly these blessings are essentially spiritual. But which would you rather have — a spiritual blessing or a bigger bank account — inner contentment or a new yacht?

Third, you must keep in mind that giving which pleases God is generous and sacrificial. As we have seen, the Macedonians gave out of their deep poverty. We can also profitably reflect on what Jesus said about the poor widow who humbly gave only a fraction of a penny: "I tell you the truth, this poor widow has put more into the treasury than all the others" (Mark 12:43).

Fourth, you must understand that what you give is to be determined between you and God. Giving should never be decided casually or flippantly, but through serious prayer — asking God what He wants you to give.

Volitional Discipline

With the mental disciplines of giving firmly in mind, the way is ready for the act of giving.

To begin with, the act of giving should be accompanied by offering oneself to the Lord, just as did the Macedonians who "gave themselves first to the Lord" (2 Corinthians 8:5). This should be done silently, not so someone will see our pious act of worship. And giving oneself to God is indeed worship (Romans 12:1).

Second, it is strongly recommended, in light of the great giving requirements imposed on God's ancient people Israel, that everyone should at least consider the first 10 percent as a starting point in giving — a minimum. And in the case of the Macedonians' grace giving, the amount must have been way over 10 percent because 10 percent of their "extreme poverty" (2 Corinthians 8:2) would not have helped anyone.

Third, your giving ought to be regular. Paul advised this same Corinthian church on another occasion, "On the first day of every week, each one of you should set aside a sum of money in keeping with his income, saving it up, so that when I come no collections will have to be made" (1 Corinthians 16:2). The apostle knew that regular, systematic giving would help the people meet their regular obligations and most emergencies.

Fourth, you must begin giving now. The natural tendency is to put giving off until you feel able to give. Such thinking keeps many from ever giving. A preacher came to see a farmer and asked him,

> "If you had $200, would you give $100 of it to the Lord?"
> "I would."
> "If you had two cows, would you give one of them to the Lord?"
> "Sure."
> "If you had two pigs, would you give one of them to the Lord?"
> The farmer said, "Now that isn't fair! You know I have two pigs."[5]

Giving should not only be regular, but responsive to need, spontaneous, like that of the Macedonians and Mary of Bethany who in anointing Jesus so lavishly poured out her resources.

> *High Heaven rejects the lore*
>   *Of nicely calculated less and more.*[6]

Finally, your giving should be joyous — "for God loves a cheerful giver" (2 Corinthians 9:7). As we have been so often reminded, "cheerful" can be translated "hilarious," suggesting a joy which leaps over all restraints.

The act of giving is a blessed state. We do well to remember that our Lord Jesus Himself said, "It is more blessed to give than to receive" (Acts 20:35). May we be faithful and disciplined in giving ourselves and all we have to God!

Food for Thought

What does the phrase "grace giving" mean to you? What does grace have to do with giving? When you give to the church or various Christian ministries, do you generally do so out of obligation or willingness?

How much of your income do you believe God wants you to give to Him? Support your answer with Scripture; then ask God in prayer whether He agrees.

What does Malachi 3:8ff. say to you about giving to God? Are you generally obeying or disobeying this passage?

Should we give only when we have it to spare, so to speak — during times when God has "blessed us"? Compare 2 Corinthians 8:1, 2.

What does Matthew 6:19, 20, 21, 24 mean for *your* life? What are some specific ways you can apply these verses?

What example is found in 2 Corinthians 8:9? What does this verse say to you?

Application/Response

What did God speak to you about most specifically, most powerfully in this chapter? Talk to Him about it right now!

Think About It!

What principles stand out on this topic in 2 Corinthians 8:1-9? List as many as you can, then rate yourself on each one.

17

DISCIPLINE OF WITNESS

WHEN MY WIFE and I are in Southern California, we ritually arrange to drive out to Newport Beach's Crab Cooker for a delicious seafood dinner served on paper plates. After eating we stroll over to surfside and watch surfers, then drive out the Peninsula and board the ferry to Balboa Island for dessert — a Balboa Bar — what else? As we cross the harbor, I invariably think of Jim ("Big Jim" as his friends called him) because as a college boy in the early 1930s Jim captained these same boats during his summers. I usually say to my wife, "Jim used to run these boats," and then she and I engage in some pleasant memories which have nothing at all to do with the ocean.

When I first met Jim in 1975, he was a proud, self-sufficient business executive entering retirement who had little use for Christianity and was often even belligerent. The nickname "Big Jim" was not because of his size — he was perhaps 5'5" — but because of the force of his personality. He was suspicious of me and critical of those who had faith in Christ. But we became sparring partners, and then friends. Conversations revealed that he did have conscious spiritual needs and a cryptic interest in Christ.

And so it came about that in August 1976 I witnessed Jim's remarkable conversion in the privacy of his own living room. Tears brimmed in his eyes and began to course down his cheeks as he said, "I'm no good. But I want Christ if He'll have me." Then we prayed together. Jim was rough. The first few times he came to church he commented, "Pastor, that was a hell of a sermon." But he was a learner, and he became a disciple, and some of the rough edges began to disappear.

My favorite memory of Jim is of him sitting crossed-legged on the dirt in cut-offs, shirtless and tanned (ever the beach boy), working on the church sprinkling system, refusing all advice to go home and rest, saying, "After all Christ has done for me, this is the least I can do." It is, in fact, my last memory of him because a week later as I was about to pick up the phone to invite him out to dinner, it rang and I was told that Jim had passed away sitting in the same chair in which I had seen him come to know Christ.

"AVERAGE" JOYS

What a sweet, sweet memory. And it is even sweeter because it is not professional, but so intensely personal. In retrospect, my family's most enduring spiritual joys have come through everyday personal witness to people like Susie, our daughter Holly's kindergarten teacher who weekly promised Holly she would come to church — and finally came — and returned again and again, becoming our good friend and finding Christ.

There was our neighbor John, the industrial arts teacher, the nicest man on the block, who after several years of mutual family friendship became a Christian and then a deacon in our church.

Another particularly treasured memory is of our letter carrier, Damon, an ex-Marine, and his young wife Bobbie. Our daily greetings evolved into a friendship which culminated in Bobbie coming to Christ through a women's Bible study and Damon doing the same at a men's retreat.

Nothing in my years of productive ministry has given my wife and me more joy than being a part of seeing our neighbors, Jamie and Deby Fellowes, grow into a deep relationship with Christ and then become authentic witnesses in the church, the community, and the business world. (You can read their testimony in the Resources section of this book — "James and Deby Fellowes's Witness to Their Faith.")

It has been an increasing revelation to my wife and me that the greatest joys in pastoral ministry have come not in the extraordinary events (such as an exceptional worship service or ground-breaking on a great building project), but in the normal, "average" avenues of everyday person-to-person witness — the things any Christian can do, regardless of gifts or calling.

In this respect, it is highly significant that Andrew, one of the names most associated with witness in the Bible, was an average man who shared Christ in patently ordinary ways. In fact, there appears to be some intentional divine poetry in his name, for "Andrew" comes from the Greek root *andros*, which means "man." Thus he is an example for everyone who would follow Christ.

Andrew is what every man ought to be in witnessing for Christ. Thus, a glance at his life will properly challenge and motivate us all.

The Gospels tell us that Andrew was in on the ground floor of Jesus' ministry. When he met Jesus, he was already a devotee to the prophetic cause of John the Baptist (John 1:35ff.), which indicates he was a spiritually sensitive man who realized the days were evil, a man who had been baptized in repentance for sin and was awaiting the Messiah. He also had the distinction of being the brother of Simon Peter, the soon-to-be leader of the apostolic band (John 1:40).

But Andrew's initial claim to fame was that he, along with John, was the very first of the twelve disciples to follow Jesus. The Early Church recognized this and gave him the honored title *Protokletos*, which means "First-called."[1]

However, despite his enviable beginning Andrew never achieved prominence among the disciples. He was excluded from the inner circle of Peter, James, and John and missed the great experiences they shared with the Master — the Transfiguration, the healing of Jairus' daughter, Jesus' sorrow in Gethsemane. Moreover, he was not much of a leader. He preached no sermons deemed worth recording. He wrote no epistles and performed no recorded miracles. He appears to have had none of the bold audacity of his brother Peter and never appears in the foreground. But he did have one distinction, a grand distinction: *he excelled in bringing others to Christ!*

Interestingly, this humble distinction has endeared him to whole cultures so that today he is the patron saint of three diverse nations.[2] Eusebius in his *Ecclesiastical History* (3, 1, 1) alleges that Andrew later went to Scythia, the country north of the Black Sea between the Danube and Tanais Rivers, which today is part of modern Russia. Another tradition makes him the patron saint of Greece, for it says that he was martyred there on an X-shaped cross, where he hung for three days praising God and praying for his enemies. The third country which claims Andrew is Scotland, on the fanciful supposition that after the eighth-century monk Regulus brought Andrew's relics (three fingers from his right hand, an arm bone, one tooth, and a kneecap) to what is today St. Andrew's, Scotland, the Scots were led into battle by a white X-shaped cross levitating above them in the blue sky. Since then, the white St. Andrew's cross on a sky-blue background has been the standard of Scotland.

Did Andrew actually go to Greece or Russia or Scotland? No one knows. Why do three countries, therefore, claim him? The answer rests in Andrew's winsome character as it is recorded in Scripture. He was a great-hearted man of average abilities who loved to introduce others to Christ. Average Andrew's extraordinary evangelistic heart has made his name one of such fadeless beauty that whole nations want to claim him.

Andrew's heart commends itself to every man. His heart is meant to model what ought to be the ordinary experience of the average Christian.

AVERAGE ANDREW'S EXTRAORDINARY HEART

A Knowledgeable Heart

Andrew met Christ personally and developed an intimate knowledge of Him. It had happened as Andrew and another disciple were standing beside John the Baptist when Jesus passed by and the Baptist cried out, "Look, the Lamb of God!" (John 1:35) — thus precipitating their following Jesus and spending the remainder of the day in conversation with him (vv. 39, 40). Though unrecorded, that conversation was a spiritual watershed for Andrew. The winsome humanity of God incarnate elevated Andrew's spiritual horizons and galvanized his allegiance. Andrew heard Jesus speak words that were the truest he had ever heard, and his heart was set aflame. Andrew now knew and loved Jesus Christ!

The immediate reflex of Andrew's heart from his newfound knowledge of Christ was that *everyone* must know him, and it has been likewise with all who really meet Christ. When John Bunyan's Pilgrim met Christ at the foot of the cross, his joy was so great he wanted to shout it to the trees and stars and brooks and birds — to breathe it to everything and everyone.[3]

George Whitefield, the evangelist of the Great Awakening, records in his diary the same phenomenon when he met Christ:

> O! with what joy — joy unspeakable — even joy that was full and big with glory, was my soul filled. . . . Surely it was the day of mine espousals — a day to be had in everlasting remembrance! At first my joys were like a spring tide, and overflowed the banks![4]

My heart resonates with this because that was precisely my experience when I met Christ. In fact, some of my well-meaning friends tried to tone me down, saying, "We are happy for you . . . But take it easy!" The reality is, I simply could not keep it in, for in meeting Jesus I had experienced the primary motivation and qualification for sharing him. Men, we must not let the self-evident nature of the truth dull us to its profundity, which is this: the more immediate and personal one's knowledge of Christ, the more natural it is to share Him with others. This is why those who have newly met Christ are often so verbal and successful in leading others to Him despite the absence of learned arguments.

If you know Christ, you, like average Andrew, have the essential heart qualification to share him — even if you do not have all the answers. And the key to ongoing effectiveness is a perpetual freshness in your growing knowledge of Him.

A Magnetized Heart

The second characteristic of ordinary Andrew's extraordinary heart was that it had been magnetized by Christ. He was so drawn to Christ, he was sure that if others could just once be exposed to Jesus, it would be enough. "The first thing Andrew did," the Scripture tells us, "was to find his brother Simon and tell him, 'We have found the Messiah'" (John 1:41).

Certainly Andrew had the right idea! For unlike the caricatures of Christ, the Christ of Scripture is so winsome, so radically different, so utterly unlike the stereotypes, that when He is truly seen, He draws the most resistant to Himself. Though men and women have always resisted Christ, and will continue to do so, there are untold thousands who will be magnetized to Him when they understand the truth about Him.

If we want Andrew-like hearts, we must repeatedly expose ourselves to the raw realities of Christ as they are recorded in the Gospels. Magnetized hearts draw others to Christ.

A Selfless Heart

Andrew had a knowledgeable heart, a magnetized heart, and a remarkably selfless heart — as John's Gospel shows:

> Andrew, Simon Peter's brother, was one of the two who heard what John had said and who had followed Jesus. The first thing Andrew did was to find his brother Simon and tell him, "We have found the Messiah" (that is, the Christ). Then he brought Simon to Jesus, who looked at him and said, "You are Simon son of John. You will be called Cephas" (which, when translated, is Peter). (John 1:40-42)

What we observe here, and it is substantiated by the other Gospels, is that Andrew was commonly identified as "Simon Peter's brother" and not vice versa. The official apostolic lists in Matthew 10:2-4 and Luke 6:14-16 both identify him in this way. John's account of the feeding of the 5,000 likewise identifies him as "Simon Peter's brother" (6:8).

Everyone knew swaggering, ebullient Peter. He naturally drew people to himself, but Andrew faded into the wallpaper — especially when the big guy was around. "Andrew? Oh, you know who he is. Peter's brother. Sort of mauve-colored. Easy to miss." A lesser man would have stumbled here. Having lived with Peter all his life, he knew there would be only one seat for him once he brought Peter to Christ — the backseat! But Andrew was unencumbered by self and introduced Peter to Christ anyway. And Peter became a major player indeed!

There are men who join the army only if they can be officers, who will do evangelism if *they* are the evangelists. But the true evangelist's heart is a self-less heart. Andrew's heart was ordinary perhaps, but extraordinary in its self-lessness.

An Optimistic Heart

The fourth element of Andrew's heart was its optimism about what would happen when problems were brought to Christ. It was Andrew who, while Philip expressed dismay at the possibility of feeding the 5,000, suggested to Christ the lad's five loaves and two fishes (John 6:5-9). Andrew may have appeared fool-ish in his suggestions, but he knew Christ can mightily use all that is given to Him. The result was stupendous — the all-time picnic of the ages! After this, Andrew's optimism knew no bounds.

Our attitude makes all the difference in bringing people to Christ. Belief in the sufficiency of Christ fueled the great works of Wesley and Whitefield. In fact, every great evangelical work has had this optimism at its core.

Are we optimistic about what Christ can do? If so, we will see Him turn the ordinary into the extraordinary, just like average Andrew.

An Expansive Heart

The final characteristic we will note in Andrew's heart is its expansiveness. John 12:20-22 preserves a vignette which showcases this aspect:

> Now there were some Greeks among those who went up to worship at the Feast. They came to Philip, who was from Bethsaida in Galilee, with a request. "Sir," they said, "we would like to see Jesus." Philip went to tell Andrew; Andrew and Philip in turn told Jesus.

The Greeks who wanted to see Jesus were, of course, Gentiles and thus accursed in traditional Jewish eyes. Philip was unsure what to do with their request, so he approached Andrew — and Andrew, without hesitation, went straight to Jesus. Andrew has the great distinction of being the first disciple to understand that Jesus is the answer for *everyone* and to apply the universality of Jesus' ministry. No wonder he is the patron saint of the Greeks and the Russians and the Scots.

EXTRAORDINARY ENCOURAGEMENT

What encouragement there is here for all of us, because Andrew was a *bona fide* average guy. He did not have an education like Dr. Luke. He did not possess a great intellect like the Apostle Paul. He had nothing of the force of personality and oratorical gifts of his celebrated brother. But in his own way he helped shape the Christian world — much to his own surprise, we can be sure.

When we think of people being brought to Christ, we think of Andrew. Every city of any size has several churches named St. Andrew's. The Billy Graham Association has rightly encouraged us to bring others to its Crusades through "Operation Andrew." *Andrew* is one of the sweetest names in Christendom.

Ordinary Andrew's extraordinary heart is a heart we should all emulate: a knowledgeable heart, a magnetized heart, a selfless heart, an optimistic heart, and an expansive heart — a heart which any ordinary Christian can have if he wants it, as he yields to the work of the Spirit. Average Andrew's heart not only challenges but *hallows* everyday, ordinary, average life. The greatest joys are not in the extraordinary events of ministry, but in the normal avenues of everyday witness — in bringing people to Christ.

ORDINARY ANDREW EVANGELISM

Statistics demonstrate that ordinary Andrew relational evangelism is the most effective way to go. Recently The American Institute of Church Growth surveyed some 8,000 church attenders and found that 1 to 2 percent were people with special needs; 2 to 3 percent were walk-ins; 5 to 6 percent were influenced to come by a particular preacher; 2 to 3 percent came because they liked the church program; 1 to 2 percent came because they responded to a visitation effort; 4 to 5 percent were reached by Sunday school; .5 percent came through evangelistic crusades/TV programs; and a whopping 75 to 90 percent came through the influence of friends or relatives.[5] Clearly, the personal ordinary Andrew approach is the most important aspect of evangelism, far outweighing institutional approaches many times over.

In addition, Search Ministries, an organization dedicated to equipping the Church for lifestyle evangelism, tells us that about .01 percent of Christians are gifted to do proclamational preaching evangelism, about .05 to 10 percent for confrontational witness, while 100 percent can do relational evangelism.[6] The implication is clear: while all forms of evangelism are important to the Church, by far the most important is the ordinary Andrew "each one win one" style.

DISCIPLINE OF WITNESS

This means, assuming one knows how to lead another to Christ, those of us who have been enfolded by the Church need to prayerfully work at being Andrews — practicing the discipline of witness.

The Value of Relationships[7]

We must understand that we have a sovereign God who orders all of life, including our relationships, and that our friendships, as well as casual encounters, are not a list of social accidents. God has placed us in our particular families, neighborhoods, and workplaces for a reason: He has put us next to people He wants us to influence for Christ. Susie, our daughter's kindergarten teacher, was not a relational accident. Neither was Damon, our letter carrier, or Jamie and Deby, our neighbors and dear friends. Everyone we encounter is an eternal soul of immense value whom we ought to regard with the same weight with which God regards them. As C. S. Lewis, the great Oxford don, memorably said:

> It is a serious thing to live in a society of possible gods and goddesses, to remember that the dullest and most uninteresting person you talk to may one day be a creature which, if you saw it now, you would be strongly tempted to worship, or else a horror and a corruption such as you now meet, if at all, only in a nightmare. All day long we are, in some degree, helping each other to one or other of these destinations. It is in the light of these overwhelming possibilities, it is with the awe and the circumspection proper to them, that we should conduct all our dealings with one another, all friendships, all loves, all play, all politics. There are no ordinary people. You have never talked to a mere mortal. Nations, cultures, arts, civilization — these are mortal, and their life is to ours as the life of a gnat. But it is immortals whom we joke with, work with, marry, snub, and exploit — immortal horrors or everlasting splendors.[8]

Identifying Relationships⁹

All of us have a complex network of relationships built around four natural contacts: biological (relatives and family, and by extension church family), geographical (where we live), vocational (who we work with), and recreational (where we play). We need to discover our networks, make a list of likely contacts, and begin to pray for them.

Investing in Relationships¹⁰

Finally, as we pray, we must invest our time, talent, and treasure in relationships.

- Become personally involved in the lives of others. Plan to spend significant time with those you would like to reach, and then make sure your plan is represented on your calendar.
- Invite your friends out for lunch or dinner, or to your home for coffee.
- Do things together. Attend plays, sporting events, art exhibits. Go fishing.
- Use special days to share your interests — birthdays, graduations, holidays, weddings, births. Visit, call, or write a note.
- Join a service club such as Rotary, Kiwanis, or Lions.
- Join an interest club: gardening, hunting, cooking, woodworking.
- Volunteer to coach a boys' or girls' athletic team, to be a teacher's aide, to give your time to the hospital or one of the many charitable organizations.
- Open your home to the neighborhood. Be the most hospitable home on the block to children and adults.

Every day they pass me by,
I can see it in their eyes;
Empty people filled with care,
Headed who knows where.
On they go through private pain,
Living fear to fear.
Laughter hides the silent cries,
Only Jesus hears.

People need the Lord.
People need the Lord.
At the end of broken dreams,
He's the open door.

People need the Lord.
   People need the Lord.
When will we realize
   People need the Lord.

—Greg Nelson and Phill McHugh

Food for Thought

Why do the people you know need to hear the message of John the Baptist — "Look, the Lamb of God!" (John 1:36)?

"If you know Christ, you . . . have the essential heart qualification to share him — even if you do not have all the answers." Do you agree with this statement? Does not having all the answers make you hesitant to speak up for Christ? How can you overcome this?

With what individuals has God given you a relationship so you can be a witness by life or word? Pray for them daily for the next month, and be alert for opportunities to share Christ with them.

What is "lifestyle evangelism"? Do you use this kind of personal outreach? Why or why not?

If you are like many Christians, the people you find most difficult to witness to are family members or relatives. Why? How can you build bridges with them?

"We must invest our time, talent, and treasure in relationships." Should we do this only so we can win others to Christ? What other reasons should we have? Practically, how can we invest in relationships?

Application/Response

What did God speak to you about most specifically, most powerfully in this chapter? Talk to Him about it right now!

Think About It!

Analyze the example of Andrew and his witness for Christ in Matthew 10; Luke 6; John 1, 6 and 12. What made his witness so effective? Why did he witness? What was his message? Now compare his experience in this area with your own. Be honest.

18

DISCIPLINE OF MINISTRY

FOR MEN WHO claim the name of Christ, there are two distinct courses of life available. One is to cultivate a small heart. This by far seems the safest way to go because it minimizes the sorrows of life. If our ambition is to dodge the troubles of human existence, the formula is simple: avoid entangling relationships, do not give yourself to others, and be sure not to seriously embrace elevated and noble ideals. If we do this, we will escape a host of afflictions.

This life principle bears out in other logics of life as well. Cultivate deafness and we will be spared hearing the discords of life. Cultivate blindness and we will be shielded from seeing ugliness. If we want to get through life with a minimum of trouble, all we have to do is wear blinders. This is how so many people, even those who profess to be Christians, get through life with such ease — they have successfully nurtured smallness of heart.

The other path is to cultivate a ministering heart. Open yourself to others, and you will become susceptible to an index of sorrows scarcely imaginable to a shriveled heart. Enlarge and ennoble your ideals, and your vulnerability will increase proportionately.

There is a sentence in the diary of James Gilmour, pioneer missionary to Mongolia, written at the sunset of his career, which speaks to this point: "In the shape of converts I have seen no result. I have not, as far as I am aware, seen anyone who even wanted to be a Christian." Painful words. But the depth of Gilmour's pain can only be seen dimly until one turns to the opening words of his diary, written when he first arrived in Mongolia: "Several huts in sight. When shall I be able to speak to the people? O Lord, suggest by the Spirit how I should come among them, and in preparing myself to teach the life and love of Christ Jesus." "I have not, as far as I am aware, seen anyone who even wanted to be a Christian."[1]

His throbbing words ooze his life's blood. We naturally think "poor Gilmour." But in truth the cause lay in Gilmour himself, for he had a "problem" — an enlarged heart. Gilmour would never have penned those pathos-filled lines if he had not cultivated a ministering heart, if he had not cared. If he had listened to the counsel of his friends, he would have remained in comfortable England instead of going to that hostile land.

Enlarge your heart, cultivate your heart, discipline yourself for ministry, and you will enlarge your experience of pain. This is an irrefragable spiritual axiom. No one has ever cultivated a ministering heart and lived to tell of a life of ease.

Of course, the effects of these two kinds of hearts are drastically different. Little hearts, though safe and protected, never contribute anything. No one benefits from their restricted sympathies and vision. On the other hand, hearts that have embraced the disciplines of ministry — though they are vulnerable — are also the hearts which possess the most joy and leave their heartprint on the world.

Cultivate deafness and we will never hear discord, but neither will we hear the glorious strains of a great symphony. Cultivate blindness and we will never see ugliness, but we also will never see the beauty of God's creation. Or, to put this in terms of our common experience, never play baseball and you will never strike out, but you will also never hit a home run in the bottom of the ninth with bases loaded to win the game! Never climb a mountain and you will never get banged up on the mountain's side, but you will also never stand on an alpine peak exulting in abundant natural beauty.

Years ago I experienced the grand reality of this principle. My wife, Barbara, informed me that she had received a call from our local youth soccer league, with which my boys were signed up to play, notifying her there was a shortage of coaches and that some boys would have to be left out — unless some fathers (like me!) would take a team. Barbara indicated I might be interested.

My response was that I was too busy and that she would have to tell them so. She replied that I could do it myself, and that a call was coming that evening. I said, "Fine, no problem."

The fateful call came during dinner with all my family as witnesses. As the caller explained the league's plight, I found myself nodding assent and committing myself to be coach of the Awesome Aztecs.

The Scriptures wisely say, "[I]f the trumpet does not sound a clear call, who will get ready for battle?" (1 Corinthians 14:8) — and that was the initial experience of my poor Aztecs. I did not even know what a fullback was, the offside rule remained inscrutable for most of the season, and we got clobbered in our first few games.

Humbled and desperate, I checked out soccer films and spent some evenings late in frantic reading. I also recruited a retired Scotsman who had once played professionally and persuaded another father to assist me. We discovered we had some good athletes, and we began to win. We did so well that we went to the play-offs. And it was here that I had one of the great experiences in my life when we played Mr. G.'s team in the opening round. Mr. G. was the founder of the league and a perennial winner.

But, miracle of miracles, we were ahead 1-0 at halftime. In the third quarter Mr. G.'s team tied it up, and the 1-1 tie held deep into the fourth quarter. Five minutes were left — then three — then one — thirty seconds — ten — two — and we scored just before time ran out! There is no describing the thrill of that moment.

Never coach soccer and you will never know the ignominy of being the league doormat, but you will never know the thrill of beating Mr. G. either!

Cultivate a small heart and life may be smooth sailing, but you will never know the heady wind of the Holy Spirit in your sails and the exhilaration of being used by God. Cultivate a small heart and you will never be the heroic likes of Gilmour of Mongolia, and you will certainly never have the heart God desires for you.

We only have to glance at a newspaper to be reminded that we live in a time when there is an urgent need for enlarged, caring hearts which are disciplined for ministry. Some of you are experiencing the elevating, frightening stirrings which accompany the enlarging of the heart, and you need to be encouraged to cultivate your expanding sympathies and broadening horizons. If so, the Biblical account we are about to consider — the story of Jesus' encounter with the woman at the well — is for you because it brilliantly showcases Jesus' own discipline of ministry, one we are to imitate as His followers.

DISCIPLINED TO LABOR

John's Gospel informs us that when Jesus completed His baptizing ministry in Judea and decided to return to Galilee, He deemed it necessary to go through Samaria, which brought him to the ancient town of Sychar. Specifically, John tells us that "Jacob's well was there, and Jesus, tired as he was from the journey, sat down by the well. It was about the sixth hour" (John 4:6). The sixth hour was noon, midday, time for a meal. So the Lord sent His disciples into town for groceries while He wearily sat down by the well for some needed rest. The words "tired as he was" seem to indicate that he sat down just as a tired man collapses in a motionless heap after a hard day's work.[2]

He was exhausted, and for good reason. A glance at the Gospels reveals that He rarely had any time for Himself unless he stole away. When not being pressed by the multitudes, He was ministering to the Twelve or the inner circle of three or to irrepressible Peter. And He was always on the dusty road. At one point He had Himself said, "Foxes have holes and birds of the air have nests, but the Son of Man has no place to lay his head" (Matthew 8:20). No wonder He was more weary than His disciples, for when mental fatigue and physical weariness meet, there you find an exhausted man. So Jesus plopped down motionless.

It was so nice to be alone in the warm sun and not moving. It is quite possible that the Lord had His eyes closed when He heard approaching steps and looked up to see a Samaritan woman. It would have been so easy for Him to sleepily close his eyes, saying to Himself, "I have been ministering to thousands . . . she's alone . . . just one person. And I have got to relax. If I do not take care of My body, who will?"

But not Jesus! Our Lord went for her heart in one of the grandest cases of spiritual aggression ever recorded. Jesus' heart was so given to the care of souls that He mustered up the strength to minister even when He was at the edge of His physical capacity. People who share the disciplines of Christ's heart will likewise reach out even when exhausted.

It has been said that the world is run by tired men, and it is true, for we daily see that America is run by tired political leaders — and that wars are won by exhausted generals — and that peace is secured by tired diplomats — and that great legislation is accomplished by weary legislators. The reason for this is that such leaders are willing to put themselves out whenever necessary in order to accomplish their noteworthy tasks.

Likewise, the Christian world is ministered to by tired people. Eastern Europe is being evangelized by tired missionaries who are making the most of the fleeting day of opportunity. Show me a great church and I'll show you some tired people, both up front and behind the scenes, because greatness depends on a core of people who are willing to put out as the situation demands. Men, we have to understand that we will never do great things for God without the willingness to extend ourselves for the sake of the gospel even when bone-tired.

Christ's example teaches us that a ministering heart must of necessity be a laboring heart. The Apostle Paul had a heart like that: "Surely you remember, brothers," he says, "our toil and hardship; we worked night and day in order not to be a burden to anyone while we preached the gospel of God to you" (1 Thessalonians 2:9). This apostolic work ethic is a prominent theme with Paul: "I have labored and toiled," he told the Corinthians, "and have often gone without sleep . . ." (2 Corinthians 11:27).

The fact is, anyone who has ever done anything for God has had a laboring heart — no exceptions. Luther is said to have worked so hard that he often fell into bed, not even taking time to change his sheets for a whole year! D. L. Moody's bedtime prayer on one occasion, as he rolled his bulk into bed, was, "Lord, I'm tired! Amen."

Big hearts, the enlarged hearts that God uses, are *laboring hearts* which, though weary, will willingly be expended as necessary. You may fancy that you have a ministering heart, but if you are not laboring for the gospel in the place God where has put you, and do not find yourself being inconvenienced by your commitment, you are deluding yourself. Ministering hearts are disciplined to labor, for they regularly move beyond their comfort zones, they put themselves in vulnerable spots, they make commitments which cost, they get tired for Christ's sake, they pay the price, they encounter rough seas. But their sails billow full of God's Spirit.

DISCIPLINED TO REACH OUT

Jesus' ensuing conversation with the Samaritan woman shows us further that a heart which is disciplined to minister not only works hard, but crosses difficult relational barriers to reach out to others. The narrative continues: "When a Samaritan woman came to draw water, Jesus said to her, 'Will you give me a drink?' (His disciples had gone into the town to buy food.) The Samaritan woman said to him, 'You are a Jew and I am a Samaritan woman. How can you ask me for a drink?' (For Jews do not associate with Samaritans.)" (vv. 7-9). Racial differences form some of the most daunting barriers in this world.

Australian Anglican Bishop John Reed relates that early in his ministry he was driving a bus carrying a full mix of black aboriginal boys and white boys on an outing. As they filed in, the white boys took one side and the blacks the other. And as the trip went on, they exchanged jibes with increasing intensity.

Finally Reed could take it no longer. He stopped the bus and ordered everyone off. Then he stood at the bus door and made every boy say, "I'm green" before allowing him back on.

It took some doing, but at last the bus was full. Bishop Reed was feeling pretty good about his accomplishment until he heard someone in the back of the bus say, "Alright, light green on this side, dark green on the other!"

The Samaritan woman was amazed at Jesus' forward conduct. But to the Jews it was an even more astounding story. The hatred between Judea and Samaria went back over 400 years and centered around racial purity, for while the Jews had kept their purity during the Babylonian Captivity, the Samaritans had lost theirs by intermarrying with the Assyrian invaders. This, in Jewish eyes, was unforgivable. They looked down with disgust on the compromising mongrel Samaritans. Predictably, the Samaritans built a rival temple on Mt. Gerizim only to have it destroyed by the Jews in Maccabean times.

So in Jesus' day the hatred was ingrained and utterly implacable. The rabbis said, "Let no man eat the bread of the Cuthites [Samaritans], for he who eats their bread is as he who eats swine's flesh." And the crowning vilification came in a sulphurous Jewish prayer which concluded, ". . . and do not remember the Cuthites in the Resurrection." Thus we see that Jesus' reaching out to this woman was a radical breach of racial and religious convention.

Piled upon this ignominy was the disgraceful fact that the Samaritan was a woman. Strict rabbis forbade other rabbis to greet women in public. There were even Pharisees who piously designated themselves "the bruised and bleeding Pharisees" because when they saw a woman they shut their eyes and thus stumbled into walls and fell over whatever was in their holy paths. Yet, Jesus spoke to a woman — a woman who was also a despicable Samaritan! And then, to add sin upon sin, Jesus scandalously requested the use of her drinking cup, thus becoming ceremonially defiled.[3]

Jesus' bold attempt to reach out to the soul of the lost Samaritan woman radically hurdled the conventional barriers of the day — and blew people's minds.

In His grand gesture Jesus modeled one of the crowning glories of the Church — that it crosses barriers, be they ethnic or social or economic or psychological. This is exactly what the Early Church did when Jew and Gentile, rich and poor, slave and free, men and women all met together at one table as one family in Christ. This was so radical that the ancient world began to accuse the Church of magic and sorcery. Such barrier-breaking was incomprehensible in Jesus' world.

We are all naturally more comfortable when we are reaching out to others like us — likes winning likes — the rich winning the rich, lawyers lawyers, basketball players basketball players, clerks clerks. But that is not the ideal set by

Jesus and the Early Church. Rather, we are to have a heart so filled with love, so willing to go the extra mile, that we reach out to anybody we come in contact with, regardless of any barriers.

How are we to go about this? We must first understand that it is never to be done in a patronizing "do-gooder" manner, but rather with a relational egalitarianism informed by God's Word, understanding that we reach across barriers as sinner to sinner, equal to equal. The opportunities are virtually limitless: lonely foreign students who long for contact with someone who genuinely cares; immigrant refugees desperately seeking to find a foothold in an alien culture; pregnant women alone and in need of sanctuary and protection; the ever-present people at the bottom of the salary scale — those who park and wash cars, clean homes, bus dishes, pump gas, and mow lawns, whom most people pass by with no more notice than they give the telephone poles along the highway.

It is not natural to cross barriers. It takes the supernatural heart of Christ, a heart which can only come through conscious prayer and discipline. Every believer is called to have a heart that reaches out. Will you pray for this heart for yourself? Will you discipline your heart to reach out? Jesus longs for your heart to beat with His.

DISCIPLINED IN PERSPECTIVE

Jesus' exchange with the woman at the well suggests one other quality of a ministering heart: a perspective disciplined to see one's life, as it passes from person to person, as a series of divine appointments. This is implicit in the expression in verse 4, "Now he had to go through Samaria," which indicates that God's will or plan was involved.[4] In a sense, Jesus did not have to go through Samaria. He could have gone around it, but He was aware of the sovereign ordering of His life and the people who would come His way.

Ministering hearts are aware of this dimension. They know there are no relational accidents.

In 1968 I took twenty-five high-school students to Parker, Arizona, to share their faith with the tens of thousands of young Californians who had traveled to Arizona for Easter vacation. My plans were carefully laid out because a friend and I had flown by small plane to Parker, had taken aerial photographs of the Colorado River from Parker to the dam, and had then driven both sides of the river as I selected a camp site. However, upon arrival I found that the locale I

chose was not available. As a result I spent the rest of the hot day leading my
caravan from spot to spot and getting a series of rejections until finally, near
sunset, we found an opening where we pitched our tents twenty feet from the
camp of five high-school seniors — four of whom made professions of faith by
the week's end, three of whom continue following Christ today, two in the
ministry!

It is a hallowed realization to know that "The steps of a good man are
ordered by the Lord" (Psalm 37:23, KJV) and that the people who pass our way
are divine appointments. A holy sobering takes place as we realize that none of
our appointments are with mere mortals, but that everyone (the woman at the
well and at the laundromat, the religious leader and the pizza delivery boy) will
continue eternally as glorious beings or lost souls. The ministering heart, like
Jesus' heart, senses this and treats all souls accordingly.

The luminous display of Jesus' ministering heart in engaging the Samaritan
woman has showcased for all time the disciplines which are necessary for a life
of ministry.

First, it is a heart which is *disciplined to labor*. The man who has this
heart puts out for Christ and His Church. He is willingly inconvenienced. He
allows his comfort zone to be invaded. Sometimes he will work to the point
of exhaustion.

Second, the heart that ministers is a heart that is *disciplined to reach out*.
For the sake of the gospel it hurdles social barriers and even risks the oppro-
brium of others in doing so. It humbly goes after people who are quite different from itself.

Third, the heart God uses is *disciplined in perspective*, seeing all its human
relationships as sovereignly ordered encounters with eternal beings. To this
heart, all life's relationships are shrouded with the numinous — pulsating with
spiritual potential — part of an eternal drama in which each Christian has a
special part to play.

The heart which is disciplined to labor, to reach out, and to see life's relationships full of divine potential is, above all, a dangerously enlarged heart. Its
high ideals and expanded sympathies make it susceptible to a list of sorrows
unknown to a small heart, but it is also open to a catalogue of joys the shriveled heart will never know.

Never coach soccer and you will never be the league doormat, but you will
also never beat Mr. G. just before time runs out. And you will also never have
the heart-pounding joy of having the Awesome Aztecs and their parents surprise
you by showing up in the front row at church.

Cultivate a small heart and life may be smooth sailing, but you will never experience the exhilaration of the wind of the Spirit in your sails.

Men, the choice is ours. May we discipline ourselves for ministry.

Food for Thought

Do you have a little heart or a ministering heart, as the author described the two? Describe, in your own words, these two hearts.

What reasons could Jesus have found, humanly speaking, to not minister to the Samaritan woman (John 4)? Why did He reach out to her?

What lesson do we learn from 1 Thessalonians 2:9 and 2 Corinthians 11:27? How you do match up here? What barriers or distractions hold you back?

What kind of prejudices interfere with effective Christian ministry? What prejudices do you practice, even occasionally? What ministries are being aborted because of this? What will you do about this?

"It is a hallowed realization to know that 'The steps of a good man are ordered by the Lord' (Psalm 37:23, KJV) and that the people who pass our way are divine appointments." Is this how you see the many people you rub shoulders with at work, down the block, at church, in rush-hour traffic, in a restaurant, etc.?

"The heart which is disciplined to labor, to reach out, and to see life's relationships full of divine potential is, above all, a dangerously enlarged heart." What's so dangerous, for you, in having a ministering heart? What might serving God and reaching out to others cost you?

Application/Response

What did God speak to you about most specifically, most powerfully in this chapter? Talk to Him about it right now!

Think About It!

What ministries are you currently involved in for Christ? List them; then evaluate your service, positive and negative. What ministries do you feel God might want you to withdraw from? What additional ministries might God want you to enter? What preparation is necessary to do so?

DISCIPLINE

19

GRACE OF DISCIPLINE

A S WE LEARNED in the opening study of this book, the word *discipline* in "discipline yourself for the purpose of godliness" (1 Timothy 4:7, NASB) is a word with the smell of the gym in it — the sweat of a good workout. It is an unabashed call to spiritual sweat.

The rich etymology of "discipline" suggests a conscious *divestment* of all encumbrances, and then a determined *investment* of all of one's energies. Just as ancient athletes discarded everything and competed *gumnos* (naked), so must the disciplined Christian man divest himself of every association, habit, and tendency which impedes godliness. Then, with this lean spiritual nakedness accomplished, he must invest all his energy and sweat in the pursuit of godliness.

The lithe, sculpted figure of the classic Greek runner gives the idea. Stripped naked, he has put his perspiration into thousands of miles for the purpose of running well. Even so, the successful Christian life is always, without exception, a stripped-down, disciplined, sweaty affair.

The understanding that vigorous spiritual discipline is essential to godliness accords with the universal understanding that discipline is necessary to accomplish anything in this life. The legendary success of Mike Singletary, two-time NFL Defensive Player of the Year, is testimony to his remarkably disciplined life. Ernest Hemingway's massive literary discipline transformed the way people throughout the English-speaking world use language. Michangelo's, da Vinci's, and Tintoretto's billion sketches, the *quantitative* discipline of their work, prepared the way to the enduring *cosmic* quality of those works. Winston Churchill, speaker of the century, was anything but a natural — unless by "natural" we mean a naturally disciplined man who overcame his remarkable impediments through much hard work and extra effort. Ignace Jan Paderewski, the brilliant pianist, said it all when he remarked to an overardent admirer, "Madam, before I was a genius, I was a drudge."

It is an immutable fact that we will never get anywhere in life without discipline — especially in spiritual matters. There are some who have innate athletic or musical advantages. But none of us can claim an innate spiritual advantage. None of us are inherently righteous, none of us naturally seek God or are reflexively good. Therefore, as children of grace, our spiritual discipline is everything.

No *discipline, no discipleship!*
    No *sweat, no sainthood!*
No *perspiration, no inspiration!*
    No *pain, no gain!*
No *manliness, no maturity!*

This grand spiritual axiom has provided the basis for our examination of sixteen disciplines which are essential to a godly life — the disciplines of: *Purity, Marriage, Fatherhood, Friendship, Mind, Devotion, Prayer, Worship, Integrity, Tongue, Work, Church, Leadership, Giving, Witness,* and *Ministry.*

It is an intimidating list, to say the least! And it is made even more daunting — in that each of the disciplines has been presented in an intentionally prescriptive "do this" manner. In fact, each of the sixteen headings contains an average of seven recommended disciplines — which amounts to over 100 "do's!"

THE CORRECT RESPONSE

How then are we to respond? Certainly not with the "do nothing" *passivity* which has become increasingly characteristic of the American male. For many men, a challenge is an opportunity to duck — to pull up the covers and stay in bed — "There is so much to do . . . I don't know where to begin . . ." — the paralysis of analysis.

On the other hand, an equally deadly response is self-sufficient *legalism.* Admittedly, it is less a statistical danger than passivity. Nevertheless, there are many whose mind-sets could easily appropriate the sixteen disciplines and their multiplied "do's" as a Draconian structure for a harsh legalistic hybrid. Oh, what possibilities we have for a list! "So you missed some days reading the Bible this week? Shame! Remember, five pages a day puts the Bible away." — "If Harry really is the husband he says he is, he would have gotten the door."

God save us from the *reductionism* of such legalism which enshrines spirituality as a series of wooden laws and then says, "If you can do these six, sixteen or sixty-six things, you will be godly." Christianity, godliness, is far more than a checklist. Being "in Christ" is a relationship, and like all relationships it deserves disciplined maintenance, but never legalistic reductionism.

God save us also from self-righteous *judgmentalism*. How easily our sinful hearts can imagine our lists to elevate us, while at the same time providing us with a merciless rack on which to stretch others in judgment.

As we said when we began, there is a universe of difference between the motivations behind legalism and discipline. Legalism says, "I will do this thing to gain merit with God," while discipline says, "I will do this because I love God and want to please Him." Legalism is man-centered; discipline is God-centered. Paul, the arch anti-legalist, said, "[D]iscipline [train] yourself to be godly"!

WISDOM FOR DISCIPLINE

Throughout this book I have kept before me a personal mental picture of the young men in my family, my sons and sons-in-laws, sitting across the coffee table from me as we discuss the disciplines of a godly man. Now they say, "How are we to go about it? Tell us how to discipline ourselves for godliness without being legalistic." In response, I become intensely personal.

Prioritize

I would begin, I tell them, by reviewing the sixteen disciplines and dividing them into separate lists — a list of those areas in which I am doing well and another list of the areas where I need help. If I were married, I would seek the help of my spouse in objectifying the lists. If not, then a trusted friend who is spiritually mature.

I would then number my areas of need in order of importance, say: 1) Purity, 2) Mind, 3) Prayer, 4) Witness, 5) Giving, 6) Work, 7) Friendship, and 8) Leadership. Then, beginning with the first need, Purity, I would look over the suggested sub-disciplines and choose one to three things which I think would best help me improve. In doing this, I would resist the temptation to commit myself to too many disciplines. Better to succeed in a few than to assure failure by overcommitment. Perhaps, regarding the discipline of Purity, I would choose to commit myself, first, to memorizing Scriptures which will help steel me to temptations, and, second, to not watching anything sensual on TV or at the movies. Perhaps under Witness, I would make commitments to pray that

God would give me someone to share Christ with and to join an interest club to meet unchurched people.

After going through my list I would have perhaps twenty specific things which I could do to improve my eight weakest areas.

Be Realistic

But before commitment to the specifics, I would look at the whole list with honest realism, asking, "Are the things which I am about to commit to really within my reach with the help of God?" Perhaps, regarding the discipline of Mind, I have become so convicted that I am considering committing myself to reading the Old Testament once and the New Testament twice, plus reading *War and Peace* in January. Think again! Since I have not been doing much reading, how about setting a goal of reading the New Testament through once in a year and *War and Peace* in January through April? Make sure your commitments make you sweat, but also make sure that taken together they are manageable. It is better to increase your commitments as you succeed than to bite off more than you can do. Success begets success.

Pray

Before setting your commitments in concrete, give yourself a week to think about them and pray over them. Seek the Holy Spirit's guidance for other ways of personal discipline not mentioned in this book.

Be Accountable

Ask your spouse or friend to hold you accountable for your disciplines. Make sure you regularly confer and pray — even if it has to be over the phone. Be honest about your successes and failures. And be willing to take advice and make adjustments.

If You Stumble . . .

You will, no doubt, stumble and even fail outright at times. When this happens, wounded pride and embarrassment can make you want to take your marbles and go home. We do not like to do things at which we fail. But we must realize that failure is a part of succeeding, provided we admit our failures and go at it again. Moreover, we are not under Law but grace. God is not counting our failures against us, and we are not building a treasury of merit with our successes. We are simply trying to live a disciplined life which pleases our loving Father — and He understands our failures better than we understand our own children's.

GRACE OF DISCIPLINE

The man who wisely disciplines himself for godliness understands the necessity of *prioritizing* and *realism* and *prayer* and *accountability* and that *failure* is part of success, but his greatest wisdom and impetus comes from his understanding of *grace*. Everything in his life comes from God's grace — *sola gratia* — grace alone!

Salvation itself is by grace alone. We were dead in our transgressions and sins, captive to dark powers, no more capable of effecting our own salvation than a corpse. "But . . . God, who is rich in mercy, made us alive with Christ even when we were dead in transgressions — it is *by grace* you have been saved. . . . For it is *by grace* you have been saved, through faith — and this not from yourselves, it is the gift of God — not by works, so that no one can boast" (Ephesians 2:4, 8, 9, italics added). We are saved by God's grace, His unmerited favor. Even the smallest percentage of works debases saving grace, as Paul made so pointedly clear: "And if by grace, then it is no longer by works; if it were, grace would no longer be grace" (Romans 11:6). *Sola gratia.*

Salvation is by grace alone, and living the Christian life is by grace alone also. James makes this stunning declaration regarding the believer's universal experience in this world: "[B]ut he gives us more grace" (4:6). This is not saving grace, but grace to live our lives as we ought in this fallen world — literally, "greater grace." There is always "more grace."[1]

An artist once submitted a painting of Niagara Falls to an exhibition, but neglected to give it a title. The gallery, faced with the need to supply one, came up with these words: "More to Follow." Old Niagara Falls, spilling over billions of gallons per year for thousands of years, has more than met the needs of those below and is a fit emblem of the floods of God's grace He showers upon us. There is always more to follow! The Apostle John referred to this reality, saying, "For of His fulness we have all received, and grace upon grace" (John 1:16, NASB) — literally, "grace instead of grace," or as others have rendered it, "grace following grace" or "grace heaped upon grace." "For daily need there is daily grace; for sudden need, sudden grace; for overwhelming need, overwhelming grace," says John Blanchard.[2]

As we tackle the disciplines of a godly man, we must remember it is a matter of grace from beginning to end.

Consider slowly and carefully Paul's words, "But by the *grace* of God I am what I am, and his *grace* to me was not without effect. No, I worked harder than all of them — yet not I, but the *grace* of God that was with me" (1

Corinthians 15:10, italics added). You see, there is no contradiction between grace and hard work. In fact, grace produces spiritual sweat!

It is God's grace that energizes us to live out the disciplines of a godly man. There is always more grace.

> *Grace for Purity*
> *Grace for Marriage*
> *Grace for Fatherhood*
> *Grace for Friendship*
> *Grace for Mind*
> *Grace for Devotion*
> *Grace for Prayer*
> *Grace for Worship*
>
> *Grace for Inegrity*
> *Grace for Tongue*
> *Grace for Work*
> *Grace for Church*
> *Grace for Leadership*
> *Grace for Giving*
> *Grace for Witness*
> *Grace for Ministry*

Brothers, when we attempt to do His will, He always gives more grace.

> *When we have exhausted our store of endurance,*
> *When our strength has failed ere the day is half done;*
> *When we reach the end of our hoarded resources,*
> *Our Father's full giving is only begun.*
> *His love has no limits, His grace has no measure,*
> *His power has no boundary known unto men;*
> *For out of His infinite riches in Jesus,*
> *He giveth, and giveth, and giveth again.*

> —Annie Johnson Flint

Food for Thought

What responses do you sometimes make to the challenge of 1 Timothy 4:7? What does God think of those responses?

Review the sixteen disciplines studied in this book, then prioritize them in relation to your own life — the abilities and interests God has given you, the opportunities before you, your own level of spiritual understanding and maturity, your willingness to move forward.

Do you more often have a problem with promising God or the church too little and being a lazy Christian, or promising too much and being unable to do it all?

How do you feel about asking a close Christian friend to hold you accountable? Does the thought of this encourage you or scare you? Why do we need to hold each other accountable? Isn't being accountable to God enough?

How do you generally respond when you stumble spiritually? What usually causes you to fall or get off track? What can you do to allow God to help you to not stumble as often?

What do *discipline* and *grace* have to do with each other? Define each term carefully. What is the importance of each for your life? What aspect of the character of God most encourages you and keeps you going?

Application/Response

What did God speak to you about most specifically, most powerfully in this chapter? Talk to Him about it right now!

Think About It!

Make a complete list of all the areas of your life in which you need greater discipline. Then, for each, write down what you can do to experience increased discipline. Since you cannot accomplish this in your own strength and must have God's help, your answers should include ways you can receive divine assistance and enabling.

RESOURCES

$\overline{\text{A}}$

THE BIBLE ON AUDIOCASSETTE

Among the selections of the Bible on cassette tape, your local Christian bookstore will have available the following:

NIV — Old and New Testaments (Zondervan), $119.95; New Testament, $39.95.

KJV — Old and New Testaments (Christian Duplicate), $79.95; New Testament, $17.95.

NKJ — Old and New Testaments (read by Alexander Scourby), $119.95; New Testament, $29.98; Psalms/Proverbs, $16.98.

Living Bible, Old and New Testaments (Tyndale House), $89.95; New Testament, $19.95.

BIBLE MEMORIZATION PROGRAMS

NIV — *Hiding the Word* (60-minute cassettes/cards), $8.98.

Navigators, *The Topical Memory System*, $8.95/box (four versions)

B

JAMES AND DEBY FELLOWES'S
WITNESS TO THEIR FAITH

James: My wife Deby and I are glad to give witness to the change that came into our lives when we accepted Jesus Christ as our Lord and Savior. We are grateful for those who stood tall in their faith and were instrumental in our decision for Christ.

During our courtship and early years of marriage, we never attended church, nor do I recall ever discussing God or what we believed. We were too busy with our careers and each other.

I had been born into a churchgoing family. My parents were and are marvelous examples of the Christian ideal. They are generous, loving, gracious, compassionate, kind, and humble. But, as good as their example was, in my youth I never really understood Jesus' life, death, or resurrection. I figured I was a Christian because I went to church and tried to be a good person just like my mom and dad.

Deborah: Like Jamie, I grew up going to church. My mother was a Sunday school teacher for many years, and she made sure my brother and I attended every Sunday. It was in church, I believe, that the three of us found comfort and strength to deal with difficult family problems.

In the midst of a time of uncertainty and insecurity during my junior-high years, I remember having a keen interest in spiritual matters. I felt a strong desire to go to church, but could find no answers. I recall a stained-glass window in our church depicting an angel kneeling with its wing outstretched. How I yearned to crawl under that wing for security, protection and peace.

When I fell in love with Jamie, it seemed like I could find all these things I was searching for in him and our relationship. We had each other, and I turned my back on God. We lived for the moment and for ourselves.

James: On December 23, 1975, at 2:00 in the afternoon, our first child, Jennifer, was born. Experiencing childbirth in the delivery room was more than this new father could handle. I cried uncontrollably, overcome with the emotions of joy, awe, and thankfulness. This magnificent moment of birth tugged the spiritual chords within me.

In the hours and days afterwards, I thought a lot about God and the creation of a baby. Only God can create a baby, I thought. I wanted to know God. I had seen His great and powerful work.

The next Sunday we searched for a neighborhood church in the Lincoln Park area of Chicago, where we lived, and finally found one that we liked. I really enjoyed this new dimension in my life. I began to learn about Christianity as an adult. I liked the people and being part of the church community. In time I became an usher, then an elder, then chairman of the board of elders.

Deborah: While Jamie was finding a new dimension and fulfillment in his life, I became resentful of this new interest. He now had more meetings to attend and obligations to fill which did not include me. Knowing how much this church meant to Jamie, however, I became somewhat involved along with him.

On a spiritual level, however, I was needy. Singing hymns alone would bring me to the brink of tears. I wanted to know what to believe in. I was searching for meaning in my life, but was looking in the wrong places. Material possessions and worldly success were far too important to me. And these were attainable goals since Jamie's responsibilities and stature were growing in his family's business. In spite of our material success, though, I felt an emptiness in my life.

Both Jamie's and my background made us leery of evangelical churches. When we moved to Wheaton (Illinois) in 1979, we looked for a house far removed from the Wheaton College campus. However, the house of our dreams happened to be one block from the area we were trying to avoid.

Five months after we moved in, the new pastor of College Church — Kent Hughes — and his family moved in across the street from us. I became friends with his wife, Barbara. She invited me to come to a Bible study at their church on Wednesday mornings, and I decided I would give it a try. From the moment I walked into that room, I sensed a difference in this group. The women seemed to sincerely care about each other. There was not the superficiality I had encountered at so many other social and business groups. Before long the Bible study became a highlight of my week. I admired these women's strength of character that I sensed was lacking in myself. I began to recognize these women were different because of the teachings of the Scripture. They were committed to displaying through their lives what the Bible taught — acting upon what they had learned. They trusted Christ to rule their lives instead of themselves. That was so contrary to the way we were living our lives.

It was during this time that Jamie and I received an invitation to a dinner being held at a country club by a business acquaintance of Jamie's. It was to feature a testimony by a business executive and his wife on what their relationship with Christ has meant in their lives. Out of respect for our friend, we went. Here I heard what I had been hearing at Bible study but by a business executive's wife, someone who had been struggling with many of the things that I was struggling with. I could definitely identify with her. I realized that Revelation 3:20 was speaking to *me*: "Here I am! I stand at the door and knock. If anyone hears my voice and opens the door, I will come in and eat with him, and he with me."

That night was one of the most stressful for me. In a moment of anxiety I prayed that my friend Barbara would come speak to me the next day. And she did. After explaining to her the previous evening's events, she could sense the struggle I was having. She offered to lead me through the Scriptures and explain Jesus' claims. Through her leading, I took a step of faith and surrendered my life to Christ. I knew my commitment would make a big change in our marriage, but I knew this was what I had to do.

James: I went to the same dinner, of course. At the end of the testimony, we were given cards to fill out. I checked the box "don't call me." I distrusted the "born-again" types. I thought they were self-righteous and often a lot worse than the rest of us. Besides that, I had been chairman of the board of elders and served our church in other ways. Was that not religious enough?

It made me sick that my susceptible wife had been drawn into this "born-again" business. Maybe it would die away.

Soon a division between Deby and me began to open. She read the Bible all the time. If not that, she was reading Chuck Swindoll, C. S. Lewis, or Kent Hughes, our neighbor. She spent all her time in Bible studies and prayer groups. She accepted party invitations, and they were boring. I felt out of it, and I didn't want "in." In many ways we began to grow apart.

Deborah: Actually what I had feared would happen did happen. Jamie could not understand how my priorities could change overnight. Where did he now fit into the scheme of things? Although our relationship was as important to me as it had always been, a new relationship was deepening within me — one with Christ. My desire to follow, serve, and obey Christ had become first in my life. With that decision I wanted to spend my time differently. Lifestyle preferences changed. The division in our marriage opened wider. I simply had to trust Christ.

James: I was trying to be understanding and patient, but I often found myself resentful and angry. I felt lonely in my own house. If God is good, how could He be the center of a heretofore successful, happy marriage? I was very confused.

I had my own views about God based on I know not what. I figured I had a reasonable shot at Heaven because I was a pretty good person. God graded on a curve, no doubt — hopefully a generous one. Deby refuted my arguments based on Scripture. She spoke of salvation through faith and God's grace.

In the interest of family unity, I decided to go to a Sunday evening service with Deby. My experience was rather similar to Deby's the first time she visited the women's Bible study. I sensed something different than other church experiences I'd had. I decided to go back the next Sunday. I sensed the presence of Christ in a new and deeper way.

Maybe there was some good in all this, I thought, difficult as it might be to admit. For all that I resented about our new lifestyle, Deby had changed positively in many ways. For openers she was at peace with our relationship. I was the one in emotional stress. She definitely was a stronger, more independent person. She was less argumentative and more forgiving. Irony of ironies, she was somehow more romantic through this period of marital tension.

I decided I might read some of her books that were lying around — *In His Steps* by Charles Sheldon, *Mere Christianity* by C. S. Lewis, then *Loving God* by Chuck Colson. Kent Hughes and I read *Basic Christianity* by John Stott. We began to talk about our faith. On a difficult business trip to San Francisco I read the Gospel of John from a Gideon Bible in the motel desk drawer. The power of Scripture was beginning to take root for the first time in my life.

Deborah: Jamie had changed. It was not an overnight experience as it had been with me, but I sensed a gradual open and sensitive spirit to know the Lord. Our relationship grew in a way it never had before — on a spiritual level. We began to trust God for our daily decisions. We realized that God was sovereign and in control of our lives. We became happier and closer than we ever had been before. Looking back over the years, we could see how God had gently yet firmly pulled us to Himself, and in the process drew us closer to each other. God had done what He promised in Ezekiel 11:19, 20: "I will give them an undivided heart and put a new spirit in them; I will remove from them their heart of stone and give them a heart of flesh. Then they will follow my decrees and be careful to keep my laws. They will be my people, and I will be their God."

James: There had been an emptiness to my life, despite a great marriage, kids, and all the nice things we could afford. How do you define an emptiness or void? It's hard. Most of the time we suppress it, or feebly attempt to fill it with something superficial.

As I began to understand the claims of Christ and why He had come to earth and died for me, I looked at my life. It was embarrassing when I reflected upon God's riches in my life and compared it to the selfishness and downright wickedness of my heart. I was ashamed.

I journeyed frequently to the foot of the cross and begged forgiveness. I prayed in detail, sickening as it was. The more I read and listened, the better I understood where I had gone wrong. More importantly, I discovered how to get on track. Through God's forgiveness and grace I began to feel free and alive in a new way.

In those early days God seemed to fill me with a new power and a totally new sense of self-worth. By trusting in Him, things seemed to work out better. Trying to please Him instead of myself somehow took the pressure off and made me feel better about my life.

Jesus Christ has made all the difference in our lives. Our lives are a living testimony to His power. Through countless trials, struggles, and everyday events He has guided our path. He has blessed us beyond our hopes. We are grateful to the many who prayed for, nurtured, and discipled us.

As a businessman by profession, a healthy skepticism comes naturally. My own conversion was slow and deliberate, unlike Deby's. But I discovered the Way, the Truth, and the Life — the Lord Jesus Christ. I've learned where to put my trust. God is faithful. He loves you, and He loves me. Trust in Him.

C

PERSONAL READING SURVEY

What we read affects us deeply, with long-term results. What books have influenced you the most? The following are the responses given to a survey of Christian leaders, sent out by R. Kent Hughes. Specific questions asked on the survey were:

> 1. What are the five books, secular or sacred, which have influenced you the most?
> 2. Of the spiritual/sacred books which have influenced you, which is your favorite?
> 3. What is your favorite novel?
> 4. What is your favorite biography?

JOHN W. ALEXANDER

1. Charles Sheldon, *In His Steps*; H. B. Wright, *The Will of God and a Man's Life Work*; H. J. Carnell, *An Introduction to Christian Apologetics*; William Manchester, *American Caesar*; Garth Lean, *God's Politician*.
2. H. J. Carnell, *An Introduction to Christian Apologetics*.
3. Charles Dickens, *David Copperfield*.
4. William Manchester, *American Caesar*.

HUDSON T. ARMERDING

1. *The Bible*; Calvin's *Institutes*; J. I. Packer, *Knowing God*; J. O. Buswell, *A Systematic Theology of the Christian Religion*; S. E. Morison, *History of the U.S. Navy in World War Two*.

2. After the *Bible*, Calvin's *Institutes*.

3. Dostoyevski, *Crime and Punishment* and Ernest Gordon, *Through the Valley of the Kwai*.

4. Pollock, *Hudson Taylor*.

JAMES M. BOICE

1. John Calvin, *Institutes of the Christian Religion* (2 vols.); B. B. Warfield, *Inspiration and Authority of the Bible*; T. M. Lindsay, *History of the Reformation* (2 vols.); John Stott, *Basic Christianity*; Donald Grey Barnhouse, *Romans* (10 vols.).

2. Calvin's *Institutes*.

3. Ernest Hemingway, *Over the River and into the Trees*.

4. Arnold Dallimore, *George Whitefield*.

BRYAN CHAPELL

1. C. S. Lewis, *Mere Christianity*.

2. Calvin's *Institutes*.

3. J. Oliver Buswell, *A Systematic Theology of Christian Religion*.

4. John Bunyan, *Pilgrim's Progress*.

5. Sidney Greidanus, *Sola Scriptura*.

RICHARD CHASE

1. Charles Colson, *Loving God*; Werner Jaeger, *Paideia: The Ideals of Greek Culture* (3 vols.); Sir Robert Anderson, *The Silence of God*; David J. Hassel, *City of Wisdom*; Nathan Hatch, *The Democritization of American Christianity*.

2. Charles Colson, *Loving God*.

3. Mary Stewart's novels: *The Crystal Cave*, *The Hollow Hills*, *The Last Enchantment* (favorite).

4. Charles Colson, *Born Again*.

CHARLES COLSON

1. C. S. Lewis, *Mere Christianity*; St. Augustine, *Confessions*; Armando Valladares, *Against All Hope*; Alexander Solzhenitsyn, *The Gulag Archipelago*; Richard John Neuhaus, *The Naked Public Square*; Donald Bloesch, *Crumbling*

Foundations; Harry Blamires, *The Christian Mind*; Dietrich Bonhoeffer, *The Cost of Discipleship*; St. Augustine, *The City of God*; Jonathan Edwards, *Treatise on Religious Affections*; R. C. Sproul, *Knowing Scripture*; William Wilberforce, *Real Christianity*; Jacques Ellul, *The Political Illusion* and *The Presence of the Kingdom*; J. I. Packer, *Knowing God*; Paul Johnson, *Modern Times*; John Bunyan, *Pilgrim's Progress*.

3. John Bunyan, *Pilgrim's Progress*; Dostoyevski, *Brothers Karamazov*.

4. St. Augustine, *Confessions*.

JAMES C. DOBSON

Rather than select several books which exceed all others in their impact on my life, I prefer to commend the authors whose collection of writings are most highly prized. This is easier because the best writers require several books to state their cases and leave their mark. First, I admire the memory of Dr. Francis Schaeffer and the anthology he left to us. Second, I have great appreciation for the writings of Chuck Colson. His best book, I believe, is *Loving God*. His life is a demonstration of its theme.

LYLE DORSETT

1. Besides the *Bible*, which I would, of course, rank #1, E. M. Bounds, *Power Through Prayer*; George Müller, *A Life of Trust*; G. K. Chesterton, *Orthodoxy*; Oswald Chambers, *My Utmost for His Highest*; Robert E. Coleman, *The Master Plan of Evangelism*.

2. Oswald Chambers, *My Utmost for His Highest*.

3. C. S. Lewis, *The Great Divorce*.

4. Catherine Marshall, *A Man Called Peter*.

ELISABETH ELLIOT

1. Romano Guardini, *The Lord*; George MacDonald, *Salted with Fire*; Amy Carmichael, *Toward Jerusalem*; Janet Erskine Stuart, *Life and Letters*; Evelyn Underhill, *The Mystery of Charity*.

2. Impossible to say.

3. Sigrid Undeset, *Kristin Lavransdatter*.

4. St. Augustine, *Confessions*.

LTG. HOWARD G. GRAVES

1. *The Bible*; Oswald Chambers, *My Utmost for His Highest*; Francis Schaeffer, *How Should We Then Live?*; J. I. Packer, *Knowing God*; James Stockdale, *A Vietnam Experience, Ten Years of Reflection*; Charles Swindoll, *Growing Strong in the Seasons of Life*.
2. Oswald Chambers, *My Utmost for His Highest*.
3. Herman Wouk's series, *Winds of War* and *Remembrance*.
4. *The Personal Memoirs of U. S. Grant*.

HOWARD G. HENDRICKS

1. C. S. Lewis, *Mere Christianity*.
2. Adler Mortimer, *How to Read a Book*.
3. Calvin's *Institutes*.
4. Lewis Sperry Chafer, *He That Is Spiritual*.
5. A. W. Tozer, *The Pursuit of God*.

CARL F. H. HENRY

1. *The Bible*; James Orr, *The Christian View of God and the World*; John Calvin, *The Institutes of the Christian Religion*.
2. *The Bible* and James Orr, *The Christian View of God and the World*.

DAVID M. HOWARD

1. John Stott, *The Baptism and Fulness of the Holy Spirit*; Earle Cairns, *Christianity Through the Centuries*; Alexander Whyte, *Bible Characters*; Carolina Maria de Jesus, *Child of the Dark*; Dwight Eisenhower, *Crusade in Europe*.
2. Earle Cairns, *Christianity Through the Centuries*.
3. Leo Tolstoy, *Anna Karenina*.
4. Elisabeth Elliot, *Shadow of the Almighty*.

JERRY JENKINS

1. Roger Kahn, *The Boys of Summer*.
2. Charles Colson, *How Now Shall We Live?*
3. Charles Colson, *Born Again*.

4. Elisabeth Elliot, *Shadow of the Almighty.*
5. Elisabeth Elliot, *Through Gates of Splendor.*

KENNETH S. KANTZER

1. St. Augustine, *The City of God*; John Calvin, *Institutes*; Edwards, *The Distinguishing Marks of a Revival of the Spirit of God*; James Orr, *The Christian View of God and the World*; Leo Tolstoy, *Anna Karenina.*
2. St. Augustine, *The City of God.*
3. Leo Tolstoy, *Anna Karenina.*
4. Carl F. H. Henry, *The Confessions of a Theologian.*

JAY KESLER

1. Jacques Ellul, *The Presence of the Kingdom*; John Bright, *The Kingdom of God*; Alan Paton, *Too Late the Phalarope*; Carl Sandburg, *Lincoln*; C. S. Lewis, *Mere Christianity*; Fyodor Dostoyevski, *Crime and Punishment.*
2. Jacques Ellul, *The Presence of the Kingdom.*
3. Alan Paton, *Too Late the Phalarope.*
4. Carl Sandburg, *Lincoln*; see also *Lee, Jefferson, Sadat, Wesley, Judson, Truman, Churchill.*

DENNIS F. KINLAW

1. Clarence Hall, *Portrait of a Prophet: The Life of Samuel Logan Brengle*; *Hudson Taylor's Spiritual Secret*; *The Standard Sermons of John Wesley*; Yehekel Kaufmann, *The Religion of Israel*; A. W. Tozer, *The Pursuit of God.*
2. *The Standard Sermons of John Wesley.*
3. Charles Dickens, *A Tale of Two Cities.*
4. Clara H. Stuart, *Latimer, Apostle to the English.*

HAROLD LINDSELL

1. John Calvin, *Institutes*; Oswald Chambers, *My Utmost for His Highest*; Philip Schaff, *History of the Christian Church*; Matthew Henry, *Commentary*; Martyn Lloyd-Jones, *Spiritual Depression — Its Causes and Its Cure.*
2. Oswald Chambers, *My Utmost for His Highest.*

3. None.

4. Hudson Taylor, *Spiritual Secrets*.

DUANE LITFIN

(Most influential authors rather than most influential books)

1. C. S. Lewis, *The Great Divorce*; *Mere Christianity*; *God in the Dock*.

2. A. W. Tozer, *The Pursuit of God*.

3. J. I. Packer, *Knowing God*.

4. St. Augustine, *De Doctrina Christiana* (*On Christian Doctrine*).

5. Haddon Robinson, *Biblical Preaching*.

WAYNE MARTINDALE

1. C. S. Lewis, *The Great Divorce*; C. S. Lewis, *The Problem of Pain*; C. S. Lewis, *Mere Christianity*; Charles Sheldon, *In His Steps*; Elisabeth Elliot, *Through Gates of Splendor*.

2. Elisabeth Elliot, *Through Gates of Splendor*.

3. Fyodor Dostoyevski, *Brothers Karamazov*.

4. Elisabeth Elliot, *Through Gates of Splendor*.

ROBERTSON MCQUILKIN

1. *Romans, John, Luke, 2 Timothy*; C. S. Lewis, *Miracles*; Warfield, *Inspiration and Authority of Scripture*; Johnstone, *Operation World*; Pollock, *Course of Time*.

2. Pollock, *Course of Time*.

3. C. S. Lewis, *Till We Have Faces*; Tolkien, *Lord of the Rings*; many of Shakespeare's plays.

4. Robert McQuilkin, *Always in Triumph*.

CALVIN MILLER

1. Dallas Willard, *The Spirit of the Disciplines*; Bill Moyers, *World of Ideas II*; Virginia Stem Owens, *If You Do Love Old Men*; Larsen, *Passions*; Williams, *Islam*.

2. Jean Pierre de Causade, *The Sacrament of the Present Moment* or Mother Teresa's *Life in the Spirit*.

3. *War and Peace*, *Anna Karenina*, anything by Dickens, Dostoyevski, Tolkien.

4. Troyat's *Tolstoy* or Massie's *Nicholas and Alexandra*.

HAROLD MYRA

1. C. S. Lewis, *Mere Christianity*; C. S. Lewis, *Perelandra*; Paul Tournier, *The Meaning of Persons*; Helmut Thielicke, *The Waiting Father*; Thomas a Kempis, *The Imitation of Christ*; Oswald Chambers books.

2. C. S. Lewis, *Perelandra*.

3. Fyodor Dostoyevski, *Brothers Karamazov*.

4. William Manchester, *The Last Lion*.

STEPHEN F. OLFORD

1. Alvin Toffler, *Future Shock*; Carl Henry, *God, Revelation and Authority*; Thomas a Kempis, *The Imitation of Christ*; A. J. Gordon, *The Ministry of the Spirit*; John Stott, *The Cross of Christ*.

2. Dr. and Mrs. Howard Taylor, *Hudson Taylor in the Early Years: The Growth of a Soul*.

3. Lloyd Douglas, *The Robe* and Lew Wallace, *Ben Hur*.

4. Dr. and Mrs. Howard Taylor, *Hudson Taylor in the Early Years: The Growth of a Soul*.

J. I. PACKER

1. John Calvin, *Institutes*; John Bunyan, *Pilgrim's Progress*; Goold, *John Owen Works* (Vols. 3, 6, 7); Richard Baxter, *Reformed Pastor*; Luther, *Bondage of the Will*.

2. John Bunyan, *Pilgrim's Progress*.

3. Fyodor Dostoyevski, *The Brothers Karamazov*.

4. Arnold Dallimore, *George Whitefield*.

PAIGE PATTERSON

1. F. W. Krummacher, *The Suffering Savior*.

2. Leonard Verduin, *The Reformers and Their Stepchildren*.

3. Courtney Anderson, *To the Golden Shore*.

4. Roland Bainton, *Here I Stand*.

5. Francis Schaeffer, *Escape from Reason*.

EUGENE H. PETERSON

1. Karl Barth, *Epistle to the Romans*; Fyodor Dostoyevski, *The Idiot*; Charles Williams, *Descent of the Dove*; Herman Melville, *Moby Dick*; George Herbert, *Country Parson and the Temple*.

2. Karl Barth, *Epistle to the Romans*.

3. Fyodor Dostoyevski, *The Brothers Karamazov*.

4. Meriol Trevor, 2 volumes on *Newman: The Pillar of the Cloud* and *Light in Winter*.

C. WILLIAM POLLARD

1. C. S. Lewis, *Mere Christianity*.

2. C. S. Lewis, *Surprised by Joy*.

3. Francis Schaeffer, *How Should We Then Live?*

4. Dorothy Sayers, *The Mind of the Maker*.

5. Peter Drucker, *Managing for Results* and *Managing for the Future*.

JIM REAPSOME

1. W. H. Griffith Thomas, *Christianity Is Christ*; C. S. Lewis, *Mere Christianity*; A. W. Tozer, *The Pursuit of God*; Dr. and Mrs. Hudson Taylor, *Hudson Taylor's Spiritual Secret*; D. Martyn Lloyd-Jones, *Spiritual Depression — Its Causes and Its Cure*.

2. W. H. Griffith Thomas, *Christianity Is Christ*.

HADDON ROBINSON

1. Richard Halvorsen, *Christian Maturity*; H. Grady Davis, *Design for Preaching*; S. I. Hayakawa, *Language in Thought and Action*; Robert Alter, *The Art of Biblical Narrative*; C. S. Lewis, *Mere Christianity*.

2. James Stuart, *Heralds of God*.

3. Olov Hartman, *Holy Masquerade*.

4. Stockford Brooks, *Life and Letters of F. W. Robertson*.

R.C. SPROUL

1. J. Edwards, *Freedom of the Will*; M. Luther, *Bondage of the Will*; J. Calvin, *Institutes of the Christian Religion*; James Collins, *God and Modern Philosophy*; William Simon, *A Time for Truth*; Ben Hogan, *Power Golf*.
2. *Bondage of the Will* because of its theological insight and its literary style.
3. H. Melville, *Moby Dick*.
4. W. Manchester, *American Caesar*.

CHARLES R. SWINDOLL

John Bunyan, *Pilgrim's Progress*; A. W. Tozer, *The Pursuit of God*; J. I. Packer, *Knowing God*; Elisabeth Elliot, *Through Gates of Splendor*; J. Oswald Sanders, *Spiritual Leadership*; Charles H. Spurgeon, *Lectures to My Students*; Philip Yancey, *Where Is God When It Hurts?*

BILL WALDROP

1. *The Bible*; A. W. Tozer, *The Pursuit of God*; A. W. Tozer, *Knowledge of the Holy*; Elisabeth Elliot, *Shadow of the Almighty*; Richard Foster, *Celebration of Discipline*.
2. A. W. Tozer, *Knowledge of the Holy*.
3. Leo Tolstoy, *War and Peace*.
4. William Manchester, *The Last Lion*.

WARREN WIERSBE

1. A. W. Tozer, *The Pursuit of God*; Jill Morgan, *Campbell Morgan, A Man and the Word*; Thomas a Kempis, *The Imitation of Christ*; Henry David Thoreau, *Walden*; Phillips Brooks, *Yale Lectures on Preaching*.
2. Thomas a Kempis, *The Imitation of Christ*.
3. Herman Melville, *Moby Dick*.
4. Boswell's *Life of Samuel Johnson*.

OTHER THAN THE BIBLE, BOOKS MENTIONED MORE THAN ONCE

C. S. Lewis, *Mere Christianity* (10)

John Calvin, *Institutes of the Christian Religion* (8)
A. W. Tozer, *The Pursuit of God* (6)
Oswald Chambers, *My Utmost for His Highest* (5)
Fyodor Dostoyevski, *Brothers Karamazov* (5)
Leo Tolstoy, *Anna Karenina* (5)
John Bunyan, *Pilgrim's Progress* (5)
Elisabeth Elliot, *Shadow of the Almighty* (4)
Dr. and Mrs. Howard Taylor, *Hudson Taylor's Spiritual Secret* (3)
Thomas a Kempis, *The Imitation of Christ* (3)
C. S. Lewis, *The Great Divorce* (3)
Charles Sheldon, *In His Steps* (2)
James Orr, *The Christian View of God and the World* (2)
William Manchester, *American Caesar* (2)
William Manchester, *The Last Lion* (2)
Herman Melville, *Moby Dick* (2)
Leo Tolstoy, *War and Peace* (2)
Charles Colson, *Loving God* (2)
St. Augustine, *Confessions* (2)
Elisabeth Elliot, *Through Gates of Splendor* (2)
J. I. Packer, *Knowing God* (2)

D

M'CHEYNE'S CALENDAR FOR DAILY READINGS

A concise course whereby one can read through the whole Bible once a year — the Psalms and the New Testament twice.

Arranged by Robert Murray M'Cheyne.

Publisher's note: This adapted calendar is published by the Banner of Truth Trust as an aid to systematic Bible reading and is available in quantities (minimum order 10 copies, 60 cents; 25 copies, $1.35) from: The Banner of Truth Trust, P.O. Box 621, Carlisle, Pennsylvania 17013.

1   This reading schedule gives the day of the month, as well as chapters to be read in the family, and portions to be read in secret.
2   The head of the family should previously read over the chapter indicated for the family worship, and mark two or three of the most prominent verses, upon which he may dwell, giving a few explanatory thoughts, and asking several simple questions.
3   The portions read, both for family and private reading, would be greatly illuminated if they were preceded by a moment's silent prayer: 'Open Thou mine eyes, that I may behold wondrous things out of Thy law' [Ps 119:18].
4   Let the conversation at the family meals frequently turn upon the chapter read; thus every meal will be a sacrament, being sanctified by the Word and prayer.
5   Let our private reading precede the dawning of the day. Let God's voice be the first we hear in the morning. Mark two or three of the richest verses and pray over every word and line of them.

6   Above all, use the Word as a lamp to your feet and a light to your path — your guide in perplexity, your armour in temptation, your food in times of faintness.

JANUARY

This is my beloved Son, in whom I am
well pleased; hear ye him.

FAMILY

DAY	BOOK AND CHAPTER	
☐ 1	Genesis 1	Matthew 1
☐ 2	Genesis 2	Matthew 2
☐ 3	Genesis 3	Matthew 3
☐ 4	Genesis 4	Matthew 4
☐ 5	Genesis 5	Matthew 5
☐ 6	Genesis 6	Matthew 6
☐ 7	Genesis 7	Matthew 7
☐ 8	Genesis 8	Matthew 8
☐ 9	Genesis 9, 10	Matthew 9
☐ 10	Genesis 11	Matthew 10
☐ 11	Genesis 12	Matthew 11
☐ 12	Genesis 13	Matthew 12
☐ 13	Genesis 14	Matthew 13
☐ 14	Genesis 15	Matthew 14
☐ 15	Genesis 16	Matthew 15
☐ 16	Genesis 17	Matthew 16
☐ 17	Genesis 18	Matthew 17
☐ 18	Genesis 19	Matthew 18
☐ 19	Genesis 20	Matthew 19
☐ 20	Genesis 21	Matthew 20
☐ 21	Genesis 22	Matthew 21
☐ 22	Genesis 23	Matthew 22
☐ 23	Genesis 24	Matthew 23
☐ 24	Genesis 25	Matthew 24
☐ 25	Genesis 26	Matthew 25
☐ 26	Genesis 27	Matthew 26
☐ 27	Genesis 28	Matthew 27
☐ 28	Genesis 29	Matthew 28
☐ 29	Genesis 30	Mark 1
☐ 30	Genesis 31	Mark 2
☐ 31	Genesis 32	Mark 3

SECRET

DAY	BOOK AND CHAPTER	
☐ 1	Ezra 1	Acts 1
☐ 2	Ezra 2	Acts 2
☐ 3	Ezra 3	Acts 3
☐ 4	Ezra 4	Acts 4
☐ 5	Ezra 5	Acts 5
☐ 6	Ezra 6	Acts 6
☐ 7	Ezra 7	Acts 7
☐ 8	Ezra 8	Acts 8
☐ 9	Ezra 9	Acts 9
☐ 10	Ezra 10	Acts 10
☐ 11	Nehemiah 1	Acts 11
☐ 12	Nehemiah 2	Acts 12
☐ 13	Nehemiah 3	Acts 13
☐ 14	Nehemiah 4	Acts 14
☐ 15	Nehemiah 5	Acts 15
☐ 16	Nehemiah 6	Acts 16
☐ 17	Nehemiah 7	Acts 17
☐ 18	Nehemiah 8	Acts 18
☐ 19	Nehemiah 9	Acts 19
☐ 20	Nehemiah 10	Acts 20
☐ 21	Nehemiah 11	Acts 21
☐ 22	Nehemiah 12	Acts 22
☐ 23	Nehemiah 13	Acts 23
☐ 24	Esther 1	Acts 24
☐ 25	Esther 2	Acts 25
☐ 26	Esther 3	Acts 26
☐ 27	Esther 4	Acts 27
☐ 28	Esther 5	Acts 28
☐ 29	Esther 6	Romans 1
☐ 30	Esther 7	Romans 2
☐ 31	Esther 8	Romans 3

FEBRUARY

I have esteemed the words of his mouth
more than my necessary food.

FAMILY				SECRET			
DAY	**BOOK AND CHAPTER**			**DAY**	**BOOK AND CHAPTER**		
☐	1	Genesis 33	Mark 4	☐	1	Esther 9, 10	Romans 4
☐	2	Genesis 34	Mark 5	☐	2	Job 1	Romans 5
☐	3	Genesis 35, 36	Mark 6	☐	3	Job 2	Romans 6
☐	4	Genesis 37	Mark 7	☐	4	Job 3	Romans 7
☐	5	Genesis 38	Mark 8	☐	5	Job 4	Romans 8
☐	6	Genesis 39	Mark 9	☐	6	Job 5	Romans 9
☐	7	Genesis 40	Mark 10	☐	7	Job 6	Romans 10
☐	8	Genesis 41	Mark 11	☐	8	Job 7	Romans 11
☐	9	Genesis 42	Mark 12	☐	9	Job 8	Romans 12
☐	10	Genesis 43	Mark 13	☐	10	Job 9	Romans 13
☐	11	Genesis 44	Mark 14	☐	11	Job 10	Romans 14
☐	12	Genesis 45	Mark 15	☐	12	Job 11	Romans 15
☐	13	Genesis 46	Mark 16	☐	13	Job 12	Romans 16
☐	14	Genesis 47	Luke 1 v 38	☐	14	Job 13	1 Cor 1
☐	15	Genesis 48	Luke 1 v 39	☐	15	Job 14	1 Cor 2
☐	16	Genesis 49	Luke 2	☐	16	Job 15	1 Cor 3
☐	17	Genesis 50	Luke 3	☐	17	Job 16, 17	1 Cor 4
☐	18	Exodus 1	Luke 4	☐	18	Job 18	1 Cor 5
☐	19	Exodus 2	Luke 5	☐	19	Job 19	1 Cor 6
☐	20	Exodus 3	Luke 6	☐	20	Job 20	1 Cor 7
☐	21	Exodus 4	Luke 7	☐	21	Job 21	1 Cor 8
☐	22	Exodus 5	Luke 8	☐	22	Job 22	1 Cor 9
☐	23	Exodus 6	Luke 9	☐	23	Job 23	1 Cor 10
☐	24	Exodus 7	Luke 10	☐	24	Job 24	1 Cor 11
☐	25	Exodus 8	Luke 11	☐	25	Job 25, 26	1 Cor 12
☐	26	Exodus 9	Luke 12	☐	26	Job 27	1 Cor 13
☐	27	Exodus 10	Luke 13	☐	27	Job 28	1 Cor 14
☐	28	Exodus 11, 12 v 21	Luke 14	☐	28	Job 29	1 Cor 15

MARCH

Mary kept all these things,
and pondered them in her heart.

FAMILY				SECRET			
DAY	**BOOK AND CHAPTER**			**DAY**	**BOOK AND CHAPTER**		
☐	1	Exodus 12 v 22	Luke 15	☐	1	Job 30	1 Cor 16
☐	2	Exodus 13	Luke 16	☐	2	Job 31	2 Cor 1
☐	3	Exodus 14	Luke 17	☐	3	Job 32	2 Cor 2
☐	4	Exodus 15	Luke 18	☐	4	Job 33	2 Cor 3

☐	5	Exodus 16	Luke 19		☐	5	Job 34	2 Cor 4
☐	6	Exodus 17	Luke 20		☐	6	Job 35	2 Cor 5
☐	7	Exodus 18	Luke 21		☐	7	Job 36	2 Cor 6
☐	8	Exodus 19	Luke 22		☐	8	Job 37	2 Cor 7
☐	9	Exodus 20	Luke 23		☐	9	Job 38	2 Cor 8
☐	10	Exodus 21	Luke 24		☐	10	Job 39	2 Cor 9
☐	11	Exodus 22	John 1		☐	11	Job 40	2 Cor 10
☐	12	Exodus 23	John 2		☐	12	Job 41	2 Cor 11
☐	13	Exodus 24	John 3		☐	13	Job 42	2 Cor 12
☐	14	Exodus 25	John 4		☐	14	Proverbs 1	2 Cor 13
☐	15	Exodus 26	John 5		☐	15	Proverbs 2	Galatians 1
☐	16	Exodus 27	John 6		☐	16	Proverbs 3	Galatians 2
☐	17	Exodus 28	John 7		☐	17	Proverbs 4	Galatians 3
☐	18	Exodus 29	John 8		☐	18	Proverbs 5	Galatians 4
☐	19	Exodus 30	John 9		☐	19	Proverbs 6	Galatians 5
☐	20	Exodus 31	John 10		☐	20	Proverbs 7	Galatians 6
☐	21	Exodus 32	John 11		☐	21	Proverbs 8	Ephesians 1
☐	22	Exodus 33	John 12		☐	22	Proverbs 9	Ephesians 2
☐	23	Exodus 34	John 13		☐	23	Proverbs 10	Ephesians 3
☐	24	Exodus 35	John 14		☐	24	Proverbs 11	Ephesians 4
☐	25	Exodus 36	John 15		☐	25	Proverbs 12	Ephesians 5
☐	26	Exodus 37	John 16		☐	26	Proverbs 13	Ephesians 6
☐	27	Exodus 38	John 17		☐	27	Proverbs 14	Philippians 1
☐	28	Exodus 39	John 18		☐	28	Proverbs 15	Philippians 2
☐	29	Exodus 40	John 19		☐	29	Proverbs 16	Philippians 3
☐	30	Leviticus 1	John 20		☐	30	Proverbs 17	Philippians 4
☐	31	Leviticus 2, 3	John 21		☐	31	Proverbs 18	Colossians 1

APRIL

O send out thy light and thy truth;
let them lead me.

FAMILY

DAY		BOOK AND CHAPTER	
☐	1	Leviticus 4	Psalms 1, 2
☐	2	Leviticus 5	Psalms 3, 4
☐	3	Leviticus 6	Psalms 5, 6
☐	4	Leviticus 7	Psalms 7, 8
☐	5	Leviticus 8	Psalms 9
☐	6	Leviticus 9	Psalms 10
☐	7	Leviticus 10	Psalms 11, 12
☐	8	Leviticus 11, 12	Psalms 13, 14
☐	9	Leviticus 13	Psalms 15, 16
☐	10	Leviticus 14	Psalms 17
☐	11	Leviticus 15	Psalms 18
☐	12	Leviticus 16	Psalms 19
☐	13	Leviticus 17	Psalms 20, 21
☐	14	Leviticus 18	Psalms 22

SECRET

DAY		BOOK AND CHAPTER	
☐	1	Proverbs 19	Colossians 2
☐	2	Proverbs 20	Colossians 3
☐	3	Proverbs 21	Colossians 4
☐	4	Proverbs 22	1 Thess 1
☐	5	Proverbs 23	1 Thess 2
☐	6	Proverbs 24	1 Thess 3
☐	7	Proverbs 25	1 Thess 4
☐	8	Proverbs 26	1 Thess 5
☐	9	Proverbs 27	2 Thess 1
☐	10	Proverbs 28	2 Thess 2
☐	11	Proverbs 29	2 Thess 3
☐	12	Proverbs 30	1 Timothy 1
☐	13	Proverbs 31	1 Timothy 2
☐	14	Eccles 1	1 Timothy 3

☐	15	Leviticus 19	Psalms 23, 24	☐	15	Eccles 2	1 Timothy 4
☐	16	Leviticus 20	Psalms 25	☐	16	Eccles 3	1 Timothy 5
☐	17	Leviticus 21	Psalms 26, 27	☐	17	Eccles 4	1 Timothy 6
☐	18	Leviticus 22	Psalms 28, 29	☐	18	Eccles 5	2 Timothy 1
☐	19	Leviticus 23	Psalms 30	☐	19	Eccles 6	2 Timothy 2
☐	20	Leviticus 24	Psalms 31	☐	20	Eccles 7	2 Timothy 3
☐	21	Leviticus 25	Psalms 32	☐	21	Eccles 8	2 Timothy 4
☐	22	Leviticus 26	Psalms 33	☐	22	Eccles 9	Titus 1
☐	23	Leviticus 27	Psalms 34	☐	23	Eccles 10	Titus 2
☐	24	Numbers 1	Psalms 35	☐	24	Eccles 11	Titus 3
☐	25	Numbers 2	Psalms 36	☐	25	Eccles 12	Philemon 1
☐	26	Numbers 3	Psalms 37	☐	26	Song 1	Hebrews 1
☐	27	Numbers 4	Psalms 38	☐	27	Song 2	Hebrews 2
☐	28	Numbers 5	Psalms 39	☐	28	Song 3	Hebrews 3
☐	29	Numbers 6	Psalms 40, 41	☐	29	Song 4	Hebrews 4
☐	30	Numbers 7	Psalms 42, 43	☐	30	Song 5	Hebrews 5

MAY

From a child thou hast known the holy Scriptures.

FAMILY   SECRET

	DAY	BOOK AND CHAPTER			DAY	BOOK AND CHAPTER	
☐	1	Numbers 8	Psalms 44	☐	1	Song 6	Hebrews 6
☐	2	Numbers 9	Psalms 45	☐	2	Song 7	Hebrews 7
☐	3	Numbers 10	Psalms 46, 47	☐	3	Song 8	Hebrews 8
☐	4	Numbers 11	Psalms 48	☐	4	Isaiah 1	Hebrews 9
☐	5	Numbers 12, 13	Psalms 49	☐	5	Isaiah 2	Hebrews 10
☐	6	Numbers 14	Psalms 50	☐	6	Isaiah 3, 4	Hebrews 11
☐	7	Numbers 15	Psalms 51	☐	7	Isaiah 5	Hebrews 12
☐	8	Numbers 16	Psalms 52-54	☐	8	Isaiah 6	Hebrews 13
☐	9	Numbers 17, 18	Psalms 55	☐	9	Isaiah 7	James 1
☐	10	Numbers 19	Psalms 56, 57	☐	10	Isaiah 8, 9 v 7	James 2
☐	11	Numbers 20	Psalms 58, 59	☐	11	Isaiah 9 v 8, 10 v 4	James 3
☐	12	Numbers 21	Psalms 60, 61	☐	12	Isaiah 10 v 5	James 4
☐	13	Numbers 22	Psalms 62, 63	☐	13	Isaiah 11, 12	James 5
☐	14	Numbers 23	Psalms 64, 65	☐	14	Isaiah 13	1 Peter 1
☐	15	Numbers 24	Psalms 66, 67	☐	15	Isaiah 14	1 Peter 2
☐	16	Numbers 25	Psalms 68	☐	16	Isaiah 15	1 Peter 3
☐	17	Numbers 26	Psalms 69	☐	17	Isaiah 16	1 Peter 4
☐	18	Numbers 27	Psalms 70, 71	☐	18	Isaiah 17, 18	1 Peter 5
☐	19	Numbers 28	Psalms 72	☐	19	Isaiah 19, 20	2 Peter 1
☐	20	Numbers 29	Psalms 73	☐	20	Isaiah 21	2 Peter 2
☐	21	Numbers 30	Psalms 74	☐	21	Isaiah 22	2 Peter 3
☐	22	Numbers 31	Psalms 75, 76	☐	22	Isaiah 23	1 John 1
☐	23	Numbers 32	Psalms 77	☐	23	Isaiah 24	1 John 2
☐	24	Numbers 33	Psalms 78 v 37	☐	24	Isaiah 25	1 John 3
☐	25	Numbers 34	Psalms 78 v 38	☐	25	Isaiah 26	1 John 4
☐	26	Numbers 35	Psalms 79	☐	26	Isaiah 27	1 John 5

☐	27	Numbers 36	Psalms 80	☐	27	Isaiah 28	2 John 1
☐	28	Deut 1	Psalms 81, 82	☐	28	Isaiah 29	3 John 1
☐	29	Deut 2	Psalms 83, 84	☐	29	Isaiah 30	Jude 1
☐	30	Deut 3	Psalms 85	☐	30	Isaiah 31	Rev 1
☐	31	Deut 4	Psalms 86, 87	☐	31	Isaiah 32	Rev 2

JUNE

Blessed is he that readeth and they that hear.

FAMILY

DAY		BOOK AND CHAPTER	
☐	1	Deut 5	Psalms 88
☐	2	Deut 6	Psalms 89
☐	3	Deut 7	Psalms 90
☐	4	Deut 8	Psalms 91
☐	5	Deut 9	Psalms 92, 93
☐	6	Deut 10	Psalms 94
☐	7	Deut 11	Psalms 95, 96
☐	8	Deut 12	Psalms 97, 98
☐	9	Deut 13, 14	Psalms 99-101
☐	10	Deut 15	Psalms 102
☐	11	Deut 16	Psalms 103
☐	12	Deut 17	Psalms 104
☐	13	Deut 18	Psalms 105
☐	14	Deut 19	Psalms 106
☐	15	Deut 20	Psalms 107
☐	16	Deut 21	Psalms 108, 109
☐	17	Deut 22	Psalms 110, 111
☐	18	Deut 23	Psalms 112, 113
☐	19	Deut 24	Psalms 114, 115
☐	20	Deut 25	Psalms 116
☐	21	Deut 26	Psalms 117, 118
☐	22	Deut 27, 28 v. 19	Psalms 119 v 24
☐	23	Deut 28 v. 20	Psalms v 25-48
☐	24	Deut 29	Psalms v 49-72
☐	25	Deut 30	Psalms v 73-96
☐	26	Deut 31	Psalms v 97-120
☐	27	Deut 32	Psalms v 121-144
☐	28	Deut 33, 34	Psalms v 145-176
☐	29	Joshua 1	Psalms 120-122
☐	30	Joshua 2	Psalms 123-125

SECRET

DAY		BOOK AND CHAPTER	
☐	1	Isaiah 33	Rev 3
☐	2	Isaiah 34	Rev 4
☐	3	Isaiah 35	Rev 5
☐	4	Isaiah 36	Rev 6
☐	5	Isaiah 37	Rev 7
☐	6	Isaiah 38	Rev 8
☐	7	Isaiah 39	Rev 9
☐	8	Isaiah 40	Rev 10
☐	9	Isaiah 41	Rev 11
☐	10	Isaiah 42	Rev 12
☐	11	Isaiah 43	Rev 13
☐	12	Isaiah 44	Rev 14
☐	13	Isaiah 45	Rev 15
☐	14	Isaiah 46	Rev 16
☐	15	Isaiah 47	Rev 17
☐	16	Isaiah 48	Rev 18
☐	17	Isaiah 49	Rev 19
☐	18	Isaiah 50	Rev 20
☐	19	Isaiah 51	Rev 21
☐	20	Isaiah 52	Rev 22
☐	21	Isaiah 53	Matthew 1
☐	22	Isaiah 54	Matthew 2
☐	23	Isaiah 55	Matthew 3
☐	24	Isaiah 56	Matthew 4
☐	25	Isaiah 57	Matthew 5
☐	26	Isaiah 58	Matthew 6
☐	27	Isaiah 59	Matthew 7
☐	28	Isaiah 60	Matthew 8
☐	29	Isaiah 61	Matthew 9
☐	30	Isaiah 62	Matthew 10

JULY

They received the word with all readiness of mind,
and searched the Scriptures daily.

FAMILY				SECRET			
DAY		**BOOK AND CHAPTER**		**DAY**		**BOOK AND CHAPTER**	
☐	1	Joshua 3	Psalms 126-128	☐	1	Isaiah 63	Matthew 11
☐	2	Joshua 4	Psalms 129-131	☐	2	Isaiah 64	Matthew 12
☐	3	Joshua 5, 6 v 5	Psalms 132-134	☐	3	Isaiah 65	Matthew 13
☐	4	Joshua 6 v 6	Psalms 135, 136	☐	4	Isaiah 66	Matthew 14
☐	5	Joshua 7	Psalms 137, 138	☐	5	Jeremiah 1	Matthew 15
☐	6	Joshua 8	Psalms 139	☐	6	Jeremiah 2	Matthew 16
☐	7	Joshua 9	Psalms 140, 141	☐	7	Jeremiah 3	Matthew 17
☐	8	Joshua 10	Psalms 142, 143	☐	8	Jeremiah 4	Matthew 18
☐	9	Joshua 11	Psalms 144	☐	9	Jeremiah 5	Matthew 19
☐	10	Joshua 12, 13	Psalms 145	☐	10	Jeremiah 6	Matthew 20
☐	11	Joshua 14, 15	Psalms 146, 147	☐	11	Jeremiah 7	Matthew 21
☐	12	Joshua 16, 17	Psalms 148	☐	12	Jeremiah 8	Matthew 22
☐	13	Joshua 18, 19	Psalms 149, 150	☐	13	Jeremiah 9	Matthew 23
☐	14	Joshua 20, 21	Acts 1	☐	14	Jeremiah 10	Matthew 24
☐	15	Joshua 22	Acts 2	☐	15	Jeremiah 11	Matthew 25
☐	16	Joshua 23	Acts 3	☐	16	Jeremiah 12	Matthew 26
☐	17	Joshua 24	Acts 4	☐	17	Jeremiah 13	Matthew 27
☐	18	Judges 1	Acts 5	☐	18	Jeremiah 14	Matthew 28
☐	19	Judges 2	Acts 6	☐	19	Jeremiah 15	Mark 1
☐	20	Judges 3	Acts 7	☐	20	Jeremiah 16	Mark 2
☐	21	Judges 4	Acts 8	☐	21	Jeremiah 17	Mark 3
☐	22	Judges 5	Acts 9	☐	22	Jeremiah 18	Mark 4
☐	23	Judges 6	Acts 10	☐	23	Jeremiah 19	Mark 5
☐	24	Judges 7	Acts 11	☐	24	Jeremiah 20	Mark 6
☐	25	Judges 8	Acts 12	☐	25	Jeremiah 21	Mark 7
☐	26	Judges 9	Acts 13	☐	26	Jeremiah 22	Mark 8
☐	27	Judges 10, 11 v 11	Acts 14	☐	27	Jeremiah 23	Mark 9
☐	28	Judges 11 v 12	Acts 15	☐	28	Jeremiah 24	Mark 10
☐	29	Judges 12	Acts 16	☐	29	Jeremiah 25	Mark 11
☐	30	Judges 13	Acts 17	☐	30	Jeremiah 26	Mark 12
☐	31	Judges 14	Acts 18	☐	31	Jeremiah 27	Mark 13

AUGUST

Speak, Lord; for thy servant heareth.

FAMILY				SECRET			
DAY		**BOOK AND CHAPTER**		**DAY**		**BOOK AND CHAPTER**	
☐	1	Judges 15	Acts 19	☐	1	Jeremiah 28	Mark 14
☐	2	Judges 16	Acts 20	☐	2	Jeremiah 29	Mark 15

☐	Day	Book and Chapter		☐	Day	Book and Chapter	
☐	3	Judges 17	Acts 21	☐	3	Jeremiah 30, 31	Mark 16
☐	4	Judges 18	Acts 22	☐	4	Jeremiah 32	Psalms 1, 2
☐	5	Judges 19	Acts 23	☐	5	Jeremiah 33	Psalms 3, 4
☐	6	Judges 20	Acts 24	☐	6	Jeremiah 34	Psalms 5, 6
☐	7	Judges 21	Acts 25	☐	7	Jeremiah 35	Psalms 7, 8
☐	8	Ruth 1	Acts 26	☐	8	Jeremiah 36, 45	Psalms 9
☐	9	Ruth 2	Acts 27	☐	9	Jeremiah 37	Psalms 10
☐	10	Ruth 3, 4	Acts 28	☐	10	Jeremiah 38	Psalms 11, 12
☐	11	1 Samuel 1	Romans 1	☐	11	Jeremiah 39	Psalms 13, 14
☐	12	1 Samuel 2	Romans 2	☐	12	Jeremiah 40	Psalms 15, 16
☐	13	1 Samuel 3	Romans 3	☐	13	Jeremiah 41	Psalms 17
☐	14	1 Samuel 4	Romans 4	☐	14	Jeremiah 42	Psalms 18
☐	15	1 Samuel 5, 6	Romans 5	☐	15	Jeremiah 43	Psalms 19
☐	16	1 Samuel 7, 8	Romans 6	☐	16	Jeremiah 44	Psalms 20, 21
☐	17	1 Samuel 9	Romans 7	☐	17	Jeremiah 46	Psalms 22
☐	18	1 Samuel 10	Romans 8	☐	18	Jeremiah 47	Psalms 23, 24
☐	19	1 Samuel 11	Romans 9	☐	19	Jeremiah 48	Psalms 25
☐	20	1 Samuel 12	Romans 10	☐	20	Jeremiah 49	Psalms 26, 27
☐	21	1 Samuel 13	Romans 11	☐	21	Jeremiah 50	Psalms 28, 29
☐	22	1 Samuel 14	Romans 12	☐	22	Jeremiah 51	Psalms 30
☐	23	1 Samuel 15	Romans 13	☐	23	Jeremiah 52	Psalms 31
☐	24	1 Samuel 16	Romans 14	☐	24	Lamen 1	Psalms 32
☐	25	1 Samuel 17	Romans 15	☐	25	Lamen 2	Psalms 33
☐	26	1 Samuel 18	Romans 16	☐	26	Lamen 3	Psalms 34
☐	27	1 Samuel 19	1 Cor 1	☐	27	Lamen 4	Psalms 35
☐	28	1 Samuel 20	1 Cor 2	☐	28	Lamen 5	Psalms 36
☐	29	1 Samuel 21, 22	1 Cor 3	☐	29	Ezekiel 1	Psalms 37
☐	30	1 Samuel 23	1 Cor 4	☐	30	Ezekiel 2	Psalms 38
☐	31	1 Samuel 24	1 Cor 5	☐	31	Ezekiel 3	Psalms 39

SEPTEMBER

The law of the Lord is perfect,
converting the soul.

FAMILY

☐	DAY	BOOK AND CHAPTER	
☐	1	1 Samuel 25	1 Cor 6
☐	2	1 Samuel 26	1 Cor 7
☐	3	1 Samuel 27	1 Cor 8
☐	4	1 Samuel 28	1 Cor 9
☐	5	1 Samuel 29, 30	1 Cor 10
☐	6	1 Samuel 31	1 Cor 11
☐	7	2 Samuel 1	1 Cor 12
☐	8	2 Samuel 2	1 Cor 13
☐	9	2 Samuel 3	1 Cor 14
☐	10	2 Samuel 4, 5	1 Cor 15
☐	11	2 Samuel 6	1 Cor 16
☐	12	2 Samuel 7	2 Cor 1

SECRET

☐	DAY	BOOK AND CHAPTER	
☐	1	Ezekiel 4	Psalms 40, 41
☐	2	Ezekiel 5	Psalms 42, 43
☐	3	Ezekiel 6	Psalms 44
☐	4	Ezekiel 7	Psalms 45
☐	5	Ezekiel 8	Psalms 46, 47
☐	6	Ezekiel 9	Psalms 48
☐	7	Ezekiel 10	Psalms 49
☐	8	Ezekiel 11	Psalms 50
☐	9	Ezekiel 12	Psalms 51
☐	10	Ezekiel 13	Psalms 52-54
☐	11	Ezekiel 14	Psalms 55
☐	12	Ezekiel 15	Psalms 56, 57

☐	13	2 Samuel 8, 9	2 Cor 2	☐	13	Ezekiel 16	Psalms 58, 59
☐	14	2 Samuel 10	2 Cor 3	☐	14	Ezekiel 17	Psalms 60, 61
☐	15	2 Samuel 11	2 Cor 4	☐	15	Ezekiel 18	Psalms 62, 63
☐	16	2 Samuel 12	2 Cor 5	☐	16	Ezekiel 19	Psalms 64, 65
☐	17	2 Samuel 13	2 Cor 6	☐	17	Ezekiel 20	Psalms 66, 67
☐	18	2 Samuel 14	2 Cor 7	☐	18	Ezekiel 21	Psalms 68
☐	19	2 Samuel 15	2 Cor 8	☐	19	Ezekiel 22	Psalms 69
☐	20	2 Samuel 16	2 Cor 9	☐	20	Ezekiel 23	Psalms 70, 71
☐	21	2 Samuel 17	2 Cor 10	☐	21	Ezekiel 24	Psalms 72
☐	22	2 Samuel 18	2 Cor 11	☐	22	Ezekiel 25	Psalms 73
☐	23	2 Samuel 19	2 Cor 12	☐	23	Ezekiel 26	Psalms 74
☐	24	2 Samuel 20	2 Cor 13	☐	24	Ezekiel 27	Psalms 75, 76
☐	25	2 Samuel 21	Galatians 1	☐	25	Ezekiel 28	Psalms 77
☐	26	2 Samuel 22	Galatians 2	☐	26	Ezekiel 29	Psalms 78 v 37
☐	27	2 Samuel 23	Galatians 3	☐	27	Ezekiel 30	Psalms 78 v 38
☐	28	2 Samuel 24	Galatians 4	☐	28	Ezekiel 31	Psalms 79
☐	29	1 Kings 1	Galatians 5	☐	29	Ezekiel 32	Psalms 80
☐	30	1 Kings 2	Galatians 6	☐	30	Ezekiel 33	Psalms 81, 82

OCTOBER

O how I love thy law!
it is my meditation all the day.

FAMILY

DAY	BOOK AND CHAPTER	
☐ 1	1 Kings 3	Ephesians 1
☐ 2	1 Kings 4, 5	Ephesians 2
☐ 3	1 Kings 6	Ephesians 3
☐ 4	1 Kings 7	Ephesians 4
☐ 5	1 Kings 8	Ephesians 5
☐ 6	1 Kings 9	Ephesians 6
☐ 7	1 Kings 10	Phil 1
☐ 8	1 Kings 11	Phil 2
☐ 9	1 Kings 12	Phil 3
☐ 10	1 Kings 13	Phil 4
☐ 11	1 Kings 14	Coloss 1
☐ 12	1 Kings 15	Coloss 2
☐ 13	1 Kings 16	Coloss 3
☐ 14	1 Kings 17	Coloss 4
☐ 15	1 Kings 18	1 Thess 1
☐ 16	1 Kings 19	1 Thess 2
☐ 17	1 Kings 20	1 Thess 3
☐ 18	1 Kings 21	1 Thess 4
☐ 19	1 Kings 22	1 Thess 5
☐ 20	2 Kings 1	2 Thess 1
☐ 21	2 Kings 2	2 Thess 2
☐ 22	2 Kings 3	2 Thess 3
☐ 23	2 Kings 4	1 Timothy 1

SECRET

DAY	BOOK AND CHAPTER	
☐ 1	Ezekiel 34	Psalms 83, 84
☐ 2	Ezekiel 35	Psalms 85
☐ 3	Ezekiel 36	Psalms 86
☐ 4	Ezekiel 37	Psalms 87, 88
☐ 5	Ezekiel 38	Psalms 89
☐ 6	Ezekiel 39	Psalms 90
☐ 7	Ezekiel 40	Psalms 91
☐ 8	Ezekiel 41	Psalms 92, 93
☐ 9	Ezekiel 42	Psalms 94
☐ 10	Ezekiel 43	Psalms 95, 96
☐ 11	Ezekiel 44	Psalms 97, 98
☐ 12	Ezekiel 45	Psalms 99-101
☐ 13	Ezekiel 46	Psalms 102
☐ 14	Ezekiel 47	Psalms 103
☐ 15	Ezekiel 48	Psalms 104
☐ 16	Daniel 1	Psalms 105
☐ 17	Daniel 2	Psalms 106
☐ 18	Daniel 3	Psalms 107
☐ 19	Daniel 4	Psalms 108, 109
☐ 20	Daniel 5	Psalms 110, 111
☐ 21	Daniel 6	Psalms 112, 113
☐ 22	Daniel 7	Psalms 114, 115
☐ 23	Daniel 8	Psalms 116

☐	24	2 Kings 5	1 Timothy 2	☐	24	Daniel 9	Psalms 117, 118
☐	25	2 Kings 6	1 Timothy 3	☐	25	Daniel 10	Psalms 119 - v 24
☐	26	2 Kings 7	1 Timothy 4	☐	26	Daniel 11	Psalms v 25-48
☐	27	2 Kings 8	1 Timothy 5	☐	27	Daniel 12	Psalms v 49-72
☐	28	2 Kings 9	1 Timothy 6	☐	28	Hosea 1	Psalms v 73-96
☐	29	2 Kings 10	2 Timothy 1	☐	29	Hosea 2	Psalms v 97-120
☐	30	2 Kings 11, 12	2 Timothy 2	☐	30	Hosea 3, 4	Psalms v 121-144
☐	31	2 Kings 13	2 Timothy 3	☐	31	Hosea 5, 6	Psalms v 145-176

NOVEMBER

*As new-born babes, desire the sincere milk of
the word, that ye may grow thereby.*

FAMILY

DAY		BOOK AND CHAPTER	
☐	1	2 Kings 14	2 Timothy 4
☐	2	2 Kings 15	Titus 1
☐	3	2 Kings 16	Titus 2
☐	4	2 Kings 17	Titus 3
☐	5	2 Kings 18	Philemon 1
☐	6	2 Kings 19	Hebrews 1
☐	7	2 Kings 20	Hebrews 2
☐	8	2 Kings 21	Hebrews 3
☐	9	2 Kings 22	Hebrews 4
☐	10	2 Kings 23	Hebrews 5
☐	11	2 Kings 24	Hebrews 6
☐	12	2 Kings 25	Hebrews 7
☐	13	1 Chr 1, 2	Hebrews 8
☐	14	1 Chr 3, 4	Hebrews 9
☐	15	1 Chr 5, 6	Hebrews 10
☐	16	1 Chr 7, 8	Hebrews 11
☐	17	1 Chr 9, 10	Hebrews 12
☐	18	1 Chr 11, 12	Hebrews 13
☐	19	1 Chr 13, 14	James 1
☐	20	1 Chr 15	James 2
☐	21	1 Chr 16	James 3
☐	22	1 Chr 17	James 4
☐	23	1 Chr 18	James 5
☐	24	1 Chr 19, 20	1 Peter 1
☐	25	1 Chr 21	1 Peter 2
☐	26	1 Chr 22	1 Peter 3
☐	27	1 Chr 23	1 Peter 4
☐	28	1 Chr 24, 25	1 Peter 5
☐	29	1 Chr 26, 27	2 Peter 1
☐	30	1 Chr 28	2 Peter 2

SECRET

DAY		BOOK AND CHAPTER	
☐	1	Hosea 7	Psalms 120-122
☐	2	Hosea 8	Psalms 123-125
☐	3	Hosea 9	Psalms 126-128
☐	4	Hosea 10	Psalms 129-131
☐	5	Hosea 11	Psalms 132-134
☐	6	Hosea 12	Psalms 135, 136
☐	7	Hosea 13	Psalms 137, 138
☐	8	Hosea 14	Psalms 139
☐	9	Joel 1	Psalms 140, 141
☐	10	Joel 2	Psalms 142
☐	11	Joel 3	Psalms 143
☐	12	Amos 1	Psalms 144
☐	13	Amos 2	Psalms 145
☐	14	Amos 3	Psalms 146, 147
☐	15	Amos 4	Psalms 148-150
☐	16	Amos 5	Luke 1 - v 38
☐	17	Amos 6	Luke 1 v 39
☐	18	Amos 7	Luke 2
☐	19	Amos 8	Luke 3
☐	20	Amos 9	Luke 4
☐	21	Obadiah 1	Luke 5
☐	22	Jonah 1	Luke 6
☐	23	Jonah 2	Luke 7
☐	24	Jonah 3	Luke 8
☐	25	Jonah 4	Luke 9
☐	26	Micah 1	Luke 10
☐	27	Micah 2	Luke 11
☐	28	Micah 3	Luke 12
☐	29	Micah 4	Luke 13
☐	30	Micah 5	Luke 14

DECEMBER

The law of his God is in his heart;
none of his steps shall slide.

FAMILY

SECRET

DAY	BOOK AND CHAPTER		DAY	BOOK AND CHAPTER	
☐	1	1 Chr 29	2 Peter 3	☐	1	Micah 6	Luke 15
☐	2	2 Chr 1	1 John 1	☐	2	Micah 7	Luke 16
☐	3	2 Chr 2	1 John 2	☐	3	Nahum 1	Luke 17
☐	4	2 Chr 3, 4	1 John 3	☐	4	Nahum 2	Luke 18
☐	5	2 Chr 5, 6 - v 11	1 John 4	☐	5	Nahum 3	Luke 19
☐	6	2 Chr 6 v 12	1 John 5	☐	6	Habakkuk 1	Luke 20
☐	7	2 Chr 7	2 John 1	☐	7	Habakkuk 2	Luke 21
☐	8	2 Chr 8	3 John 1	☐	8	Habakkuk 3	Luke 22
☐	9	2 Chr 9	Jude 1	☐	9	Zephaniah 1	Luke 23
☐	10	2 Chr 10	Rev 1	☐	10	Zephaniah 2	Luke 24
☐	11	2 Chr 11, 12	Rev 2	☐	11	Zephaniah 3	John 1
☐	12	2 Chr 13	Rev 3	☐	12	Haggai 1	John 2
☐	13	2 Chr 14, 15	Rev 4	☐	13	Haggai 2	John 3
☐	14	2 Chr 16	Rev 5	☐	14	Zech 1	John 4
☐	15	2 Chr 17	Rev 6	☐	15	Zech 2	John 5
☐	16	2 Chr 18	Rev 7	☐	16	Zech 3	John 6
☐	17	2 Chr 19, 20	Rev 8	☐	17	Zech 4	John 7
☐	18	2 Chr 21	Rev 9	☐	18	Zech 5	John 8
☐	19	2 Chr 22, 23	Rev 10	☐	19	Zech 6	John 9
☐	20	2 Chr 24	Rev 11	☐	20	Zech 7	John 10
☐	21	2 Chr 25	Rev 12	☐	21	Zech 8	John 11
☐	22	2 Chr 26	Rev 13	☐	22	Zech 9	John 12
☐	23	2 Chr 27, 28	Rev 14	☐	23	Zech 10	John 13
☐	24	2 Chr 29	Rev 15	☐	24	Zech 11	John 14
☐	25	2 Chr 30	Rev 16	☐	25	Zech 12, 13 - v 1	John 15
☐	26	2 Chr 31	Rev 17	☐	26	Zech 13 v 2	John 16
☐	27	2 Chr 32	Rev 18	☐	27	Zech 14	John 17
☐	28	2 Chr 33	Rev 19	☐	28	Malachi 1	John 18
☐	29	2 Chr 34	Rev 20	☐	29	Malachi 2	John 19
☐	30	2 Chr 35	Rev 21	☐	30	Malachi 3	John 20
☐	31	2 Chr 36	Rev 22	☐	31	Malachi 4	John 21

E

THROUGH THE BIBLE

Daily Readings Covering the Entire Bible in a Year

Publisher's Note: This reading schedule has been adapted from a publication of the National Association of Evangelicals. Copies may be ordered in quantities as follows: 25/$4.00, 50/$6.00, 100 or more $9.00 per 100. Prices include postage and handling. Write to: National Association of Evangelicals, 450 Gundersen Drive, Carol Stream, IL 60188.

JANUARY

DAY		BOOK AND CHAPTER
☐	1	John 1:1-18
☐	2	Gen. 1-4
☐	3	Gen. 5-8
☐	4	Gen. 9-12
☐	5	Gen. 13-16
☐	6	Psalms 1-3
☐	7	Gen. 17-19
☐	8	Gen. 20-22
☐	9	Job 1-4
☐	10	Job 5-8
☐	11	Job 9-12
☐	12	Job 13-16
☐	13	Psalms 4-7
☐	14	Job 17-20
☐	15	Job 21-24
☐	16	Job 25-28
☐	17	Job 29-32
☐	18	Job 33-36
☐	19	Job 37-39
☐	20	Psalms 8-11
☐	21	Job 40-42
☐	22	Gen. 23-26
☐	23	Gen. 27-30
☐	24	Gen. 31-34
☐	25	Gen. 35-38
☐	26	Gen. 39-42
☐	27	Psalms 12-14
☐	28	Gen. 43-46
☐	29	Gen. 47-50
☐	30	Ex. 1-3
☐	31	Ex. 4-6

FEBRUARY

DAY		BOOK AND CHAPTER
☐	1	Ex. 7-9
☐	2	Ex. 10-12
☐	3	Psalms 15-17
☐	4	Ex. 13-15
☐	5	Ex. 16-18
☐	6	Ex. 19-21
☐	7	Ex. 22-24
☐	8	Ex. 25-27

☐	9	Ex. 28-30
☐	10	Psalms 18-20
☐	11	Ex. 31-33
☐	12	Ex. 34-37
☐	13	Ex. 38-40
☐	14	Lev. 1-3
☐	15	Lev. 4-6
☐	16	Lev. 7-9
☐	17	Psalms 21-23
☐	18	Lev. 10-12
☐	19	Lev. 13-15
☐	20	Lev. 16-18
☐	21	Lev. 19-21
☐	22	Lev. 22-24
☐	23	Lev. 25-27
☐	24	Psalms 24-26
☐	25	Num. 1-3
☐	26	Num. 4-6
☐	27	Num. 7-10
☐	28	Num. 11-12

MARCH

DAY		BOOK AND CHAPTER
☐	1	Num. 13-15
☐	2	Num. 16-18
☐	3	Psalms 27-29
☐	4	Num. 19-21
☐	5	Num. 22-24
☐	6	Num. 25-27
☐	7	Num. 28-30
☐	8	Num. 31-33
☐	9	Num. 34-36
☐	10	Psalms 30-32
☐	11	Deut. 1-3
☐	12	Deut. 4-6
☐	13	Deut. 7-9
☐	14	Deut. 10-12
☐	15	Deut. 13-15
☐	16	Deut. 16-18
☐	17	Psalms 33-35
☐	18	Deut. 19-21
☐	19	Deut. 22-24
☐	20	Deut. 25-27
☐	21	Deut. 28-30
☐	22	Deut. 31-34
☐	23	Joshua 1-3
☐	24	Psalms 36-38
☐	25	Joshua 4-6
☐	26	Joshua 7-9

☐	27	Joshua 10-12
☐	28	Joshua 13-15
☐	29	Joshua 16-18
☐	30	Joshua 19-21
☐	31	Psalms 39-41

APRIL

DAY		BOOK AND CHAPTER
☐	1	Joshua 22-24
☐	2	Judges 1-3
☐	3	Judges 4-6
☐	4	Judges 7-9
☐	5	Judges 10-12
☐	6	Judges 13-15
☐	7	Psalms 42-44
☐	8	Judges 16-18
☐	9	Judges 19-21
☐	10	Ruth 1-4
☐	11	1 Sam. 1-3
☐	12	1 Sam. 4-6
☐	13	1 Sam. 7-9
☐	14	Psalms 45-47
☐	15	1 Sam. 10-13
☐	16	1 Sam. 14-16
☐	17	1 Sam. 17-19
☐	18	1 Sam. 20-22
☐	19	1 Sam. 23-25
☐	20	1 Sam. 26-28
☐	21	Psalms 48-50
☐	22	1 Sam. 29-21
☐	23	2 Sam. 1-3
☐	24	2 Sam. 4-6
☐	25	2 Sam. 7-9
☐	26	2 Sam. 10-12
☐	27	2 Sam. 13-15
☐	28	Psalms 51-53
☐	29	2 Sam. 16-18
☐	30	2 Sam. 19-21

MAY

DAY		BOOK AND CHAPTER
☐	1	2 Sam. 22-24
☐	2	1 Kings 1-4
☐	3	Prov. 1-3
☐	4	Prov. 4-6

☐	5	Psalms 54-56
☐	6	Prov. 7-9
☐	7	Prov. 10-12
☐	8	Prov. 13-15
☐	9	Prov. 16-18
☐	10	Prov. 19-21
☐	11	Prov. 22-24
☐	12	Psalms 57-59
☐	13	Prov. 25-27
☐	14	Prov. 28-31
☐	15	S. of Sol. 1-4
☐	16	S. of Sol. 5-8
☐	17	1 Kings 5-7
☐	18	1 Kings 8-11
☐	19	Psalms 60-62
☐	20	Eccl. 1-4
☐	21	Eccl. 5-8
☐	22	Eccl. 9-12
☐	23	1 Kings 12-14
☐	24	1 Kings 15-17
☐	25	1 Kings 18-20
☐	26	Psalms 63-65
☐	27	1 Kings 21, 22; 2 Kings 1
☐	28	2 Kings 2-4
☐	29	2 Kings 5-7
☐	30	2 Kings 8-10
☐	31	2 Kings 11:1-14:25

JUNE

DAY		BOOK AND CHAPTER
☐	1	Jonah
☐	2	Psalms 66-68
☐	3	2 Kings 14:26-29; Amos 1-3
☐	4	Amos 4-6
☐	5	Amos 7-9
☐	6	2 Kings 15-17
☐	7	2 Kings 18-21
☐	8	2 Kings 22-25
☐	9	Psalms 69-71
☐	10	1 Chron. 1-3
☐	11	1 Chron. 4-6
☐	12	1 Chron. 7-9
☐	13	1 Chron. 10-12
☐	14	1 Chron. 13-16
☐	15	1 Chron. 17-19
☐	16	Psalms 72-74
☐	17	1 Chron. 20-22
☐	18	1 Chron. 23-25
☐	19	1 Chron. 26-29

☐	20	2 Chron. 1-3
☐	21	2 Chron. 4-6
☐	22	2 Chron. 7-9
☐	23	Psalms 75-77
☐	24	2 Chron. 10-12
☐	25	2 Chron. 13-15
☐	26	2 Chron. 16-18
☐	27	2 Chron. 19-22
☐	28	Joel 1-3; Obadiah
☐	29	2 Chron. 23:1-26:8
☐	30	Psalms 78-80

JULY

DAY		BOOK AND CHAPTER
☐	1	Isaiah 1-3
☐	2	Isaiah 4-6; 2 Chron. 26:9-23
☐	3	2 Chron. 27-29
☐	4	2 Chron. 30-32
☐	5	Isaiah 7-9
☐	6	Isaiah 10-12
☐	7	Psalms 13-15
☐	8	Isaiah 13-15
☐	9	Isaiah 16-18
☐	10	Isaiah 19-21
☐	11	Isaiah 22-24
☐	12	Isaiah 25-27
☐	13	Isaiah 28-30
☐	14	Psalms 84-86
☐	15	Isaiah 31-33
☐	16	Isaiah 34-36
☐	17	Isaiah 37-39
☐	18	Isaiah 40-42
☐	19	Isaiah 43-45
☐	20	Isaiah 46-48
☐	21	Psalms 87-90
☐	22	Isaiah 49-51
☐	23	Isaiah 52-54
☐	24	Isaiah 55-57
☐	25	Isaiah 58-60
☐	26	Isaiah 61-63
☐	27	Isaiah 64-66
☐	28	Psalms 91-93
☐	29	Hosea 1-3
☐	30	Hosea 4-6
☐	31	Hosea 7-9

AUGUST

DAY	BOOK AND CHAPTER
☐ 1	Hosea 10-12
☐ 2	Hosea 13, 14; Micah 1
☐ 3	Micah 2-4
☐ 4	Psalms 94-96
☐ 5	Micah 5-7
☐ 6	Nahum 1-3
☐ 7	2 Chron. 33, 34; Zeph. 1
☐ 8	Zeph. 2, 3; 2 Chron. 35
☐ 9	Hab. 1-3
☐ 10	Jer. 1-3
☐ 11	Psalms 97-99
☐ 12	Jer. 4-6
☐ 13	Jer. 11, 12, 26
☐ 14	Jer. 7-9
☐ 15	Jer. 10, 14, 15
☐ 16	Jer. 16-18
☐ 17	Jer. 19, 20, 35
☐ 18	Psalms 100-102
☐ 19	Jer. 25, 36, 45
☐ 20	Jer. 46-49
☐ 21	Jer. 13, 22, 23
☐ 22	Jer. 24, 27, 28
☐ 23	Jer. 29, 50-51
☐ 24	Jer. 30-33
☐ 25	Psalms 103-105
☐ 26	Jer. 21, 34, 37
☐ 27	Jer. 38, 39, 52
☐ 28	Jer. 40-42
☐ 29	Jer. 43, 44; Lam. 1
☐ 30	Lam. 2-5
☐ 31	2 Chron. 36:1-8; Daniel 1-3

SEPTEMBER

DAY	BOOK AND CHAPTER
☐ 1	Psalms 106-108
☐ 2	Daniel 4-6
☐ 3	Daniel 7-9
☐ 4	Daniel 10-12
☐ 5	2 Chron. 36:9-21; Ezekiel 1-3
☐ 6	Ezekiel 4-6
☐ 7	Ezekiel 7-9
☐ 8	Psalms 109-111
☐ 9	Ezekiel 10-12
☐ 10	Ezekiel 13-16

☐ 11	Ezekiel 17-20
☐ 12	Ezekiel 21-24
☐ 13	Ezekiel 25-28
☐ 14	Ezekiel 29-32
☐ 15	Psalms 112-114
☐ 16	Ezekiel 33-36
☐ 17	Ezekiel 37-40
☐ 18	Ezekiel 41-44
☐ 19	Ezekiel 45-48
☐ 20	2 Chron. 36:22, 23; Ezra 1-3
☐ 21	Ezra 4; Haggai 1, 2
☐ 22	Psalms 115-117
☐ 23	Zech. 1-3
☐ 24	Zech. 4-6
☐ 25	Zech. 7-9
☐ 26	Zech. 10-12
☐ 27	Zech. 13, 14
☐ 28	Ezra 5-7
☐ 29	Psalms 118-119:16
☐ 30	Ezra 8-10

OCTOBER

DAY	BOOK AND CHAPTER
☐ 1	Esther 1-3
☐ 2	Esther 4-6
☐ 3	Esther 7-10
☐ 4	Neh. 1-3
☐ 5	Neh. 4-6
☐ 6	Psalms 119:17-72
☐ 7	Neh. 7-9
☐ 8	Neh. 10-13
☐ 9	Malachi
☐ 10	Matthew 1-3
☐ 11	Matthew 4-7
☐ 12	Matthew 8-10
☐ 13	Psalms 119:73-120
☐ 14	Matthew 11-13
☐ 15	Matthew 14-16
☐ 16	Matthew 17-19
☐ 17	Matthew 20-22
☐ 18	Matthew 23-25
☐ 19	Matthew 26-28
☐ 20	Psalms 119:121-176
☐ 21	Mark 1-4
☐ 22	Mark 5-8
☐ 23	Mark 9-12
☐ 24	Mark 13-16
☐ 25	Luke 1-4
☐ 26	Luke 5-8

☐ 27 Psalms 120-122
☐ 28 Luke 9-12
☐ 29 Luke 13-16
☐ 30 Luke 17-20
☐ 31 Luke 21-24

NOVEMBER

DAY	BOOK AND CHAPTER
☐ 1	John 1-3
☐ 2	John 4-6
☐ 3	Psalms 123-125
☐ 4	John 7-9
☐ 5	John 10-12
☐ 6	John 13-15
☐ 7	John 16-18
☐ 8	John 19-21
☐ 9	Acts 1-4
☐ 10	Psalms 126-128
☐ 11	Acts 5:1-8:3
☐ 12	Acts 8:4-11:18
☐ 13	Acts 11:19-14:28
☐ 14	James
☐ 15	Galatians
☐ 16	Acts 15-17:10
☐ 17	Psalms 129-131
☐ 18	Philippians
☐ 19	1 Thess.
☐ 20	2 Thess.; Acts 17:11;18:11
☐ 21	1 Cor. 1-3
☐ 22	1 Cor. 4-7
☐ 23	1 Cor. 8:1-11:1
☐ 24	Psalms 131-134
☐ 25	1 Cor. 11:2-14:40
☐ 26	1 Cor. 15, 16
☐ 27	2 Cor. 1-5
☐ 28	2 Cor. 6-9
☐ 29	2 Cor. 10-13
☐ 30	Acts 18:12-19:41; Eph. 1, 2

DECEMBER

DAY	BOOK AND CHAPTER
☐ 1	Psalms 135-137
☐ 2	Eph. 3-6
☐ 3	Romans 1-3
☐ 4	Romans 4-6
☐ 5	Romans 7-9
☐ 6	Romans 10-12
☐ 7	Romans 13-16
☐ 8	Psalms 138-140
☐ 9	Acts 20-22
☐ 10	Acts 23-25
☐ 11	Acts 26-28
☐ 12	Colossians
☐ 13	Heb. 1-4
☐ 14	Heb. 5-8
☐ 15	Psalms 141-144
☐ 16	Heb. 9-11
☐ 17	Heb. 12-13; Titus
☐ 18	Philemon
☐ 19	1 Tim.; 2 Tim.
☐ 20	1 Peter
☐ 21	1 John
☐ 22	Psalms 145-147
☐ 23	2 Peter; 2, 3 John; Jude
☐ 24	Rev. 1-3
☐ 25	Rev. 4-7
☐ 26	Rev. 8-10
☐ 27	Rev. 11-13
☐ 28	Rev. 14-17
☐ 29	Psalms 148-150
☐ 30	Rev. 18-20
☐ 31	Rev. 21-22

F̄

TOPICAL GUIDE TO DAILY DEVOTIONAL BIBLE READING IN A YEAR

Special Times for the Church and the Nation
Special Reading for every day of the year related to Civil Holidays, the Church Calendar and special times of the Christian Year

Publisher's note: This Bible reading schedule was prepared for use in 1991. Thus, some dates and their accompanying readings will need to be adjusted for use in other years.

Certain days of the church calendar, i.e. Christmas and Easter, have rather obvious readings. Selected civil holidays, i.e. Independence Day, suggest rather pertinent readings without great thought. Other "times of the year" have required extensive research.

We trust that these topical readings for 1991 prove helpful and meaningful to you and your family.

JANUARY

DAY   **BOOK AND CHAPTER**

A. Beginnings
New Year's Day
- ☐ 1 Gen. 1:1-31
- ☐ 2 Gen. 2:1-25
- ☐ 3 Gen. 3:1-24
- ☐ 4 John 1:1-18
- ☐ 5 Ps. 100:1-5; 101:1-8

B. Time of Epiphany
Epiphany Sunday
- ☐ 6 Eph. 3:1-13
- ☐ 7 Matt. 2:1-12
- ☐ 8 Rom. 12:1-5; Isa. 50:1-6
- ☐ 9 Luke 2:41-51
- ☐ 10 Rom. 12:6-16a; Rom. 13:8-10
- ☐ 11 John 2:1-11
- ☐ 12 Rom. 12:16c-21; Isa. 61:1-6
- ☐ 13 Matt. 8:1-13
- ☐ 14 Matt. 8:23-34

☐ 15 Col. 1:23-29; Col. 3:12-17
☐ 16 Matt. 13:24-30; John 1:29-34
☐ 17 Eccl. 12:1-8; 1 Cor. 9:24-27
☐ 18 Matt. 20:1-16
☐ 19 2 Cor. 11:19-31

C. The Sanctity of Life
Right to Life Sunday
☐ 20 Gen. 2:7; Ex. 21:22-23;
Ps. 30:1-3
☐ 21 Ps. 68:1-20
☐ 22 Ps. 104:19-30
☐ 23 Isa. 38:15-20
☐ 24 Job 27:1-6; 34:10-15
☐ 25 James 4:13-17; 1 John 3:10-15
☐ 26 John 12:23-25, 44-40; 17:2-3

D. A Time for Unity
NAE Sunday
☐ 27 1 Cor. 1:10-17
☐ 28 Rom. 12:16-18; 14:16-19; 15:4-6
☐ 29 Phil. 1:27-30; 2:1-11; 3:15-17
☐ 30 Acts 4:32-33; Ps. 133:1-3
☐ 31 1 Peter 3:8-17

FEBRUARY

DAY **BOOK AND CHAPTER**

☐ 1 John 17:1-26
☐ 2 Col. 2:1-7; 3:12-15
☐ 3 2 Chron. 30:1-12
☐ 4 1 Cor. 12:12-31
☐ 5 2 Cor. 13:7-11
☐ 6 Isa. 52:1-8
☐ 7 Eph. 4:1-16

E. A Time for Remembering Patriots
☐ 8 Ps. 85:1-13
☐ 9 Ps. 51:18-19; 122:6-9; 137:1-6
☐ 10 Judg. 5:1-23
☐ 11 2 Sam. 10:12; Neh. 1:1-11
Lincoln's Birthday
☐ 12 2 Sam. 23:3-4; Prov. 28:2, 16;
Rom. 13:1-7

F. A Time for Personal Reflection
Lent
Ash Wednesday
☐ 13 Matt. 6:5-23
☐ 14 Isa. 53:1-12
☐ 15 Isa. 55:1-9
☐ 16 Gen. 22:1-14

☐ 17 Jer. 26:1-15
☐ 18 Matt. 4:1-11
☐ 19 Zech. 9:9-12; Num. 21:4-9
☐ 20 1 Thess. 4:1-7; Heb. 9:11-15
☐ 21 Matt. 15:21-28; Phil. 2:5-11
Washington's Birthday
☐ 22 Gen. 41:33; Ex. 18:21-22;
Deut. 1:13, 16; 18-20
☐ 23 Ex. 33:12-23
☐ 24 2 Cor. 6:1-10
☐ 25 John 6:1-15
☐ 26 Eph. 5:1-14
☐ 27 Luke 11:4-28
☐ 28 John 8:46-59

MARCH

DAY **BOOK AND CHAPTER**

G. A Time for Prayer
World Day of Prayer
☐ 1 Ps. 117:1-2; 105:1-5;
Heb. 4:14-16
☐ 2 James 5:13-18; Rom. 8:18-26
☐ 3 Luke 18:1-8; Phil. 4:4-7
☐ 4 Eph. 6:10-20; Col. 4:2-6

H. A Time for Coming Together
NAE's Annual Convention
☐ 5 Ps. 19:1-11; 50:1-6
☐ 6 Matt. 28:16-20;
Acts 5:40-42; 20:22-27
☐ 7 Col. 1:15-29

Return to a Time of Prayer
☐ 8 1 Thess. 5:12-18;
Ps. 146:1-10
☐ 9 Rev. 5:8-10; 8:1-5; 14:7
☐ 10 Ps. 145:1-21
☐ 11 Eph. 3:1-21
☐ 12 Mark 9:14-29; Jude 20-23
☐ 13 Lam. 3:40-41; Luke 11:1-13
☐ 14 Ps. 148:1-14
☐ 15 Deut. 4:9, 29-31; Jer. 33:1-3
☐ 16 John 17:1-26
☐ 17 Matt. 7:7-11; 18:18-20
☐ 18 Dan. 9:5-15; Ps. 141:1-2
☐ 19 Ps. 150:1-6; Isa. 12:1-6
Spring Begins
☐ 20 Gen. 1:14; 8:22;
Song 2:11-13; Isa. 28:2-4

☐ 21   1 Kings 8:22-30; Ps. 61:1-2
☐ 22   Gen. 32:1-2, 22-31;
       Ps. 55:1-2, 16-17
☐ 23   Gen. 18:23-32

I. A Time for Celebration
Holy Week
Palm Sunday
☐ 24   Matt. 21:1-11; Mark 11:1-11;
       Luke 19:28-44; John 12:12-19
☐ 25   Matt. 21:12-46; Mark 11:12-26;
       Luke 19:45-48
☐ 26   Matt. 22:1-46; 23:1-39;
       Mark 11:27-33; 12:1-44;
       Luke 20:1-47; John 12:20-36
☐ 27   Matt. 24:1-51; 25:11-46;
       26:1-16; Mark 13:1-37;
       14:1-9; Luke 21:1-38;
       John 12:37-50
Maundy Thursday
☐ 28   Matt. 26:17-46; Mark 14:10-42;
       Luke 22:1-62; John 13:1-30
Good Friday
☐ 29   Matt. 26:47-75; 27:1-61;
       Luke 22:63-71; 23:1-49
☐ 30   Matt. 27:62-66; Luke 23:50-56;
       John 19:38-42
Easter
☐ 31   Matt. 28:1-10; Mark 16:1-11;
       Luke 24:1-12; John 20:1-18

APRIL

DAY   BOOK AND CHAPTER

J. A Time for Joy—
Remembering the Resurrection
☐ 1   Matt. 28:11-15; John 20:19-31
☐ 2   Matt. 28:16-20; John 20:1014
☐ 3   Mark 16:14-18; John 21:15-19
☐ 4   Ezek. 34:11-16; John 21:20-25
☐ 5   Luke 24:13-32
☐ 6   Luke 24:33-49
☐ 7   John 14:1-31
☐ 8   John 15:1-27
☐ 9   John 16:1-33
☐ 10   John 17:1-26
☐ 11   Acts 13:13-41
☐ 12   1 Peter 2:11-25
☐ 13   1 John 5:1-13
☐ 14   Acts 10:1-43

☐ 15   1 Cor. 15:1-19
☐ 16   1 Cor. 15:20-34
☐ 17   1 Cor. 15:35-49
☐ 18   John 21:12-22
☐ 19   Acts 2:22-36
☐ 20   Acts 17:16-34
☐ 21   Acts 26:2-23
☐ 22   Rom. 14:1-12
☐ 23   Rom. 1:1-7
☐ 24   Matt. 28:1-10
☐ 25   Matt. 28:11-20
☐ 26   Rom. 10:5-10; 2 Cor. 4:13-15
☐ 27   Matt. 12:38-45
☐ 28   John 20:11-18
☐ 29   John 20:19-29
☐ 30   John 21:1-23

MAY

DAY   BOOK AND CHAPTER

K. Another Time for Prayer
☐ 1   1 Chron. 16:7-36
       National Day of Prayer
☐ 2   2 Chron. 6:34-42; 7:12-14
☐ 3   Neh. 1:1-11
☐ 4   Neh. 4:1-9
☐ 5   Neh. 9:1-21
☐ 6   Neh. 9:22-38
☐ 7   Job 1:20-22; 17:1-9; 23:1-17
☐ 8   Job 40:1-5; 42:1-6, 12-17

L. A Time for Great Thankfulness
Ascension Day
☐ 9   Mark 16:19-20; Luke 24:50-53;
       Acts 1:1-11
☐ 10   Acts 1:12-26
☐ 11   2 Kings 2:1-15; Gen. 5:21-24

M. A Time for Showing Appreciation
Mother's Day
☐ 12   Prov. 10:1; 15:20; 31:10-31
☐ 13   Prov. 19:26-29; 20:20-22;
       23:22-25; 28:20-24
☐ 14   Prov. 29:11-15; 30:11-17
☐ 15   1 Thess. 2:7; 1 Tim. 2:9-15
☐ 16   Titus 2:3-5; 1 Peter 3:1-6
☐ 17   Rom. 16:1-7
☐ 18   Eph. 5:22-24, 33

N. A Time for Gladness
Pentecost

☐ 19 Joel 2:28-29; Acts 2:1-24
☐ 20 Acts 2:25-47
☐ 21 Isa. 57:15-21
☐ 22 1 Peter 4:7-19
☐ 23 John 3:1-21
☐ 24 Acts 8:26-40
☐ 25 Acts 10:42-48
Trinity Sunday
☐ 26 Gen. 1:26; 3:22; 1 John 4:7-21
☐ 27 Luke 16:19-31
☐ 28 Matt. 1:18, 20; 28:19;
John 16:7, 13-15
☐ 29 Rom. 1:3-4; 8:9-11, 26-27;
1 Cor. 12:3-6
Memorial Day
☐ 30 Josh. 3:1-17
☐ 31 Josh. 4:1-24

JUNE

DAY   **BOOK AND CHAPTER**

O. A Time to Look at the Nature of the Church

☐ 1 Matt. 16:13-20
☐ 2 Eph. 4:1-16
☐ 3 Col. 1:18-29
☐ 4 Eph. 3:8-21
☐ 5 Eph. 5:23-32
☐ 6 Matt. 18:15-20
☐ 7 1 Cor. 11:17-34
☐ 8 1 Cor. 5:1—6:8
☐ 9 Heb. 10:19-25
☐ 10 Acts 2:37-47
☐ 11 1 Cor. 14:26-40
☐ 12 1 Cor. 10:23-33
☐ 13 1 Cor. 12:12-31
☐ 14 Eph. 2:13-22
☐ 15 1 Peter 2:1-10
Father's Day
☐ 16 1 Tim. 2:8; 3:1-10
☐ 17 Titus 1:6-9; 2:2, 6-8
☐ 18 Eph. 5:23-33; 6:4; Col. 3:19, 21
☐ 19 Deut. 6:1-25
☐ 20 Deut. 11:13-21
Summer Begins
☐ 21 Matt. 24:32-35; Ps. 74:9-17

P. A Time to Share Our Faith
☐ 22 Luke 15:1-10
☐ 23 Luke 15:11-32

☐ 24 Rom. 10:1-17
☐ 25 1 Cor. 9:11-23
☐ 26 Col. 4:2-6
☐ 27 2 Tim. 4:1-8
☐ 28 John 4:1-42
☐ 29 Matt. 28:16-20
☐ 30 Isa. 52:7; 60:1-2

JULY

DAY   **BOOK AND CHAPTER**

☐ 1 Mark 1:14-20
☐ 2 Rom. 1:14-17; 1 Tim. 2:3-7
☐ 3 1 Thess. 2:1-9
Independence Day
☐ 4 Ex. 22:28; Acts 23:1-5
☐ 5 Ezra 6:9-10; Lev. 7:25-28
☐ 6 Eccl. 8:2-9
☐ 7 Matt. 17:24-27
☐ 8 Rom. 13:1-7
☐ 9 1 Tim. 2:1-7
☐ 10 1 Peter 2:13-20
☐ 11 Matt. 22:15-22
☐ 12 Job 34:16-20
☐ 13 Prov. 14:28, 35; 23:1-3

Q. A Time to Worship
☐ 14 1 Peter 2:1-10
☐ 15 Acts 2:37-47
☐ 16 Matt. 4:1-11
☐ 17 Acts 14:8-18
☐ 18 John 4:19-25
☐ 19 Rev. 4:1-11
☐ 20 Rev. 5:6-14
☐ 21 Isa. 6:1-7
☐ 22 Ps. 96:1-13
☐ 23 Deut. 6:4-17
☐ 24 Ps. 84:1-12
☐ 25 Isa. 29:11-24
☐ 26 Heb. 10:19-25

R. A Time to Appreciate the Nature of Jesus Christ
☐ 27 Luke 1:26-38
☐ 28 Matt. 3:1-17
☐ 29 John 3:13-21
☐ 30 John 6:52-65
☐ 31 John 8:21-30, 53-58

AUGUST

DAY	BOOK AND CHAPTER
☐ 1	John 5:16-47
☐ 2	Acts 2:22-36
☐ 3	John 1:1-18
☐ 4	Gal. 4:1-7
☐ 5	Eph. 1:3-23
	Transfiguration Sunday
☐ 6	Matt. 17:2-9; Mark 9:2-10
☐ 7	Luke 9:29-36; 2 Peter 1:16-18
☐ 8	Col. 1:15-20; 2:9-12
☐ 9	Matt. 26:57-68
☐ 10	Acts 13:16-41
☐ 11	Isa. 7:14; 9:2-7
☐ 12	Rev. 4:1-11

S. A Time to Recognize the Nature of the Atonement

☐ 13	2 Cor. 5:11-21
☐ 14	Heb. 9:11-28
☐ 15	1 Peter 1:8-19
☐ 16	1 Peter 2:21-25
☐ 17	Phil. 2:5-11
☐ 18	Heb. 12:1-3
☐ 19	Rom. 5:6-21
☐ 20	Heb. 2:5-18
☐ 21	1 John 1:5–2:2
☐ 22	1 John 4:7-17
☐ 23	John 1:26-36
☐ 24	Gal. 3:1-14
☐ 25	Matt. 20:20-28
☐ 26	1 Tim. 2:1-7
☐ 27	John 10:7-18
☐ 28	Rom. 3:21-30
☐ 29	Lev. 16:1-19
☐ 30	Lev. 16:20-34
☐ 31	Lev. 23:26-32

SEPTEMBER

DAY	BOOK AND CHAPTER
☐ 1	Num. 29:7-11
	Labor Day
☐ 2	Gen. 2:15-17; 3:1-19
☐ 3	Ex. 23:10-12; 35:2-3; Prov. 12:11-27
☐ 4	Prov. 13:4-11; 14:15-23
☐ 5	Prov. 19:22-24; 20:1-13; 28:18-19
☐ 6	Eccl. 2:10-22

☐ 7	Eccl. 9:1-10; 11:4-6
☐ 8	Eccl. 4:17-28
☐ 9	1 Thess. 4:9-12; 2 Thess. 3:6-12
☐ 10	1 Tim. 5:1-8; James 5:1-4
☐ 11	Deut. 24:14-22; 25:1-4
☐ 12	Eccl. 5:1-12
☐ 13	Jer. 22:13-17
☐ 14	Mal. 3:1-10
☐ 15	Matt. 20:1-15
☐ 16	Luke 20:17-35
☐ 17	Matt. 21:28-41
☐ 18	John 10:1-13
☐ 19	Ruth 2:1-12
☐ 20	Luke 12:35-48
☐ 21	Luke 16:1-13
☐ 22	Gal. 6:1-10
	Autumn
☐ 23	Prov. 6:6-8; 10:1-5; 27:25-27

T. A Time to Consider the Final Judgment

☐ 24	Matt. 25:31-46
☐ 25	John 5:19-29
☐ 26	Rom. 2:1-16
☐ 27	Heb. 9:27-28; 10:26-31
☐ 28	2 Peter 3:1-10
☐ 29	Rev. 20:11-15
☐ 30	Ps. 50:1-6

OCTOBER

DAY	BOOK AND CHAPTER
☐ 1	Matt. 12:30-37
☐ 2	Acts 10:38-43
☐ 3	1 Cor. 4:1-4; 2 Cor. 5:9-10
☐ 4	Matt. 13:36-50
☐ 5	Luke 12:41-48
	World Communion Sunday
☐ 6	1 Cor. 11:17-34
☐ 7	1 Cor. 10:14-31
☐ 8	John 14:1-18
☐ 9	1 Cor. 12:12-31
☐ 10	1 Cor. 13:1-13; Heb. 10:24-25
☐ 11	1 John 11:1-10; Acts 2:42-47
☐ 12	Acts 4:32-37
☐ 13	1 Cor. 12:4-31
☐ 14	Eph. 4:1-16
☐ 15	Rom. 12:1-8
☐ 16	1 Peter 4:1-11

U. A Time to Think About the Trinity

☐ 17	John 14:25-31; 15:27-27

☐ 18   Gal. 4:1-7
☐ 19   Matt. 3:13-17
☐ 20   Matt. 28:16-20
☐ 21   1 Cor. 12:4-11
☐ 22   2 Cor. 13:11-14
☐ 23   1 Peter 1:1-12
☐ 24   Gen. 1:26-27; 11:5-9
☐ 25   Acts 5:1-11
☐ 26   Luke 1:26-36
         Reformation Sunday
☐ 27   Rom. 1:1-17
☐ 28   Rom. 3:1-31
☐ 29   Rom. 4:1-25
☐   Rom. 5:1-21
         Reformation Day
☐ 31   Rom. 8:1-30

NOVEMBER

DAY	BOOK AND CHAPTER
☐ 1	Ps. 116:7-16
☐ 2	1 Cor. 15:20-25, 35-58

V. A Time to Please God

☐ 3	1 Thess. 4:1-12
☐ 4	2 Cor. 5:6-10
☐ 5	Rom. 14:13-23
☐ 6	Eph. 5:1-21
☐ 7	Col. 1:9-14
☐ 8	Rom. 6:1-14
☐ 9	Rom. 6:15-23

Stewardship Day

☐ 10	Luke 19:11-27
☐ 11	Acts 4:31-37
☐ 12	Gen. 47:13-26
☐ 13	Matt. 19:16-26
☐ 14	Matt. 25:1-13
☐ 15	Matt. 25:14-30
☐ 16	Mal. 3:6-18
☐ 17	James 5:1-6
☐ 18	John 4:31-38
☐ 19	2 Cor. 6:1-10
☐ 20	Phil. 1:12-30
☐ 21	James 4:7-17
☐ 22	Eph. 5:15-21
☐ 23	Col. 4:2-6

Thanksgiving Sunday

☐ 24	Luke 17:11-19
☐ 25	2 Cor. 9:6-15
☐ 26	Phil. 1:3-11

☐ 27   1 Tim. 4:1-10
         Thanksgiving Day
☐ 28   Ps. 75:1-10
☐ 29   Ps. 107:1-43
☐ 30   Ps. 136:1-26

DECEMBER

DAY	BOOK AND CHAPTER

First Sunday in Advent

☐ 1	John 1:1-5; Gen. 3:14-15
☐ 2	Zech. 9:9-10; 11:12-13
☐ 3	Isa. 2:2-5; 7:10-16; 8:11-18
☐ 4	Isa. 9:1-17
☐ 5	Isa. 11:1-10
☐ 6	Isa. 35:1-10
☐ 7	Isa. 40:1-11
☐ 8	Isa. 40:12-31
☐ 9	Isa. 42:1-13, 18-21
☐ 10	Isa. 45:1-25
☐ 11	Isa. 53:1-13
☐ 12	Jer. 31:31-40
☐ 13	Ps. 2:1-12
☐ 14	Ps. 22:1-31
☐ 15	Ps. 45:1-7
☐ 16	Ps. 67:1-7
☐ 17	Ps. 72:1-19
☐ 18	Dan. 7:9-14, 27; Mal. 4:1-6
☐ 19	Matt. 1:1-7
☐ 20	Luke 1:1-25
☐ 21	Luke 1:25-38
☐ 22	Luke 1:39-56
☐ 23	Luke 1:57-66
☐ 24	Luke 1:57-60

Christmas Day

☐ 25	Luke 2:1-20; Matt. 1:18-25
☐ 26	Luke 2:21-38
☐ 27	Matt. 2:2-12
☐ 28	Matt. 2:13-18; 1 John 5:1-3, 18-21
☐ 29	Luke 2:39-52
☐ 30	Matt. 2:19-23; Phil. 2:5-11
☐ 31	Luke 3:1-22

G

SELECTED PROVERBS REGARDING THE TONGUE

10:11 — "The mouth of the righteous is a fountain of life, but violence overwhelms the mouth of the widked."

10:18 — "He who conceals his hatred has lying lips, and whoever spreads slander is a fool."

10:19 — "When words are many, sin is not absent, but he who holds his tongue is wise."

10:20 — "The tongue of the righteous is choice silver, but the heart of the wicked is of little value."

10:21 — "The lips of the righteous nourish many, but fools die for lack of judgment."

10:31 — "The mouth of the righteous brings forth wisdom, but a perverse tongue will be cut out."

10:32 — "The lips of the righteous know what is fitting, but the mouth of the wicked only what is perverse."

11:9 — "With his mouth the godless destroys his neighbor, but through knowledge the righteous escape."

11:11 — "Through the blessing of the upright a city is exalted, but by the mouth of the wicked it is destroyed."

11:12 — "A man who lacks judgment derides his neighbor, but a man of understanding holds his tongue."

11:13 — "A gossip betrays a confidence, but a trustworthy man keeps a secret."

12:6 — "The words of the wicked lie in wait for blood, but the speech of the upright rescues them."

12:19 — "Truthful lips endure forever, but a lying tongue lasts only a moment."

12:22 — "The Lord detests lying lips, but he delights in men who are truthful."

13:3 — "He who guards his lips guards his soul, but he who speaks rashly will come to ruin."

14:3 — "A fool's talk brings a rod to his back, but the lips of the wise protect them."

15:1 — "A gentle answer turns away wrath, but a harsh word stirs up anger."

15:2 — "The tongue of the wise commends knowledge, but the mouth of the fool gushes folly."

15:4 — "The tongue that brings healing is a tree of life, but a deceitful tongue crushes the spirit."

15:7 — "The lips of the wise spread knowledge; not so the hearts of fools."

15:14 — "The discerning heart seeks knowledge, but the mouth of a fool feeds on folly."

15:23 — "A man finds joy in giving an apt reply — and how good is a timely word?"

15:28 — "The heart of the righteous weighs its answers, but the mouth of the wicked gushes evil."

16:1 — "To man belong the plans of the heart, but from the Lord comes the reply of the tongue."

16:13 — "Kings take pleasure in honest lips; they value a man who speaks the truth."

16:23 — "A wise man's heart guides his mouth, and his lips promote instruction."

16:24 — "Pleasant words are a honeycomb, sweet to the soul and healing to the bones."

16:27 — "A scoundrel plots evil, and his speech is like a scorching fire."

16:28 — "A perverse man stirs up dissension, and a gossip separates close friends."

17:4 — "A wicked man listens to evil lips; a liar pays attention to a malicious tongue."

17:7 — "Arrogant lips are unsuited to a fool — how much worse lying lips to a ruler!"

17:9 — "He who covers over an offense promotes love, but whoever repeats the matter separates close friends."

17:20 — "A man of perverse heart does not prosper; he whose tongue is deceitful falls into trouble."

17:27 — "A man of knowledge uses words with restraint, and a man of understanding is even-tempered."

17:28 — "Even a fool is thought wise if he keeps silent, and discerning if he holds his tongue."

18:2 — "A fool finds no pleasure in understanding but delights in airing his own opinions."

18:4 — "The words of a man's mouth are deep waters, but the fountain of wisdom is a bubbling brook."

18:6 — "A fool's lips bring him strife, and his mouth invites a beating."

18:7 — "A fool's mouth is his undoing, and his lips are a snare to his soul."

18:8 — "The words of a gossip are like choice morsels; they go down to a man's inmost parts."

18:13 — "He who answers before listening — that is his folly and his shame."

18:20 — "From the fruit of his mouth a man's stomach is filled; with the harvest from his lips he is satisfied."

18:21 — "The tongue has the power of life and death, and those who love it will eat its fruit."

19:1 — "Better a poor man whose walk is blameless than a fool whose lips are perverse."

19:5 — "A false witness will not go unpunished, and he who pours out lies will not go free."

19:28 — "A corrupt witness mocks at justice, and the mouth of the wicked gulps down evil."

20:15 — "Gold there is, and rubies in abundance, but lips that speak knowledge are a rare jewel."

20:19 — "A gossip betrays a confidence; so avoid a man who talks too much."

21:6 — "A fortune made by a lying tongue is a fleeting vapor and a deadly snare."

21:23 — "He who guards his mouth and his tongue keeps himself from calamity."

21:28 — "A false witness will perish, and whoever listens to him will be destroyed forever."

23:9 — "Do not speak to a fool, for he will scorn the wisdom of your words."

24:1, 2 — "Do not envy wicked men, do not desire their company; for their hearts plot violence, and their lips talk about making trouble."

24:26 — "An honest answer is like a kiss on the lips."

24:28 — "Do not testify against your neighbor without cause, or use your lips to deceive."

25:11 — "A word aptly spoken is like apples of gold in settings of silver."

25:15 — "Through patience a ruler can be persuaded, and a gentle tongue can break a bone."

25:23 — "As a north wind brings rain, so a sly tongue brings angry looks."

26:2 — "Like a fluttering sparrow or a darting swallow, an undeserved curse does not come to rest."

26:7 — "Like a lame man's legs that hang limp is a proverb in the mouth of a fool."

26:9 — "Like a thornbush in a drunkard's hand is a proverb in the mouth of a fool."

26:20 — "Without wood a fire goes out; without gossip a quarrel dies down."

26:22 — "The words of a gossip are like choice morsels; they go down to a man's inmost parts."

26:23 — "Like a coating of glaze over earthenware are fervent lips with an evil heart."

26:24, 25 — "A malicious man disguises himself with his lips, but in his heart he harbors deceit. Though his speech is charming, do not believe him, for seven abominations fill his heart."

29:20 — "Do you see a man who speaks in haste? There is more hope for a fool than for him."

30:11, 12 — "There are those who curse their fathers and do not bless their mothers; those who are pure in their own eyes and yet are not cleansed of their filth."

31:26 — "She speaks with wisdom, and faithful instruction is on her tongue."

H

HYMNS FOR PERSONAL ADORATION AND PRAISE

The following hymns are particularly suitable for singing to the Lord because they have wonderful texts and are, for the most part, in the first person singular. This selection is culled from *Hymns for the Living Church*, edited by Don Hustad, and published by Hope Publishing (Carol Stream, IL), 1981.

122	"Of the Father's Love Begotten"	Aurelius C. Prudentius
131	"All Glory, Laud and Honor"	Theodulph of Orleans
136	"O Sacred Head, Now Wounded"	Attr. to Bernard of Clairvaux
140	"In the Cross of Christ I Glory"	John Bowring
148	"When I Survey the Wondrous Cross"	Isaac Watts
149	"Rock of Ages, Cleft for Me"	Augustus M. Toplady
156	"Alas! And Did My Savior Bleed?"	Isaac Watts
159	"Jesus Lives and So Shall I"	Christian F. Gellert
187	"Breathe on Me, Breath of God"	Edwin Hatch
194	"Holy Spirit, Light Divine"	Andrew Reed
203	"I Love Thy Kingdom, Lord"	Timothy Dwight
220	"Break Thou the Bread of Life"	Mary A. Lathbury
229	"O the Deep, Deep Love of Jesus"	S. Trevor Francis
242	"Not What These Hands Have Done"	Horatius Bonar
246	"Jesus, Lover of My Soul"	Charles Wesley
248	"And Can It Be That I Should Gain?"	Charles Wesley
260	"Just As I Am, Without One Plea"	Charlotte Elliott
288	"Amazing Grace! How Sweet the Sound"	John Newton
308	"My Hope Is in the Lord"	Norman J. Clayton
344	"Be Thou My Vision"	Irish Hymn
349	"May the Mind of Christ My Savior"	Kate B. Wilkinson
359	"More Love to Thee, O Christ"	Elizabeth P. Prentiss
360	"Speak, Lord, in the Stillness"	E. May Grimes
384	"All for Jesus! All for Jesus! "	Mary D. James
401	"When Peace Like a River Attendeth"	Horatio G. Spafford
438	"Teach Me to Pray, Lord"	Albert S. Reitz
448	"Guide Me, O Thou Great Jehovah"	William Williams
571	"Thanks to God for My Redeemer"	August L. Storm

I

CHORUSES AND SCRIPTURE SONGS FOR PERSONAL ADORATION AND PRAISE

Most of the following selections are excellent for personal devotions because they are in the first person singular. All can he found in *Maranatha! Music Praise Chorus Book* (P.O. Box 1396, Costa Mesa, California, 92626). Distributed by Word, Inc.

J

PRAISE PSALMS ESPECIALLY APPROPRIATE FOR PERSONAL WORSHIP

Psalm 8
Psalm 9:1, 2
Psalm 16:7-11
Psalm 18:1-3
Psalm 19
Psalm 23
Psalm 24
Psalm 29
Psalm 33
Psalm 34
Psalm 40:1-5
Psalm 46
Psalm 47
Psalm 63:1-7
Psalm 65
Psalm 66:1-8

Psalm 67
Psalm 68:4-6, 32-35
Psalm 72:18, 19
Psalm 84
Psalm 89:1, 2
Psalm 91
Psalm 92:1-5
Psalm 93
Psalm 95:1-7
Psalm 96
Psalm 97
Psalm 98
Psalm 99
Psalm 100
Psalm 103
Psalm 104

Psalm 105:1-6
Psalm 108:1-6
Psalm 111
Psalm 113
Psalm 115
Psalm 116
Psalm 117
Psalm 118
Psalm 126
Psalm 134
Psalm 135
Psalm 136
Psalm 138
Psalm 144:1-10

NOTES

CHAPTER ONE: *Discipline for Godliness*

1. Mike Singletary with Armen Keteyian, *Calling the Shots* (Chicago/New York: Contemporary Books, 1986), p. 57.
2. Paul Johnson, *Intellectuals* (New York: Harper & Row, 1988), pp. 168, 169.
3. Leland Ryken, *The Liberated Imagination* (Portland: Multnomah, 1989), p. 76.
4. *MD*, "Scriveners' Stances," Vol. 13, No. 7 (July 1969), pp. 245-254.
5. Ryken, *The Liberated Imagination*, p. 76.
6. Lane T. Dennis, ed., *Letters of Francis Schaeffer* (Wheaton, IL: Crossway Books, 1985), pp. 93, 94.
7. William Manchester, *The Last Lion: Winston Spencer Churchill; Visions of Glory: 1874-1932* (Boston: Little, Brown and Company, 1983), pp. 32, 33.
8. Gerhard Kittle, ed., *Theological Dictionary of the New Testament*, Vol. 1 (Grand Rapids, MI: Eerdmans, 1968), p. 775.
9. Personal correspondence with Harold Smith, executive editor of *Marriage Partnership* magazine, February 1, 1991.
10. Bill Hendricks of the Christian Booksellers Association reported on February 28, 1991 that a recent survey taken in seven Christian bookstores in different parts of the country revealed that of those customers buying Christian literature three out of four buyers are women, the average age is thirty-five years, and 70 percent of customers are married. The survey also indicated that just under half of the total customers (married and unmarried) have children at home, the average income is $32,000 per household, the amount spent per visit averages $15, and 60 percent of the customers attend church more than once a week.
11. *Ibid.*
12. Gallup Poll, *Emerging Trends*, a publication of Princeton Religion Research Center.
13. *Leadership*, Winter 1991, Vol. 12, No. 1, p. 17.
14. *Ibid.*, p. 18.

CHAPTER TWO: *Discipline of Purity*

1. Barbara Lippert, "Talk on the Wild Side," *Chicago Tribune*, September 3, 1990.
2. Robert H. Bork, *The Tempting of America* (New York: The Free Press, 1990), p. 212.
3. "How Common Is Pastoral Indiscretion?," *Leadership*, Winter 1988, p. 12, says:

   The survey probed the frequency of behavior that pastors themselves feel is inappropriate. *Since you have been in local church ministry, have you ever done anything with someone (not your spouse) that you feel was sexually inappropriate?*

The responses: 23 percent yes; 77 percent no. The "inappropriate" behavior was left undefined — possibly ranging from unguarded words to flirtation to adultery. Subsequent questions were more specific. *Have you ever had sexual intercourse with someone other than your spouse since you have been in local-church ministry?* Yes: 12 percent. No: 88 percent. And of that 88 percent, many indicated their purity had not come easily.

4. *Ibid.*:

To lend some perspective to these figures, CTi researchers also surveyed almost one thousand subscribers of *Christianity Today* magazine who are *not* pastors. Incidences of immorality were nearly double: 45 percent indicated having done something they considered sexually inappropriate, 23 percent said they had had extramarital intercourse, and 28 percent said they had engaged in other forms of extramarital sexual contact.

5. Dietrich Bonhoeffer, *Temptation* (London: SCM Press Ltd., 1961), p. 33.
6. J. Allan Peterson, *The Myth of the Greener Grass* (Wheaton, IL: Tyndale House, 1983), p. 29.
7. J. Oswald Sanders, *Bible Men of Faith* (Chicago: Moody Press, 1974), p. 13.
8. Leon Morris, *The First and Second Epistles to the Thessalonians* (Grand Rapids, MI: Eerdmans, 1959), p. 128.
9. Jerry B. Jenkins, "How to Love Your Marriage Enough to Protect It," *Marriage Partnership*, Summer 1990, pp. 16, 17, who suggests the four hedges which follow. See also his book *Hedges* (Brentwood, TN: Wolgemuth & Hyatt, 1989), pp. 75-130.

CHAPTER THREE: *Discipline of Marriage*

1. Mike Mason, *The Mystery of Marriage* (Portland: Multnomah, 1985), p. 52.
2. George Gilder, "Taming the Barbarians," in *Men and Marriage* (Gretna, LA: Pelican Publishing House, 1986), pp. 39-47.
3. Mason, *The Mystery of Marriage*, pp. 163, 164.
4. N. G. L. Hammond and H. H. Scullard, eds., *The Oxford Classical Dictionary* (London: Oxford University Press, 1978), p. 722.
5. William Shakespeare, *Merchant of Venice*, II, vi, 57.

> Lord. Beshrew me but I love her heartily;
> For she is wise, if I can judge of her,
> and fair she is, if that mine eyes be true,
> And true she is, as she hath proved herself,
> And therefore, like herself, wise, fair, and true,
> Shall she be placed in my constant soul.

6. Mason, *The Mystery of Marriage*, p. 36.
7. Robert Seizer, *Mortal Lessons: Notes on the Art of Surgery* (New York: Simon and Schuster, 1976), pp. 45, 46.
8. Walter Trobisch, *The Complete Works of Walter Trobisch* (Downers Grove, IL: InterVarsity Press, 1987), quoted in *Marriage Partnership*, Winter 1989, p. 17.
9. William Alan Sadler, Jr., ed., *Master Sermons Through the Ages* (New York: Harper & Row, 1963), p. 116.
10. Conversation with Harold Smith, editor of *Marriage Partnership*, February 19, 1991.

11. Eugene H. Peterson, *Working the Angles* (Grand Rapids, MI: Eerdmans, 1989), p. 62.
12. Howard Hendricks made this statement in a lecture delivered at College Church in Wheaton, June 1984.
13. James Humes, *Churchill, Speaker of the Century* (Briarcliff Manor, NY: Stein and Day, Scarborough House, 1980), p. 291.
14. Dante Alighieri, *The Inferno*, trans. John Ciardi (New York: New American Library, 1954), p. 42 , quoting Canto III, which reads,

> I am the way into the city of woe.
> I am the way to a forsaken people.
> I am the way into eternal sorrow.
> Sacred justice moved my architect.
> I was raised here by divine omnipotence,
> Primordial love and ultimate intellect.
> Only those elements time cannot wear
> Were made before me, and beyond time I stand.
> Abandon all hope all ye who enter here.

15. Jeanette Lauer and Robert Lauer, "Marriages Made to Last," *Psychology Today*, June 1985, p. 26.

CHAPTER FOUR: *Discipline of Fatherhood*

1. Lance Morrow, *The Chief, A Memoir of Fathers and Sons* (New York: Macmillan, 1984), pp. 6, 7.
2. Elizabeth R. Moberly, *Homosexuality: A New Christian Ethic* (Cambridge: James Clarke & Co., 1986), p. 2 writes:

> From amidst a welter of details, one constant underlying principle suggests itself: . . . the homosexual deficit in the relationship with the parent *of the same sex*; and that there is a corresponding drive to make good this deficit — through the medium of same-sex, or 'homosexual', relationships.

3. William Manchester, *The Last Lion: Winston Spencer Churchill; Visions of Glory: 1874-1932* (Boston: Little, Brown and Company, 1983), pp. 187, 188, quoting Churchill:

> I would far rather have been apprenticed as a bricklayer's mate, or run errands as a messenger boy, or helped my father to dress the front windows of a grocer's shop. It would have been real; it would have been natural; it would have taught me more; and I should have got to know my father, which would have been a joy to me.

4. Peter T. O'Brien, *Colossians, Philemon*, Word Biblical Commentary, Vol. 44 (Waco, TX: Word, 1982), p. 225.
5. *Calvin's Commentaries: The Epistles of Paul the Apostle to the Galatians, Ephesians, Philippians and Colossians*, trans. T. H. L. Parker (Grand Rapids, MI: Eerdmans, 1974), p. 213.
6. Elton Trueblood and Pauline Trueblood, *The Recovery of Family Life* (New York: Harper & Brothers, 1953), p. 94.
7. James Dobson, *Hide or Seek* (Old Tappan, NJ: Revell, 1974), pp. 82, 83, who quotes Dr. Stanley Coopersmith, associate professor of psychology at the University of California, who surveyed 1,738 normal middle-class boys and their families, beginning in the preadolescent period and following them through to

young manhood. After determining the boys with the best self-esteem, he then compared their homes and childhood influences with those boys having a lower sense of self-esteem. He found three important characteristics which distinguished them. The second was as follows:

2. The high-esteem group came from homes where parents had been significantly more strict in their approach to discipline. By contrast, the parents of the low-esteem group had created insecurity and dependence by their permissiveness. Furthermore, the most successful and independent young men during the latter period of the study were found to have come from homes that demanded the strictest accountability and responsibility. And as could have been predicted, the family ties remained the strongest . . . in the homes where discipline and self-control had been a way of life.

8. Dorothy Walsorth, "General of the Army: Evangeline Booth," *Reader's Digest*, August 1947, p. 37.

CHAPTER FIVE: *Discipline of Friendship*

1. James Wright, *Above the River: The Complete Poems* (Hanover, NH/New York: Wesleyan University Press/Farrar, Straus & Giroux, 1990), p. 122.

> There is this cave
> In the air behind my body
> That nobody is going to touch
> A cloister, a silence
> Closing around a blossom of fire
> When I stand upright in the wind,
> My bones turn to dark emeralds.

2. Alan Loy McGinnis, *The Friendship Factor* (Minneapolis: Augsburg, 1979), p. 11.
3. Harold B. Smith, "Best Friend," *Marriage Partnership*, Summer 1988, p. 126.
4. C. F. Keil and F. Delitzsch, *Biblical Commentary on the Books of Samuel* (Grand Rapids, MI: Eerdmans, 1967), p. 187.
5. McGinnis, *The Friendship Factor*, pp. 60, 61.
6. C. S. Lewis, *The Four Loves* (New York: Harcourt, Brace, Jovanovich, 1960), p. 126.

CHAPTER SIX: *Discipline of Mind*

1. Charles Malik, *The Two Tasks* (Grand Rapids, MI: Eerdmans, 1980), p. 32.
2. Harry Blamires, *The Christian Mind* (Ann Arbor, MI: Servant Books, 1978), pp. 3, 4.
3. Harry Blamires, *Recovering the Christian Mind* (Downers Grove, IL: InterVarsity Press, 1988), p. 9.
4. Charles Colson, *Who Speaks for God?* (Wheaton, IL: Crossway Books, 1985), pp. 129, 130.
5. *Television* (Northbrook, IL: Nielsen Report, 1986), pp. 6-8.
6. George Barna and William Paul McKay, *Vital Signs* (Wheaton, IL: Crossway Books, 1984), p. 51.
7. Neil Postman, "TV's 'Disastrous' Impact on Children," *U.S. News and World Report*, January 19, 1981, p. 43.
8. *Ibid.*, p. 44.
9. *Ibid.*, p. 45.

10. Barna and McKay, *Vital Signs*, p. 56, who reference Linda Lichter, S. Robert Lichter, Stanley Rothman, "Hollywood and America: The Odd Couple," *Public Opinion*, January 1983, pp. 54-58.
11. A. T. Robertson, *Paul's Joy in Christ* (Grand Rapids, MI: Baker, 1979), p. 242.
12. Personal correspondence with retired Air Force Colonel William Waldrop, February 1991.
13. Dennis Prager, "A Civilization That Believes in Nothing," *The Door*, November/December 1990, p. 15.
14. Bill Hendricks, Christian Booksellers Association, February 28, 1991, regarding recent survey taken in seven Christian bookstores in different parts of the country.

CHAPTER SEVEN: Discipline of Devotion

1. E. Stanley Jones, *A Song of Ascents* (Nashville: Abingdon, 1979), p. 383.
2. Dallas Willard, *The Spirit of the Disciplines* (San Francisco: Harper & Row, 1988), p. 186.
3. George Gallup, Jr. and Sarah Jones, *100 Questions and Answers: Religion in America* (Princeton, NJ: Princeton Religion Research Center, 1989), p. 39 says: "Most apt to cite the importance of daily prayer are women (82 percent)," and "Groups less inclined to stress daily prayer are men (69 percent)."
4. Eugene Peterson, *Working the Angles* (Grand Rapids, MI: Eerdmans, 1989), p. 70.
5. *Ibid.*
6. Edmund P. Clowney, *CM* Christian Meditation* (Nutley, NJ: Craig Press, 1978), p. 13.
7. C. H. Spurgeon, *The Treasury of David*, Vol. 1 (London: Passemore and Alabaster, 1884), p. 6.
8. C. S. Lewis, *Letters to Malcolm: Chiefly on Prayer* (New York: Harcourt, Brace & World), p. 22.
9. George Arthur Buttrick, ed., *The Interpreter's Bible*, Vol. 8 (New York: Abingdon Press, 1952), p. 725, quotes Fenelon, *Spiritual Letters to Man*, Letter LXXXVII, "To the Vidame D'Amiens: On Prayer and Meditation." See also Letter XXIV, "To One Who Had Recently Turned to God."
10. Roland Bainton, *Here I Stand* (Nashville: Abingdon, 1950), p. 41.
11. H. G. Haile, *Luther, An Experiment in Biography* (Garden City, NY: Doubleday, 1980), p. 56.
12. Annie Dillard, *Pilgrim at Tinker Creek* (New York: Bantam, 1978), p. 35.
13. C. S. Lewis, "Footnote to All Prayers," in *Poems* (New York/London: Harcourt Brace Jovanovich, 1977), p. 129.
14. A. W. Tozer, *The Knowledge of the Holy* (New York: Harper & Row, 1961), p. 128.
15. John Piper, *Desiring God* (Portland: Multnomah, 1986), p. 145, who quotes "Personal Narrative," from *Jonathan Edwards*, eds. C. H. Faust and T. H. Johnson, (New York: Hill and Wang, 1962), p. 61.
16. Peterson, *Working the Angles*, pp. 35, 36.
17. Richard J. Foster, *Celebration of Discipline* (New York: Harper & Row, 1978), p. 106.

CHAPTER EIGHT: Discipline of Prayer

1. E. M. Bounds, *The Essentials of Prayer* (Grand Rapids, MI: Baker, 1979), p. 93.
2. John Bunyan, *The Pilgrim's Progress* (Philadelphia: Universal Book and Bible House, 1935), p. 66:

> About the midst of this valley I perceived the mouth of hell to be, and it stood also hard by the wayside. Now thought Christian, what shall I do? And ever and anon the flame and smoke would come out in such abundance, with sparks and hideous noises (things that cared not for Christian's sword, as did Apollyon before), that he was forced to put up his sword, and betake himself to another weapon, called "All-Prayer."

3. J. Oswald Sanders, *Spiritual Leadership* (Chicago: Moody Press, 1978), p. 83.
4. John Bunyan, Bedford Prison, 1662.
5. Thomas Kelly, *Testament of Devotion* (New York: Harper, 1941), p. 35.
6. Brother Lawrence, *The Practice of the Presence of God* (New York: Revell, 1958), pp. 30, 31.
7. John Wesley, *Works*, VIII (Grand Rapids, MI: Zondervan, 1959), p. 343.
8. Alfred Lord Tennyson, "The Passing of Arthur," in *The Idylls of the King*, 1:26, quoted in *The Oxford Dictionary of Quotations*, p. 535.
9. Michael Mott, *The Seven Mountains of Thomas Merton* (Boston: Houghton Mifflin, 1984), p. 216.
10. H. G. Haile, *Luther, An Experiment in Biography* (Garden City, NY: Doubleday, 1980), p. 56.
11. Elisabeth Elliot, *Notes on Prayer* (Wheaton, IL: Good News Publishers, 1982), writes:

> People who ski, I suppose, are people who happen to like skiing, who have time for skiing, who can afford to ski, and who are good at skiing. Recently I found that I often treat prayer as though it were a sport like skiing — something you do if you can afford the trouble, something you do if you are good at it.

12. Excerpted from the author's personal correspondence with J. Sidlow Baxter, September 8, 1987.

CHAPTER NINE: *Discipline of Worship*

1. Paul Seabury, "Trendier Than Thou, the Many Temptations of the Episcopal Church," *Harper's Magazine*, October 1978, Vol. 257, No. 1541, pp. 39-52.
2. *Ibid.*
3. Robert G. Rayburn, *O Come, Let Us Worship* (Grand Rapids, MI: Baker, 1984), p. 15:

> Nowhere in all the Scriptures do we read of God's seeking anything else from the child of God. One often hears that Christians are "saved to serve," and there is a limited sense in which this is true, for throughout eternity as well as during our earthly life it will be our joy and privilege to serve the Lord God. But this heavenly service will itself be primarily worship (see Heb. 9:14; 12:28; Rev. 22:3). Nowhere in the Bible are we told that the Lord seeks our service. It is not servants He seeks, but true worshipers.

4. A. J. Gordon, *How Christ Came to Church, The Pastor's Dream* (Philadelphia: American Baptist Publication Society, 1895), pp. 28-30.
5. The following pamphlets are available from Chapel of the Air: #7245, *Getting Ready for Sunday* by David and Karen Mains; #7451, *Rules for the Sunday Search* by David R. Mains; #7454, *Preparation for Sunday*; #7462, *The Sunday Search: A Guide to Better Church Experiences* by Steve Bell.
6. J. I. Packer, *A Quest for Godliness* (Wheaton, IL: Crossway Books, 1990), p. 257.
7. Rayburn, *O Come, Let Us Worship*, pp. 29, 30.

8. Annie Dillard, *Teaching a Stone to Talk* (New York: Harper & Row, 1982), pp. 40, 41.

9. Eugene H. Peterson, *A Long Obedience in the Same Direction* (Downers Grove, IL: InterVarsity Press, 1980), p. 49.

10. Lawrence C. Roff, *Let Us Sing* (Norcross, GA: Great Commission Publications, 1991), p. 27.

11. Packer, *A Quest for Godliness*, p. 254.

12. *Preparation for Sunday.*

13. Peterson, *A Long Obedience in the Same Direction*, p. 50.

CHAPTER TEN: *Discipline of Integrity*

1. James Patterson and Peter Kim, *The Day America Told the Truth* (New York: Prentice Hall, 1991), pp. 200, 201, 45, 48, 136, 154, 155, 65, 66.

2. Robert A. Caro, *The Years of Lyndon Johnson: Means of Ascent* (New York: Alfred A. Knopf, 1990), pp. 46-53.

3. Thomas Mallon, *Stolen Words: Forays into the Origin and Ravages of Plagiarism* (New York: Penguin Books, 1989), p. 90.

4. Doug Sherman and William Hendricks, *Keeping Your Ethical Edge Sharp* (Colorado Springs, CO: NavPress, 1990), p. 25, quoting from the *Wall Street Journal*, October 31, 1989, p. 33.

5. Patterson and Kim, *The Day America Told the Truth*, pp. 166, 167.

6. Sherman and Hendricks, *Keeping Your Ethical Edge Sharp*, p. 26.

7. Patterson and Kim, *The Day America Told the Truth*, pp. 157, 158.

8. *Ibid.*, pp. 29-31.

9. Robert H. Bork, *The Tempting of America* (New York: The Free Press, 1990), pp. 248, 249.

10. Paul Johnson, *Intellectuals* (New York: Harper & Row, 1988), pp. 154, 155.

11. Helmut Thielicke, *Life Can Begin Again* (Philadelphia: Westminster Press, 1980), p. 55.

12. Francis Brown, S. R. Driver, Charles A. Briggs, *A Hebrew and English Lexicon of the Old Testament* (London: Oxford University Press, 1974), pp. 1070, 1071.

13. Warren W. Wiersbe, *The Integrity Crisis* (Nashville: Thomas Nelson, 1988), p. 21.

14. Sherman and Hendricks, *Keeping Your Ethical Edge Sharp*, p. 91.

15. Henry Fairlie, *The Seven Deadly Sins Today* (Notre Dame, IN: University of Notre Dame Press, 1979), p. 36.

16. Myrna Grant, ed., *Letters to Graduates* (Nashville: n.p., 1990), p. 82.

17. William James, *Principles of Psychology* (Chicago, London, Toronto: Encyclopedia Britannica, Inc., 1952), p. 83.

18. *The Oxford Dictionary of Quotations*, Second Edition (London: Oxford University Press, 1959), p. 405.

CHAPTER ELEVEN: *Discipline of Tongue*

1. Paul Aurandt, ed., *More of Paul Harvey's the Rest of the Story* (New York: Bantam Books, 1981), pp. 136-138.

2. Douglas Moo, *The Letters of James* (Grand Rapids, MI: Eerdmans, 1988), p. 125; cf. Martin, *Word Biblical Commentary, James*, Volume 8, p. 115, which says:

   . . . the phrase, and others parallel to it, were used in the Orphic religion to describe the unending cycle of reincarnations from which deliverance was sought. But there is sufficient evidence to show that what had originally been a technical religious or philosophical expression had become "popularized" and was used in James' day as a way of describing the course of human life, perhaps with an emphasis on the "ups and downs" of life.

3. John Calvin, *A Harmony of the Gospels Matthew, Mark and Luke Volume III and the Epistle of James and Jude*, trans. A. W. Morrison (Grand Rapids, MI: Eerdmans, 1972), p. 291.
4. Walter Wangerin, Jr., *Ragman and Other Cries of Faith* (San Francisco: Harper & Row, 1984), p. 26.
5. James S. Hewitt, ed., *Illustrations Unlimited* (Wheaton, IL: Tyndale House, 1988), p. 475.

CHAPTER TWELVE: Discipline of Work

1. Studs Terkel, *Working: People Talk About What They Do All Day and How They Feel About What They Do* (New York: Pantheon, 1974), p. xi.
2. James Patterson and Peter Kim, *The Day America Told the Truth* (New York: Prentice Hall, 1991), p. 155.
3. *Ibid.*
4. Leland Ryken, *Work and Leisure in Christian Perspectives* (Portland: Multnomah, 1987), p. 44.
5. Douglas LaBier, *Modern Madness* (Reading, MA: Addison-Wesley, 1986), p. 25.
6. Doug Sherman and William Hendricks, *Your Work Matters to God* (Colorado Springs, CO: NavPress, 1987), p. 27, who reference Dennis Waitley, *Seeds of Greatness* (Old Tappan, NJ: Fleming H. Revell, 1983), p. 199.
7. Sherman and Hendricks, *Your Work Matters to God*, p. 18.
8. Tim Hansel, *When I Relax I Feel Guilty* (Elgin, IL: David C. Cook, 1981), p. 34.
9. F. F. Bruce, *The Epistle to the Ephesians* (London: Pickering & Inglis, 1973), p. 52.
10. Clyde E. Fant, Jr., and William M. Pinson, Jr., eds., *Twenty Centuries of Great Preaching*, Vol. 3 (Waco, TX: Word, 1976), p. 74, which quotes from Jonathan Edwards's sermon "God Glorified the Man's Dependence."
11. Ewald M. Plass, *What Luther Says*, Vol. 3 (Saint Louis: Concordia, 1959), p. 1493.
12. Ryken, *Work and Leisure in Christian Perspectives*, p. 174, who quotes Dorothy L. Sayers, *Creed of Chaos* (New York: Harcourt, Brace and Company, 1949), p. 57.

CHAPTER THIRTEEN: Discipline of Perseverance

1. F. F. Bruce, *The Epistle to the Hebrews* (Grand Rapids, MI: Eerdmans, 1965), p. 346 writes:

   But in what sense are they "witnesses"? Not, probably, in the sense of spectators, watching their successors as they in their turn run the race for which they have entered; but rather in the sense that by their loyalty and endurance they have borne witness to the possibilities of the life of faith. It is not so much they who look at us as we look to them — for encouragement.

2. James D. Ernest, trans., Ceslas Spicq, *Theological Lexicon of the New Testament*, Vol. 2 (Peabody, MA: Hendrickson, 1994), p. 132.
3. Art Carey, "Beating Agony and the Marathon," *Philadelphia Inquirer*, April 12, 1978.
4. Brooke Foss Westcott, *The Epistle to the Hebrews* (Grand Rapids, MI: Eerdmans, 1967), pp. 294, 395.

5. John Henry Newman, *The Kingdom Within (Discourses Addressed to Mixed Congregations)* (Denville, NJ: Dimension Books, 1984), pp. 328-329.
6. Hugh Montefiore, *A Commentary on the Epistle to the Hebrews* (London: Adam & Charles Black, 1964), p. 35.

CHAPTER FOURTEEN: *Discipline of Church*

1. Robert W. Patterson, "In Search of the Visible Church," *Christianity Today*, March 11, 1991, Vol. 34, No. 3, p. 36.
2. George Barna, *The Frog in the Kettle* (Ventura, CA: Regal Books, 1991), p. 133.
3. Alexander Roberts and James Donaldson, eds., *The Ante-Nicene Fathers*, Vol. 5 (Grand Rapids, MI: Eerdmans, 1951), p. 384:

   If the name of father, which in man is commanded to be honoured, is violated with impunity in God, what will become of what Christ Himself lays down in the Gospel, and says, "He that curseth father or mother, let him die the death;" if He who bids that those who curse their parents after the flesh should be punished and slain, Himself quickens those who revile their heavenly and spiritual Father, and are hostile to the Church, their Mother?

4. *Leadership*, Winter 1991, Vol. 12, No. 1, p. 17.
5. Robert L. Saucy, *The Church in God's Program* (Chicago: Moody Press, 1972), p. 17 writes:

   As for membership in an invisible church without fellowship with any local assembly, this concept is never contemplated in the New Testament. The universal church was the universal fellowship of believers who met visibly in local assemblies.

6. Ernest Bevans, trans., *Saint Augustine's Enchiridion* (London: S.P.C.K., 1953), p. 57; see also John T. McNeill, ed., *Calvin's Institutes of Christian Religion*, Vol. 2, trans. Ford Lewis Battles (Philadelphia: Westminster Press, 1975), p. 1016, n. 10.
7. John Burnaby, *Augustine: Later Works* (Philadelphia: Westminster Press, 1955), p. 368, which quotes from Augustine's first Homily on 1 John 1:1 — 2:11.
8. Robert H. Fischer, ed., *Luther's Works*, Vol. 37 (Philadelphia: Mullenberg Press, 1961), p. 368.
9. McNeill, *Calvin Institutes of Christian Religion*, pp. 1011, 1012.
10. David W. Torrance and Thomas F. Torrance, eds., *Calvin's Commentaries, The Epistles of Paul the Apostle to the Galatians, Philippians and Colossians*, Volume 3, trans. T. H. L. Parker (Grand Rapids, MI: Eerdmans, 1974), p. 181.
11. John H. Leith, ed., *Creeds of the Churches* (Richmond, VA: John Knox, 1973), p. 147.
12. *Ibid.*, p. 222.
13. John Bunyan, *Grace Abounding to the Chief of Sinners* (Grand Rapids, MI: Zondervan, 1948), pp. 107, 108.
14. Harry Blamires, *The Christian Mind* (Ann Arbor, MI: Servant, 1963), p. 153.

CHAPTER FIFTEEN: *Discipline of Leadership*

1. Warren Bennis and Burt Nanus, *Leaders: The Strategies for Taking Charge* (New York: Harper & Row, 1985), p. 1.
2. Harold Lindsell, *The New Paganism* (San Francisco: Harper & Row, 1987), p. 231:

   The New Testament eloquently witnesses to the divine work of God after the Resurrection. Peter, Paul and the other Apostles carried on the work of evangelization with mighty power with the help of the Holy Spirit. The Apostolic period was followed by one in which there emerged eminently qualified people who left their mark on the history of the church: Augustine, Aquinas, Wycliffe, Hus, Calvin, Luther, Melanchthon, Zwingli, Latimer, Ridley, Wesley, Spurgeon, Edwards, Moody, Fuller and Graham to mention just a few. At this junction point in the history of the church, when the evangelical leadership of the last generation is moving off the stage, there is need for a new dynamic leadership that is evangelical and faithful to the Word of God.

3. Bennis and Nanus, *Leaders: The Strategies for Taking Charge*, pp. 4, 20.
4. Oswald Sanders, *Spiritual Leadership* (Chicago: Moody, 1967), pp. 11, 12 quoting E. M. Bounds, *Prayer and Praying*.
5. John Huffman, Jr., *Who's in Charge Here?* (Chappaqua, NY: Christian Herald Books, 1981), p. 63.
6. Sanders, *Spiritual Leadership*, p. 75.
7. John R. Claypool, *The Preaching Event* (Waco, TX: Word, 1980), p. 68.
8. Hugh Evan Hopkins, *Charles Simeon of Cambridge* (Grand Rapids, MI: Eerdmans, 1977), p. 111.
9. Sanders, *Spiritual Leadership*, p. 141.

CHAPTER SIXTEEN: *Discipline of Giving*

1. See John F. MacArthur, Jr., *Giving: God's Way* (Wheaton, IL: Tyndale House, 1979), pp. 60-73, where the author succinctly delineates the three mandatory tithes and two types of voluntary giving in the Old Testament.
2. Alfred Plummer, *A Critical and Exegetical Commentary on the Second Epistle of St. Paul to the Corinthians* (Edinburgh: T. & T. Clark, 1915), p. 234.
3. Kari Torjesen Malcolm, *We Signed Away Our Lives* (Downers Grove, IL: InterVarsity Press, 1990), p. 23.
4. C. S. Lewis, *Mere Christianity* (New York: Macmillan, 1976), pp. 81, 82.
5. MacArthur, *Giving: God's Way*, p. 92.
6. William Wordsworth, *Ecclesiastical Sonnets*, Part 3, 43.

CHAPTER SEVENTEEN: *Discipline of Witness*

1. William Barclay, *The Master's Man* (Nashville: Abingdon, 1978), p. 41.
2. *Ibid.*, pp. 44-46 successively discusses St. Andrew as the patron saint of Russia, Greece and Scotland.
3. James Hastings, ed., *The Greater Men and Women of the Bible*, Vol. 5 (Edinburgh: T. & T. Clark, 1915), p. 122.
4. Arnold Dallimore, *George Whitefield*, Vol. 1 (Edinburgh: Banner of Truth, 1989), p. 77.
5. Win Arn, *The Master's Plan for Making Disciples* (Monrovia, CA: Church Growth Press, 1982), p. 43.
6. *Heart for the Harvest Seminar Notebook and Study Guide* (Lutherville, MD: Search Ministries [P.O. Box 521, 21093]), p. 3.
7. *Ibid.*, p. 9.
8. C. S. Lewis, *The Weight of Glory and Other Addresses* (Grand Rapids, MI: Eerdmans, 1965), pp. 14, 15.
9. *Heart for the Harvest*, p. 10.
10. *Ibid.*, p. 11.

CHAPTER EIGHTEEN: Discipline of Ministry

1. Clyde E. Fant, Jr. and William M. Pinson, Jr., *50 Centuries of Great Preaching*, Vol. 8 (Waco, TX: Word, 1976), p. 76.
2. R. H. Strachan, *The Fourth Gospel* (London: SCM Press, 1943), p. 148 notes: "Thus = 'as he was.' 'What meaneth "thus"?' Not on a throne, not on a cushion, but simply, as He was, on the ground (Chrysostom)."
3. Leon Morris, *The Gospel According to John* (Grand Rapids, MI: Eerdmans, 1971), p. 258.
4. Raymond Brown, *The Gospel According to John (i-xii)* (New York: Doubleday, 1966), p. 169 says:

   iv 4. had to pass. This is not geographical necessity; for, although the main route from Judea to Galilee was through Samaria (Josephus *Ant.* XX. vi.I ;#1 18), if Jesus was in the Jordan valley (iii 22) he could easily have gone north through the valley and then up into Galilee through the Bethshan gap, avoiding Samaria. Elsewhere in the Gospel (iii 14), the expression of necessity means that God's will or plan is involved.

CHAPTER NINETEEN: Grace of Discipline

1. "But he giveth more grace" (KJV), "But he gives more grace" (RSV), "But He gives a greater grace" (NASB), "Yet he gives grace more and more" (Moffatt), "But He affords the more grace" (Berkeley).
2. John Blanchard, *Truth for Life* (West Sussex, England: H.E. Walter Ltd., 1982), p. 239.

SCRIPTURE INDEX

GENERAL INDEX